High Country
NAMES

High Country NAMES

Rocky Mountain National Park and Indian Peaks

Louisa Ward Arps and Elinor Eppich Kingery

assisted by

Hugh E. Kingery

Published in cooperation with the
Rocky Mountain Nature Association

Johnson Books: Boulder

9 8 7 6 5 4 3 2 1

Cover design by Bob Schram/Bookends
Cover photograph by James Frank

Library of Congress Cataloging-in-Publication Data
Arps, Louisa Ward, 1901–
    High country names : Rocky Mountain National Park and
Indian Peaks / by Louisa Ward Arps and Elinor Eppich Kingery ;
assisted by Hugh E. Kingery.
      p.   cm.
    "Published in cooperation with the Rocky Mountain Nature Association."
    Includes index.
    ISBN 1-55566-133-5 (paper)
    1. Names, Geographical—Colorado—Rocky Mountain National Park.
2. Names, Geographical—Colorado—Indian Peaks Wilderness.   3. Rocky
Mountain National park (Colo.)—History, Local.   4. Indian Peaks Wilderness
(Colo.)—History, Local.   I. Kingery, Elinor Eppich.   II. Kingery, Hugh E.
III. Title
F782.R59A73   1994
917.88'69'0014—dc20   94-18989
                                                            CIP

Maps courtesy of Trails Illustrated

Printed in United States of America by
Johnson Printing Company
1880 South 57th Court
Boulder, Colorado 80301

CONTENTS

PREFACE

Louisa Ward Arps and Elinor Eppich Kingery were legendary names in their own right. Both were well-respected historians, mountaineers, conversationists, and long-time pillars of the Colorado Mountain Club. Of the many projects on which thcy collaborated, none was dearer to their hearts than the chronicle of how the many diverse geographic features in Rocky Mountain National Park and the neighboring Indian Peaks were named.

High Country Names was first published by the Colorado Mountain Club in 1965 in celebration of Rocky Mountain National Park's 50th anniversary. A revised edition was published by the Rocky Mountain Nature Association in 1972 to coincide with the 100th anniversary of the National Park System. Johnson Books and the Rocky Mountain Nature Association are pleased to make this perennial favorite available once again.

We hope, as did Louisa Ward Arps and Elinor Eppich Kingery, that this book will be not only a valuable reference, but also an entertaining read for armchair travelers, summer visitors, and high country residents alike.

C. W. Buchholtz
Executive Director,
Rocky Mountain Nature Association

Longs Peak, from Estes Park. (Crofutt, 1881)

THE NAMERS

This book attempts to trace the origins of the place names in Rocky Mountain National Park and the high country south of it. Some of the names just happened, as names do; but when the Park was proposed, various people set out systematically to name features in the area. The story of these givers of names—these namers—may well start with the beginnings of the Park.

Camp cooking in a mountain storm is chancy. The fire under the pot which held the idea of a national park for the northern Front Range of the Colorado Rockies had to weather six years of storms before Rocky Mountain National Park was established—from about 1909 when Enos Mills kindled the fire until January 25, 1915, the day President Woodrow Wilson signed the bill.

The flame was alternately fanned by women's clubs, Chambers of Commerce, conservationists, editors, and organizations like the Colorado Mountain Club; and doused by opposition groups such as other Chambers of Commerce, the Front Range Settlers League of Estes Park, cattlemen, hunters, lumbermen, and mining men who refused to believe that the rich mineral belt of Colorado did not extend north of Boulder County.

By 1912 the heat from this fire was felt in Washington. That summer the U.S. Geological Survey sent their chief topographer, R. B. Marshall, to look over the scenery. He borrowed two men already in the field working on the Geological Survey of the Longs Peak area, and made a circle tour on horseback from Longs Peak Inn, over the Grand River Trail to Squeaky Bob's, to Grand Lake, Monarch Lake, and back to the Eastern Slope by "the wild Arapaho pass."

With the scenery of this trip shining in his eyes, Marshall came to Denver to consult with Governor John Shafroth, Governor-elect Elias Ammons, Mayor Arnold of Denver, and other citizens. One of these was a young man he had met seven years before on top of a mountain. In 1905, when Marshall was surveying for the special Georgetown quad map, the young man, James Grafton Rogers, and two companions were spending five months at Jack Truesdell's cabin on upper Bear Creek, an idyllic interlude between their graduation from Yale and the business of making a living. The day they happened to meet Marshall on a mountain was a propitious day for nomenclature in Colorado. They sat and talked of many things, including Marshall's difficulties in determining the right names for mountains on the Bear Creek watershed. Rogers helped solve the problems, one of which was Mount Evans. After years of jumping from summit to summit, Governor John Evans's name at this time came to rest on the highest peak, the highest of the three sentinels of the Front Range—Pikes, Evans, and Longs.

Seven years later when Marshall returned to Colorado with problems of a national park on his mind, he looked up Jim Rogers. He found the young lawyer not only more interested in mountains than he had been in 1905, but the president of an organization of like-minded men and women. The Colorado Mountain Club had been organized in April of 1912.

Suggesting to Rogers that a map with many named peaks might interest the U.S. Congress in authorizing a national park more than a map full of unnamed mountains, Marshall returned to Washington. His report, published in January 1913, stated that turning the northern Front Range into a national park was both feasible and desirable. Two things he suggested changing from the original proposal. He commended the name Rocky Mountain National Park instead of Estes National Park, and reduced the acreage of the original dream which embraced all the country from the Poudre on the north to Rollins Pass on the south, from Grand Lake to the eastern plains, and a noncontiguous section around Mount Evans.

THE COLORADO MOUNTAIN CLUB

After Marshall's report, the Colorado Mountain Club decided to turn all its considerable energy into forwarding the formation of Rocky Mountain National Park. It decided it should learn first hand the area it was sponsoring. In 1913 it held an outing at Bear Lake and the next year essayed a movable outing, camping at Grand Lake in the rain, at Shipler Park in the rain, at Fall River Ranger Station in the rain, and at Horseshoe Park in the rain. Despite this unusual weather, the club descended to the flatland determined to help create the national park. As president, James Grafton Rogers led the campaign, drawing up each bill presented to Congress. Anyone interested in the birth pangs of Rocky Mountain National Park should study his papers from 1912 to 1914 on file in the Colorado state archives.

The Colorado Mountain Club took to heart Marshall's suggestion that the mountains needed names. The rosters of the early outings of the club include persons prominent in the history of nomenclature of the Park such as James and Edmund Rogers, Roger and Oliver Toll, Morrison Shafroth, George Barnard, and Harriet Vaille. The club organized a nomenclature committee with Harriet Vaille as chairman. She formed the Colorado Reading Party, consisting of a few people who promised to research and make notes of names connected with early Colorado history—Spanish, French, explorers, mountain men. Miss Vaille's task was Indian names. She systematically undertook this study, even going to the Newberry Library in Chicago, then the closest center of Indian information.

1914 ARAPAHOS

She soon felt that books were inadequate. Why not go to the Indians themselves? But what Indians? The Utes had lived in the mountains and the Arapahos on the plains of early Colorado, but both tribes had hunted around Estes Park and Grand Lake, fighting every time they met. Miss Vaille, educated at Bryn Mawr and other eastern schools, knew the value of consulting authorities. She talked to Dr. Livingstone Farrand, president of the Unviersity of Colorado and an authority on Indians. He advised her to seek out the northern Arapahos. After much correspondence to secure official permission and letters of introduction, Miss Vaille and Miss Edna Hendrie, also of Denver—two young women venturing alone—went by train and wagon to the Wind River Reservation in Wyoming. Indian police rounded up the oldest men of the nation. At headquarters the young ladies selected the two old men they thought would best remember their youth in the Estes Park area. The young women then returned to Denver to raise money to bring the two old men and an interpreter to Estes Park. They secured $50 from the Colorado Mountain Club, $50 from the Colonial Dames, and Frederick O. Vaille, president of the telephone company and father of Miss Harriet, agreed to pay the remaining bills which amounted to almost as much as the two clubs had provided.

In July 1914 three Arapahos stepped off the train at Longmont and were driven to Longs Peak Inn in the automobiles of Mr. Vaille and Mr. Hendrie. A chauffeur drove for Mr. Hendrie, president of the Hendrie & Bolthoff Machinery Company of Denver, but Mr. Vaille drove his own touring car with the oldest Indian sitting contentedly beside him. Shep Husted of Estes Park furnished horses and a pack outfit and escorted the Indians on the regular circle tour—Grand River Trail to Squeaky Bob's—Grand Lake—Flattop—back to Bear Lake. A cousin of Harriet Vaille, Oliver Toll, fresh from college, took down every word said by the two older Indians as interpreted by the younger. Toll's report, with glossary of Arapaho words and the Indian names for innumerable points in northern Colorado, told the tale of the trip with youthful charm. In manuscript form this report was available in a few local libraries. In 1962 Oliver Toll revised and printed most of it with the title *Arapaho Names and Trails*.

ELLSWORTH BETHEL

In the spring of 1914 another person beside Harriet Vaille was studying Indian names in relation to Colorado mountain nomenclature. Ellsworth Bethel (1863-1925) taught botany at East Denver High School at 19th and Stout. For twenty-five years from the window of his classroom he had watched the northern Rockies, noting their daily moods. This spring of 1914 was to be his last as a teacher, so with a certain nostalgia he saw the snow melt from the long line of peaks "imprinted in bold indentures upon the luminous margin of the sky," a phrase, he remembered, that Dr. Edwin James, Colorado's first botanist, had written in 1820. It worried Bethel that the mountains of the Snowy Range from the Arapahos on the south to Longs and Meeker on the north had no generally accepted names. There was Mount Alice, but who was Alice? And Audubon, named for the ornithologist by C. C. Parry, botanist. Perhaps he should suggest naming other peaks for naturalists. But that was riding his personal hobby-horse. The Arapaho Peaks were well named. What about using the names of other Indian tribes which had looked on these snowy peaks before the white men had seen them?

Bethel made a sketch map of the range; on each peak he wrote the name of an Indian tribe important in the history of the Great Plains. On May 14, 1914, he sent the map and a letter to the U.S. Board on Geographic Names in Washington. Though the map has not been located, the letter lists the names as Apache, Arapaho (already named), Arikaree, Cheyenne, Comanche, Kiowa, Navajo, Ogalalla, Pawnee, Shoshone, Sioux, and Ute. The board rejected five of the names—Cheyenne, Comanche, Shoshone, Sioux, and Ute. That Ute was refused must have pained Bethel because the Ute nation was the most important in western Colorado. The board pointed out that other mountains were already named Ute, and Bethel comforted himself by naming over the mountains in the Sawatch Range and the San Juans that bore the name of Ute leaders, like Shavano, Antero, and Ouray. On the Front Rage, Bethel comprised and substituted the name Paiute, a related tribe dwelling west of Colorado.

Perhaps Bethel did not grieve over the board's rejection of Sioux since the Ogalallas were a branch of that nation. He gave up trying to rename Chiefs Head for the Comanches. A mountain north of the Mummy Range had been named Comanche since 1876. (As the names stand in 1966, the Comanches are well represented by two mountains at the head of North St. Vrain Creek; both Tanima and Mahana are Comanche names.) The board's refusal to change the name of Alice to Shoshone made Bethel boil. In a red-hot letter he said the board had "spoiled the whole scheme of representing the ten tribes connected with Colorado history by peaks visible from Denver and the other Plains towns."

COLORADO GEOGRAPHIC BOARD

Thus the year 1914 was important for mountain names in Colorado. Mr. Bethel's Indian tribal names in the spring, the Colorado Mountain Club's outing from Grand Lake to Estes Park in the summer, and Harriet

Vaille's Arapaho project in July. Then in the fall Governor Ammons was approached by J. G. Rogers, president of the Colorado Mountain Club, and others on the subject of forming an official Colorado nomenclature committee. The approach was easy enough, since the Vailles were often guests at the governor's ranch in Middle Park, and the families of Rogers, Toll, and Shafroth were all influential in Colorado politics.

Governor Ammons sent out a letter to people all over the state bidding them come to a meeting "to consider the jumble of geographic names in Colorado." On October 28, 1914, in the Senate Chamber of the State Capitol, at 10:00 AM, sixty-two people signed the roster. From this initial meeting came the Colorado Geographic Society, constitution dated November 6, 1914, open to any reputable citizen, dues $1.00. An advisory committee was selected, including Enos Mills of Estes Park, Irving Howbert of Colorado Springs, J. H. Crawford of Steamboat Springs, Mrs. Gordon Kimball of Ouray, Otto Mears of Silverton, Alva Adams of Pueblo, Ansel Watrous of Fort Collins, and Max Clark of Greely. Their duty was to advise a four-man executive committee called the Colorado Geographic Board, appointed by Colorado Governor Elias Ammons, in October 1914.

The four men were J. G. Rogers, chairman, Ellsworth Bethel, Jerome Smiley, and Hugh Steele. Ex-officio, R. D. George, state geologist, was a member, though he seldom could attend meetings since he lived in Boulder which was farther away in 1914 than it is today.

Roger and Bethel were obvious choices, with Jerome C. Smiley almost as obligatory. Historian of the State Historical and Natural History Society, he had authored the classic *History of Denver* published in 1901. The fourth man on the board, a director of the same society, was white-haired, blue-eyed, ruddy-skinned Hugh R. Steele (1849-1923). His father had been governor of Jefferson Territory for a few months in 1859 before Colorado Territory was formed, so the son knew everybody of importance in early Colorado. After living in mining camps all over the state, Hugh Steele had come to Denver. In 1914 he was secretary of the society of Colorado Pioneers with an office in the Charles Building where he could hold his own as a story-teller with any old-timer who dropped in.

The secretary of the Colorado Geographic Board was not a member of the board but, being the attractive Harriet Vaille, she did not need a vote to make her influence felt.

The letterhead of the Colorado Geographic Board stated that they were "engaged in the task of recording, systematizing, and clarifying the geographical place names of the state so as to fix an appropriate and historical nomenclature." The meetings of the board were faithfully attended by all official members and recorded by the secretary. At the first meeting, November 27, 1914, they decided their mission was not to make a general revision of place names in the state, but to collect information and deal with specific problems as they arose. The urgent problems at the first meeting was the nomenclature of the proposed Rocky Mountain National Park. The U.S. Geological Survey, in the process of preparing the Longs Peak quad, would gladly accept help, especially from an official state board.

The board voted to turn this problem over to the chairman, James Grafton Rogers, and to George Barnard of the Colorado Mountain Club, leader of the two tribes the club had taken into the proposed Park area in 1913 and 1914. These two men already had ideas. Within two weeks, on December 9, 1914, they submitted revisions for the advance sheet of the Longs Peak quad. Then they continued to work. On February 21, 1915, they petitioned the U.S. Geological Survey to defer the printing of the Longs Peak quad until they could submit further suggestions.

NAMERS FROM 1820 TO 1914

Rogers and Barnard, aided especially by Miss Vaille, were thorough. They interviewed local residents and summer cottagers, read books, even lugged transits to the mountains to determine altitudes, but above all studied maps. A quick review of the many maps available to them starts with the first map showing the northern Colorado Front Range—the 1820 map of Long's expedition. On it they found two names in the area: Highest Peak and Bull Pen (present North Park). The very next maps used Longs Peak for Highest Peak. The first map of Colorado alone was that by Francis Case, surveyor general of Colorado Territory, published in 1862. On its northern Colorado Rockies two names appear—Longs Peak, and Mount Edmunds for the peak that stands at the head of the Boulder Creek. Some succeeding maps accepted Mount Edmunds, but Thayer's map of 1873 switched to Arapaho Peak. Mount Audubon appeared on detailed maps soon after 1864 when Dr. C. C. Parry and Professor J. W. Velie climbed and named it.

Then came the government surveyors, the prolific mountain namers. They were the first men to make it their business to identify mountains— what is a map without names? The face of the mountainous West is full of their christenings. To the Estes Park country first came Clarence King's surveyers who had ridden from California following, more or less, the 40th Parallel, which is today the Baseline Road that runs through Boulder. The top of Longs Peak was as far south as these surveyors got. They named Hagues Peak, Comanche Peak, and Mount Richthofen, all printed on King's atlas, published in 1876. The next year Hayden's *Atlas of Colorado* displayed names now familiar, names like Estes Park, Estes Cone, Muggins Gulch, Lillie's Mountain, Black Canyon, Fall River, and Grand Lake, a name in common use since the 1860s.

Rogers and Barnard supplemented their study of maps of the 1870s by reading the classic of Estes Park, *A Lady's Life in the Rocky Mountains,* written by a British gentlewoman named Isabella Bird who spent the autumn of 1873 at Griff Evans's cottage camp on Fish Creek. The name of

Jims Grove dates from her book. Rogers and Barnard also read reminiscences of sportsmen like the Irish Earl of Dunraven and Dr. George Kingsley, and found the reason for the name of Bierstadt Lake.

For the late 1880s they read Chapins *Mountaineering in Colorado.* Here was the book that gave the reason for names like Chapin, Hallett, and Otis, mountaineers all. For the 1890s Rogers and Barnard thought they had found a gold mine when they saw the map Abner Sprague had made when he was official surveyor for Larimer County, but were disappointed to find few names on it. However, Sprague and Stevens published a map in Loveland, later and non-officially, with more names. To find the history of these names for the Colorado Geographic Board, Harriet Vaille interviewed Abner Sprague at his hotel in Glacier Basin in August 1915. A friendly hotel keeper since 1875, Sprague had named many features for his neighbors and guests, like Andrews, McHenry and the Hayden brothers, as well as Alberta Falls for his wife.

Two other hotel men of the area who named places in the Park were Enos Mills and Dr. W. J. Workman. Their names reflect their hobbies. Enos Mills, with his love of nature, named Ouzel Lake, Marten Peak, and Storm Peak. On Mills's 1905 map he wrote Silent Place as a name for an area near present Tahosa Creek, but this name appears on no other map. Dr. Workman, the dedicated angler, amused himself by naming his many favorite fishing lakes after the numerous girls of his family or lady guests at his Fern Lake Lodge, such as Grace Workman Hansen, Helene Stidger, Marguerite Turck, and Odessa Workman. Fortunately their last names are in various records, but the identities of other feminine names in the Park have not been found, names such as Mount Alice, Lake Dorothy, Eugenia Mine, Irene Lake and Lake Irene, Olive Lake, and Lake Verna— the mystery women of the northern Front Range!

The board discarded most of the personal names from the first map of Wild Basin, "and rightly, too," says Dr. W. S. Cooper today. He made this first map in his youth, but now deplores his attempt to fasten family names on the great Rocky Mountains. (Dr. Cooper, an ecologist of note, is pleased that the Colorado Geographic Board retained the bird and flower names he gave to creeks and falls in Wild Basin.) Enos Mills had planned to publish Cooper's map in 1908, but Mills disliked two persons after whom Cooper had named lakes. When the young man refused to change the names, Mills refused to publish the map. In June 1911, Cooper and Dean Babcock, artists of Estes Park, published the map themselves. The cover reads: "The only authentic map from original survey. Price 15 cents."

The two maps that doubtless were most useful to the Colorado Geographic Board were the 1910 map published by the Burlington Railroad and a 1913 map published by F. P. Clatworthy, owner of Estes Park's first photographic studio. For the information of its prospective customers, the Burlington map located almost every resort and hotel in the area. The great puzzle on this map is Mount Barrett where Chiefs Head is today. On Clatworthy's map in large letters is printed Elkanah Valley, showing on which side he fought in the battle of Elkanah vs. Tahosa Valley.

The Colorado Geographic Board painstakingly collected names from each small community, from Glen Haven south to Allenspark, from Estes Park across the range to Grand Lake. They balanced them with the names on maps—names that seemed right against names that meant nothing except to one family, names that conflicted with other names, duplicate names, hackneyed names, and a few "great, proud, glittering names fit for the immense and lonely land they inhabit," as Thomas Wolfe wrote about names on the western landscape.

1915 DECISIONS

To find most of the names the Colorado Geographic Board left on the northern Front Range, compare the maps of the Burlington Railroad and Clatworthy's map, both studied by Rogers and Barnard, with the U.S. Geological Survey map of the Rocky Mountain National Park, edition of 1919. On the earlier maps not one Indian name appears: the later map has a rash of Indian names. This dictionary of names in the Rocky Mountain National Park area includes thirty-six Indian names, not counting names in translation like Gianttrack and Lumpy Ridge and Never Summer. This is one of the greatest concentrations of Indian names in one small area on the face of the U.S.A.

The comparison of the maps shows some of the trouble spots smoothed over by the Colorado Geographic Board. The Grand River Trail, sometimes called Squeaky Bob's Trail, or Poudre Lakes Trail, or North Fork Trail, over Tombstone Ridge becomes the Ute Trail over Trail Ridge. Lily Mountain has not only simplified its spelling but securely rests on the hill near Lily Lake, dissociated from Twin Sisters. Rogers and Barnard probably settled the argument as to which hill the Indians called Gianttrack Mountain by climbing, on a nice winter weekend, all the adjacent hills until they found the giant's tracks. In the vicinity of the Mummy Range the Colorado Geographic Board added Tileston for the author of a book named *Chiquita,* already on the map; Dunraven for the absentee landlord of Estes Park; and Dickinson for the first woman to climb Longs Peak.

Over the valley of the North Fork of the Grand River the board peppered the map with new names. The valley became the Kawuneeche Valley, the mountains became the Never Summer Mountains, and in that range Rogers named the Cloud Peaks—Cirrus, Cumulus, and Nimbus. The board added Mount Neota, Nokhu Crags, and Seven Utes Mountain. Near Grand Lake the board accepted Craig and Cairns from earlier maps, but eradicated Bald Mountain by naming it Mount Senator. (This became Mount Patterson.) It added Wescott and Irving Hale.

MOUNTAIN INDEX AT CHEESMAN PARK

When the Colorado Geographic Board was organized, the *Denver Post* pointed out that their "first duty was to fix definitely and for all time the nomenclature of the peaks in sight of Denver." James Grafton Rogers and Ellsworth Bethel worked on this. They sketched the view from Cheesman Park in a semicircle from south to north—from Pikes Peak to the Poudre. They provided a chart indicating altitudes, distances from Denver, and even the position of some unseen peaks, such as Grays and Torreys. Paul Weiss, Denver optician, cast it in bronze and added a sighting device. The club erected a pedestal on which to place the indicator, presenting it to the people of the city of Denver in March 1913.

This view-finder served for sixty-three years until, because of vandalism, the Denver Parks and Recreation Foundation (the "Parks People") replaced it. The 1976 marker, cast in bronze from a wooden sculpture by Lorn Wallace, is a relief map of the semicircle of mountains west of Denver, seen and unseen from the Cheesman Memorial. Those still seen consist mostly of Mount Evans and evirons. This limited view has been protected since 1968 by the Cheesman Mountain View Preservation Act of the Denver City Council. Those mountains unseen are hidden by foothills, high trees, and higher buildings.

THE COLORADO GEOGRAPHIC BOARD DISSOLVES

The Colorado Geographic Board worked on names for mountains in other parts of the state until its last official minutes, dated November 23, 1916. James Grafton Rogers had already resigned from the board. The secretary wrote that his resignation was "an unmitigated calamity," but Rogers pleaded that he had no time left over from being president of the Colorado Mountain Club and Civic League of Denver, which he organized. He did not mention his private law practice nor his growing family. Presently Rogers taught at the University of Denver Law School, became president of the Colorado Bar Association and the University Club of Denver. He wrote poetic dramas for the Cactus Club to perform in the open air on Lookout Mountain and two of his songs—"The Santa Fe Trail" and "Old Dolores"— have become folk songs. After serving as dean of the Law School of the University of Colorado, Rogers continued his distinguished career in the East, as professor of law at Yale, assistant to the U.S. Secretary of State, in the office of Strategic Services during World War II, and, for ten years, the president of the Foreign Bond Holders Protective Council. Yet, always, from New Haven, from Washington, from Europe, Mr. Rogers returned home to his Colorado mountains. He bought an historic house in Georgetown and twice served as mayor of that community. Until his death in April 1971, he continued activity in the State Historical Society of Colorado, still studied maps, and worked on his index to mountain names, which he gave to the society's library. "Only the elite," he said, "are interested in names."

What happened to the other members of the Colorado Geographic Board? Hugh Steele continued to tell tales of early Colorado until his death in 1923. Jerome Smiley went home to his native Ohio—practically nothing is known of the personal life of this man who contributed invaluable books to the history of Colorado. Harriet Vaille married Judge Francis Bouck of Leadville in 1917, then returned to Denver where Judge Bouck sat on the bench of the Colorado Supreme Court. They brought up three daughters in the traditions of Colorado history and mountain climbing.

Ellsworth Bethel continued longest in the business of nomenclature. Between the years of 1914 and 1917—after his retirement, aged fifty-one, from teaching at East High School, and his appointment as plant pathologist for the U.S. Forestry Department—Bethel spent much time establishing names for mountains. Weekend after weekend found him riding the Fisherman's Special up the South Platte Canyon. The engineer would let him off anywhere along the line, even where neither fishing hole nor raspberry patch was in sight, the usual reasons the engineer was asked to stop the train. Shouldering his heavy pack, the fragile-looking Bethel covered the hills, checking maps for contours and altitudes, interviewing local people for names, camping out on Saturday night to continue his work the next day. On Sunday night the engineer of the Colorado & Southern narrow gauge train watched for him standing beside the track and stopped the train for this little man with his pack full of rocks, his hand full of flowers for his wife, and his head full of names.

Bethel was science director of the State Historical and Natural History Society of Colorado. (This was before the Denver Museum of Natural History took over the science part of the State Historical Society.) In his 1919-20 report he wrote of two manuscripts concerning Colorado mountain names that he planned to deposit in some library. So far an extensive search for these documents has failed. Perhaps in them are recorded the meaning of various names added to the map of Colorado that are merely mentioned in the minutes of the Colorado Geographic Board, are not on file in Washington, and were not in the clear memory of James Grafton Rogers.

After Bethel's death in 1925 his friends both in and out of the Colorado Mountain Club asked the U.S. Board on Geographic Names to name a peak near Loveland Pass for him. Mount Bethel is a fitting memorial to a man who signed his letters, in a clear Spencerian script, "Yours for a more beautiful nomenclature, Ellsworth Bethel."

NAMERS SINCE 1915

Since the time of the Colorado Geographic Board, names have been added to the Rocky Mountain National Park and its environs, sometimes spasmodically, but with three concerted efforts. Roger Toll made the first effort. As park superintendent from 1919 to 1929 he climbed most of the mountains, named many of them, and christened lakes and creeks and glaciers. He amassed an extensive collection of local maps which, bound, are in the Park headquarters library. The card file of names there also probably dates from Toll's regime.

In 1942 the staff of Rocky Mountain National Park, under Superintendent David H. Canfield, spent a profitable winter revising names. And before 1961 another official committee, headed by a summer ranger named Phillip Ritterbush, suggested names and changes. The results appeared on the accurate and beautiful 1961 map of Rocky Mountain National Park published by the U.S. Geological Survey. All the names on that map and names selected from the Indian Peaks to the south and Lake Granby area to the southwest comprise the 428 distinctive names listed in this dictionary. The names reflect the interests of various people, the efforts of various groups, and are really a history of the northern Front Range of the Colorado Rockies, the Rockies that were once known as the Shining Mountains.

KEY TO PLACE NAMES

The entries in this dictionary are the names appearing on the Rocky Mountain National Park map published by the U.S. Geological Survey. For features south of the Park, the names are from four additional U.S. Geological Survey 1:24,000 maps—Allens Park, Isolation Peak, Monarch Lake, and Ward. These maps have also been used as authority for the spelling of names and the altitudes of mountains.

The maps in this book are reproductions of the Rocky Mountain National Park Map from the Trails Illustrated National Park series. For the Indian Peaks section and other adjacent areas, consult individual U.S.G.S. maps.

Each name in this dictionary is keyed to the map or maps on which the name appears, thus:

Flattop Mountain (12,324') GLACIER GORGE, GRAND LAKE
This means that Flattop Mountain is 12,324 feet above sea level, and appears on both the Glacier Gorge and Grand Lake maps in this book. It appears on two maps because the sectional maps were designed to overlap.

Hayden Creek, Gorge, Lake, Spire FOREST CANYON
All the features named Hayden are on the Forest Canyon map; the U.S. Geological Survey does not record the specific altitude of Hayden Spire.

Beaver Creek—NEVER SUMMER; **Beaver Brook, Meadow Point**— ESTES PARK; **Beaver Mountain** (10,491')—FOREST CANYON
The various features named Beaver are grouped together, with the map on which each appears indicated.

Olympus, Mount—East of Estes Park Village
This means that Mount Olympus is not on a map in this dictionary, but it is located east of a feature that is on one of the maps.

Horse Creek WILD BASIN
No text follows this or about sixty other names in the dictionary. We have listed these even though we know nothing about why, when, or by whom they were named. We hope our readers will write their own notes, and supply us with the information.

NOTE: 1914 Arapahos
This expression, used frequently in this dictionary, refers to the visit in 1914 of three Arapaho men brought to the Estes Park-Grand Lake region by the Colorado Mountain Club.

Achonee, Mount (12,649')

The Colorado Geographic Board left no record of its reason for choosing this name. Research has produced two possible sources, one Ute, one Cheyenne. Among the Uncompahgre Utes who now live near Randlett, Utah, Achonee is a family name pronounced A·ka·wa´·na, to rhyme with Lackawanna. The word means red edge or red line, a description that fits Mount Achonee no better than the Ute pronunciation of the word fits its English spelling. The Utes cannot trace the name to any prominent man in their history.

A sub-chief of the Cheyennes whose name was spelled almost the same—Ochanee or Ochinee—was well known to whites. He was one of the unsuspecting Arapaho and Cheyenne Indians camped on Sand Creek on November 29, 1864, when Colorado troops under Colonel John M. Chivington attacked at dawn. About this fight the granddaughter of Ochinee, Mary Prowers Hudnall, wrote:

> Grandfather Ochinee (One-Eye) escaped from the camp, but seeing that all his people were to be slaughtered, he deliberately chose to go back into the one-sided battle and die with them rather than survive alone. . . . Mother, father, and I were out at Big Timbers when we heard of the massacre . . . Mother was always very bitter about the Sand Creek Massacre. A number of years later, while she was attending a meeting of the Eastern Star in Denver, a friend brought Chivington over to introduce him to mother, saying, "Mrs. Prowers, do you know Colonel Chivington?" My mother drew herself up with that stately dignity peculiar to her people, and ignoring the outstretched hand, remarked in perfect English, audible to all in the room, "Know Colonel Chivington? I should. He was my father's murderer!"

Ochinee's daughter was named Amache. In 1861, when she was fifteen years old, she married the handsome Missourian John Wesley Prowers, trader at Bent's Fort, who is credited with bringing the first cattle into Prowers County. During World War II the relocation center where Japanese were interned was named Amache Relocation Center. Thus, on the map of Colorado a mountain (Achonee), a town (Amache), and a county (Prowers), commemorate a Cheyenne Indian, his daughter, and his son-in-law.

Acoma, Mount (10,508')   GRAND LAKE, LAKE GRANBY
The ancient pueblo of the Acoma Indians sits on a mesa in Valencia
County, New Mexico. F. H. Hodge, in his classic *Handbook of American
Indians,* states that the word comes "from the native A·kóme, 'People of
the White Rock,' now commonly pronounced A'·co·ma." Denver people,
often criticized for accenting the name of Acoma Street on the second syl-
lable, may be reverting to the original. The mountain was named by the
Colorado Geographic Board, as proposed by Ellsworth Bethel.

Adams Falls   GRAND LAKE
In 1886 Jay E. Adams of San Antonio, Texas, began to build a small
cabin on a large rock on the southeastern shore of Grand Lake, accessible only by boat. He sold it in 1891 to Stephen D. Cook. Later it became a
ghost house; youngsters rowed across the lake to picnic near the "House
on the Rock." In 1946 Dudley Abbott of Denver bought and rebuilt it.
Jay Adams built two more, much larger, houses on the eastern shore
of Grand Lake. In 1917 he entertained the Grand Lake community with a
sumptuous shore picnic, then asked his replete guests to suggest a name
for a nearby waterfall. They voted unanimously to name it Adams Falls.
Before this it had been known as Ouzel Falls, although Judge Wescott and
his young friends called it Minnehaha Falls. (See Mount Wescott.)

Adams Lake; Adams, Mount (12,121')—GRAND LAKE, LAKE GRANBY
This name may commemorate the same Jay E. Adams of San Antonio.
Enos Mills, however, thought the mountain honored another Adams family, year-round residents of Grand Lake. Alexander and Louise Adams
bought the Garrison House, built in 1881 south of the outlet of Grand
Lake, and renamed it the Grandview House. Here they ran a pleasant
resort until 1901, when the hotel with its fine furniture and gay rugs
burned. Mrs. Adams thereafter lived in a cottage close by until her death
in 1940 at the age of 101. Mrs. Adams's granddaughter, Mrs. E. E. Gem-
mill, now has a house on the site of Grandview House.

Adams Tunnel   GLACIER GORGE, GRAND LAKE
The official name for this tunnel is the Alva B. Adams Tunnel. Senator
Adams, Democrat from Colorado, introduced into the United States Senate, in June 1937, the bill that authorized the Colorado-Big Thompson Project. Water collected in Lake Granby, Shadow Mountain Lake, and Grand
Lake flows through the Continental Divide in the Adams Tunnel to empty
into the Big Thompson River. Water first rushed through the tunnel in
1947, flowing 13.1 miles from the intake below the surface of Grand Lake
to the Emerald Mountain Outlet.

Agnes, Lake   NEVER SUMMER
John Zimmerman changed the name of Island Lake to honor one of his

two daughters. In the clean Swiss tradition, Agnes and Eda Zimmerman were housekeepers for their father's famous Keystone Hotel on the upper Poudre River near the town of Home. The three-story brick building housed contented fishermen who gladly paid $10 a week for clean rooms and ample cooking. In 1946 the state of Colorado bought the hotel, razed it, and turned the area into a fish-retaining pond.

Alberta Falls   GLACIER GORGE
Named by Abner Sprague for his wife.

Albion, Mount (12,609')   INDIAN PEAKS
Albion is a Celtic word related to alp, meaning white or snowy. Poets use Albion as a name for the main British Isle. Following this custom, when homesick men from the lowlands of Scotland located the pioneer lead-silver vein in the Snowy Range Mining District, they called their lode Albion. Although discovered in 1864, the mine was not recorded until October of 1879. From the name of the mine, a town and a mountain and a lake were all called Albion.

From 1881 the Scottish Mining and Smelter Company worked the claim. After that company moved to Salina, near Gold Hill, the Cashier Company drilled the Snowy Range Tunnel on the old Albion lode.

Today's Mount Albion was in mining days known as Sheep Mountain. The miners knew Mount Albion as the higher peak, farther west, which appropriately towers over Lake Albion. This peak the Colorado Geographic Board renamed Kiowa Peak, in line with their efforts to call all the snowy summits north of the Arapaho Peaks after Indian tribes. Changing old Mount Albion to Kiowa Peak and Sheep Mountain to Mount Albion upset mining records. Kenneth I. White of Boulder, whose father and grandfather both were officers in the Scottish company, is not the only mining man who still complains in vain about the change—in vain because in 1968 the U.S. Board on Geographic Names firmly decided to keep Albion and Kiowa as named in 1915.

Alice, Mount (13,310')   GRAND LAKE, WILD BASIN
Who was Alice? The first record of this name for the mountain seems to be on Enos Mills's map published in the 1905 edition of his *Story of Estes Park*. The map is based on notes by A. E. Sprague, and if either Mills or Sprague knew who Alice was, he did not record it in any available records.

Mount Alice next appears on the Cooper-Babcock map of 1911. W. S. Cooper made the first detailed survey of Wild Basin in 1908. On his map the U.S. Board on Geographic Names based some of their decisions, including Mount Alice. Dr. Cooper, however, stated in 1965 that he merely accepted the name in general use in 1908, that he did not name Mount Alice, nor did he know who the lady was.

In the spring of 1914, when Ellsworth Bethel was trying to fasten the names of Indian tribes on the snowy peaks between the Arapahos and Longs Peak, he wished to change the name of Mount Alice to Shoshone Peak. The U.S. Board on Geographic Names refused the change. Bethel wrote back pleading his cause. He said he had been unable, after much research, to find out about Alice, but that "saloonists and lewd women camped near Longs Peak and named mountains."

Guesses about the identity of Alice proliferate. One piece of gossip was preserved for posterity by the Reverand Elkanah Lamb in his *Miscellaneous Meditations* (1912):

> On Dunraven's last visit to the Park, he was accompanied by his inamorata, who was registered at Stetson's hotel, Mr. Stetson being the proprietor of the English Hotel at that time, as Mrs. Alice Munroe, the celebrated actress from London, England, Dunraven presuming on American stupidity and credulity to hide the true facts of their connection.

Al Birch of the *Denver Post* in 1916 elaborated on the gossip by writing that the Lord, with his companion, was ejected from his own hotel because of boisterous behavior. Marshall Sprague (*Gallery of Dudes,* 1966) dismisses the gossip as "pattern folklore," but it does tie in with Bethel's objection to "saloonists and lewd women," if one can imagine the Earl of Dunraven, member of the House of Lords, labeled a "saloonist."

Many people theorize about Alice Roosevelt Longworth, daughter of President Theodore Roosevelt. She was America's darling around the turn of the century. But Mrs. Longworth herself wrote (November 26, 1971), "I have never heard of Mount Alice and I don't think it could have been named for me."

A romantic theory is that the mountain was named for the childhood sweetheart of Elkanah Lamb, Longs Peak's first guide. (See Lambs Slide.) Eleanor James Hondius of Elkhorn Lodge was irritated when Parson Lamb, in the presence of his second hard-working and faithful wife, referred frequently to this girl he left behind in Indiana as the one great love of his life. Lamb wrote in his memoirs that this early affair of the heart left "a shadow over my life which more than 50 years cannot efface." Such undying devotion could well have been memorialized by Elkanah Lamb, who was early in that part of the Longs Peak area from which Mount Alice is most conspicuous. The two catches in this logic are: (a) One who talked about the girl so often would surely have climaxed his story by pointing to the mountain he named after her; (b) No one knows the girl's name.

A favorite local candidate (but impossible) is Mrs. Kirkwood, mother of the Hewes boys of Hewes-Kirkwood Inn; impossible because (1) the name on the mountain pre-dates her advent into the Park region; and (2) her name was Mary Caroline Palmer Hewes Kirkwood.

Allens Park   WILD BASIN
In 1859 Alonzo Nelson Allen came to Colorado. He established his family in Burlington, a plains town on the St. Vrain River. While Mrs. Allen ran a stage station, her husband prospected all the way from the Dakotas to southwestern Colorado. In 1871, during one of his visits home, he helped move the hotel, along with the rest of the town of Burlington, from its original site to a new location two miles north (present Longmont).

During his first siege of mining fever, Alonzo Allen prospected in the hills around Allens Park, but his few prospect holes were disappointing. He stayed long enough to build, in 1864, a cabin about two miles east of the present town of Allenspark (the post office is spelled as one word) and helped blaze a trail from his park to Ward. The cabin's fireplace still stands on the north side of Colorado 7. This name—Allens Park—is the only one on the 1961 Rocky Mountain National Park map that dates from the gold rush days of the 1860s.

Alpine Brook   GLACIER GORGE

Andrews Creek, Glacier, Pass, Tarn—GLACIER GORGE, GRAND LAKE
Edwin B. Andrews was the widower of Abner Sprague's wife's sister. In 1897 Sprague and Andrews climbed to the glacier hanging from the Continental Divide at the head of Loch Vale. Because of this feat, but more because Andrews was one of the area's best fishermen, Sprague named the glacier. By association, nearby features bear the Andrews name.

Andrews Peak (12,565')   GRAND LAKE
This peak, which stands about three miles from Andrews Pass, was definitely not named for Edwin B. Andrews. Abner Sprague in 1915 and Edwin B. Andrews himself in 1936 both disclaimed any connection. This was after the 1915 Longs Peak quad map appeared with Andrews Peak labeled. The name was approved by the U.S. Board on Geographic Names in 1932.

Then who was this other Andrews? A likely candidate is Darwin M. Andrews, the founder of the Rockmont Nursery in Boulder, where gardeners secured mountain plants. From 1893 Andrews botanized, sending specimens to famous botanist Aven Nelson for identification. Andrews's reputation as a professional photographer led him to offer photographs as dues to the Colorado Mountain Club. Although this Andrews's name would grace a mountain, his son Philip in 1965 averred he had never heard that it did. (See Arapaho Glacier.)

Apache Peak (13,441')   INDIAN PEAKS
The word may mean "knife-whetters" or "enemies," for the various branches of Apache Indians were indeed enemies of the encroaching white men. They produced leaders like Cochise, Victorio, and the great

Geronimo. Ellsworth Bethel in 1914 proposed Apache as one of the Indian peak names.

On various maps Apache Peak and Mount George have exchanged places several times. The U.S. Geological Survey, on March 6, 1961, finally fastened Apache securely to the higher peak, the one on the Continental Divide, with Mount George to the southwest.

Apiatan Mountain—Six miles west of Grand Lake

Apiatan, a Kiowa chief, had earned the right to carry the feathered wooden ceremonial lance called an *apiatan*. In 1890, because of his standing, his tribe sent him to Nevada to investigate a new religion which was spreading through the western tribes. A Paiute Indian there was prophesying that the earth would be restored to the Indians, that the buffalo would come back, and that the dead would be resurrected if all Indians joined in the Ghost Dance. Apiatan's son had recently died, but the Paiute, Wovaka, was unable to help Apiatan communicate with the dead boy. Disillusioned with Wovaka and the Ghost Dance, Apiatan returned to his tribe. The Kiowas turned to the religion known as the Native American Religion which makes use of peyote to induce dreams of happier times.

When Apiatan was an old man, head chief of the Kiowas, his cousin, Hiamovi of the Cheyennes, brought a white woman named Natalie Curtis to see him. For her he sang the oldest songs of his tribe. Recorded in written music, they were published in 1908 in a book called *The Indian's Book.* When Harriet Vaille was looking for Indian names for mountains, she must have studied it. No other source has been found for names of two Colorado peaks—Apiatan and Hiamovi.

Arapaho Bay   LAKE GRANBY

Arapaho Indians left their names on Colorado scenery, like glaciers, passes, and peaks; on a Colorado county and a national forest; on streets in various Colorado towns; and most recently on Arapaho Bay on Lake Granby. The Arapahos were typical Plains Indians, depending for their life on the buffalo, and friendly enough to white men until they realized the whites were taking away their livelihood. The Arapahos considered places like Estes Park on the eastern slope of the northern Colorado Rockies their personal hunting ground, but stepped over the divide into Middle Park when they wanted better hunting or a small war, usually with Ute Indians, the tribe that belonged to the western mountains of Colorado.

After the white men came, the Arapahos divided into three sections. One was the Gros Ventre of the prairies on the Milk River in Montana; one was the Southern Arapahos on the Canadian River in Oklahoma. In between, in Wyoming, the third group settled in 1874 on the Wind River Reservation next to their traditional enemies, the Shoshones. These Northern Arapahos (presently numbering about 2,200) are considered the mother tribe because they hold the sacred objects of the Arapaho nation, including a pipe whose smoke acts like truth serum.

Etymologically, the word Arapaho presents problems both in its derivation and meaning, even to the Arapaho people themselves. They call their nation *Inunaina* (our people). A chief of the Southern Arapahos in 1897 said that he did not know the meaning of the word Arapaho but he did know it was a white man's word. One proof of white origin lies in the lack of the letter "r" in the Arapaho language; early Arapaho Indians pronounced the word N'appaho. If it is a white man's word, could it be derived from *arrapo* or *harapo,* two Spanish words meaning rag or tatter?

Both the Pawnees and Crows used names for the Arapaho Indians that resemble Arapaho in sound, and have different meanings. The Pawnees said *Tirapihu,* or *Harapihu,* meaning traders, which the Arapaho people were. The Crow word means "lots of tattoos"; the Arapaho Indians often tattooed scattered designs over their breasts. In sign language, the *lingua franca* of the plains, the speaker touched his breast in various places to indicate Arapahos.

Another problem connected with the word Arapaho is its spelling. Arapaho or Arapahoe? The old way was usually with the "e," although in 1847 G. F. Ruxton, an English army officer traveling in the West, wrote Arapaho, with an accent. The sovereign state of Colorado still uses the "e" in Arapahoe County, and Denver has an Arapahoe Street. The U.S. Board on Geographic Names, in its 1920-23 report, officially dropped the "e." Both the geological survey and the forest service have heeded the edict, though not always happily. When the rule was first enforced, one of the Arapaho National Forest Service men complained that people in his district thought he could not spell!

The plural spelling presents an additional problem: potatoes—Arapahoes; solos—Arapahos. The U.S. Board on Geographic Names recommends simplicity.

Arapaho Creek   INDIAN PEAKS, LAKE GRANBY

When Monarch Lake was constructed, the names of the two largest creeks that flowed into it were the East Fork and the South Fork of the Grand River. Below the lake, the stream that ran eight miles to the river was the South Fork. Now all the names have changed.

The river is the Colorado, the East Fork is Buchanan Creek, and the South Fork, even the half-mile remnant of the stream between Monarch Lake and Lake Granby, is Arapaho Creek.

Arapaho Glacier   INDIAN PEAKS

Dates are important in discussing Arapaho Glacier.

1897—Darwin M. Andrews (see Andrews Peak) was botanizing on the east side of Arapaho Pass with his brother-in-law, H. N. Wheeler. They noted a large snowbank, and the more they looked at it the more convinced they became that it was a glacier. This they reported to Junius Henderson of the University of Colorado.

1900—Willis T. Lee's description of Arapaho Glacier, written for the *Journal of Geology* on the basis of observations made on August 4, 1900, caused almost as much excitement in glacialogical circles as the discovery of Hallett Glacier in 1884 (see Rowe Glacier). In the *Denver Post* of September 16, 1900, Arnold Emch reported his recognition of the glacier on his September 3rd climb of North Arapaho Peak. Also, in 1900 Eben Fine of Boulder declared he discovered Arapaho Glacier.

1903—When H. N. Wheeler took lantern slides of Arapaho Glacier he carefully stated that this was a return trip, his first having been made in 1897.

1903-1912—Junius Henderson made annual measurements of the movement and shrinkage of Arapaho Glacier.

1919—Junius Henderson discovered the glacial characteristics of the ice bank north of Arapaho Glacier, which was named Henderson Glacier, though it is not named on the 1958 quad map.

This Junius Henderson (1865-1937) was a delightful lawyer-scientist of Boulder, called "Judge" by his friends because he was county judge while teaching part-time in the Law School of the University of Colorado. Gradually he gave up the practice of law for enthusiastic activities in the field of natural history. He was the first curator (without pay) of the natural science museum, now housed in the Henderson Building. First a teacher of paleontology, then, from 1909, professor of natural history, he contributed to magazines both popular and technical. He helped discover and name Fair and Isabelle glaciers in 1910. He worked on the Colorado Geological Survey with R. D. George—perhaps he named Mount George? Henderson's book, *Extinct and Existing Glaciers of Colorado,* published in 1910, is still the definitive work. In 1964 the University of Colorado published a definitive study on Arapaho Glacier, by Henry A. Waldrop. Laymen as well as scientists were excited about Arapaho Glacier. Boulder County and the U.S. Forest Service planned to build a road to the southern edge of Arapaho Glacier, continuing it with a figure-eight trail, equipped with hostels, which would cross the Continental Divide at Arapaho, Pawnee, and Buchanan passes. After national publicity and the appropriation of $56,000 from the forest service, the Maxwell Road was built as far as Rainbow Lakes in 1924. Then lack of funds canceled the project, but the city of Boulder is known as the "Gateway to the Glaciers," and is the only city in America, according to its Chamber of Commerce, that drinks glacial water.

Arapaho National Forest   INDIAN PEAKS
This forest was established by Theodore Roosevelt on July 1, 1908. Its acres—over a million—include lands adjacent to the Rocky Mountain

National Park on the west and southwest. In 1925 the forest service and the Park tried to bring the Arapaho Glacier region within the Park boundaries, just as the original bill had provided. The Boulder Chamber of Commerce voted against the annexation. In 1971, spurred by a new popular enthusiasm, Colorado congressmen introduced a bill to make the Indian Peaks a wilderness area. Now Boulder actively backs the measure.

Arapaho Pass (11,906')   INDIAN PEAKS
In 1904 the Colorado legislature appropriated $5,000 to turn the Arapaho Pass trail into a road. All the money was spent on the east side; on the 1915 Longs Peak quad this was still labeled a secondary road, but now it is only a broad trail.

Atop the windy pass, the traveler must choose between two trails which lead down the Western Slope on either side of Satanta Peak. One goes west, past Lake Dorothy, then utilizes a cut in the scree slope that was obviously the beginning of a road at one time. This was Grand County's effort to live up to its agreement to build a road on the west side of Arapaho Pass. For years a trail (relocated in 1922) followed its proposed route down to the old roads made by lumbermen when miles of wooden flumes scooted logs down to Sawmill Meadow.

The other trail from Arapaho Pass plunges north to Caribou Lake. The traveler, eyeing the switchbacks, thinks twice before he starts zig-zagging down. Once he enters the timber, he follows Arapaho Creek for miles and miles to Monarch Lake.

Old-timers claim the Indians used Arapaho Pass. One wonders which route they chose, and by which route Gordon and McHenry, two road builders of the 1860s, planned to have their road descend the Western Slope. Theirs was to be a military road connecting Boulder City and Middle Park. Proceeding via Sunshine and Four Mile canyons, it actually ended in the valley of North Boulder Creek.

Arapaho Peaks: North Arapaho Peak (13,502'); **South Arapaho Peak** (13,397')—INDIAN PEAKS
Who named the Arapaho Peaks, and when? No one seems to know. Certainly the German W. E. Andree and his two Hungarian companions, prospectors, who climbed one of them in July 1861 did not name them— they thought they were on Longs Peak!

The Arapahos had at least one other name. On Case's map of Colorado Territory, dated 1862, the name for the mountain at the head of Boulder Creek appears as Mount Edmunds. On June 21, 1862, a reporter for the *Rocky Mountain News* wrote that Surveyor Francis Case had, in his handsome office in Denver, a crayon sketch of Mount Edmunds, "painted by the General [Case] in his artistic manner and the mountain christened by him in honor of his friend, Edmunds, commissioner of the General

Land Office in Washington." One suspects that Commissioner Edmunds recommended Case to President Lincoln for the job of territorial surveyor of Colorado, and therefore naming the mountain was paying a political debt. Mount Edmunds appeared on the Pierce map of 1863, on Colton's 1872 and 1874 maps and Clarence King's atlas of 1876.

But F. V. Hayden, surveyor of western territories, stated that the name Arapaho for this mountain was in common use before 1873, and used it in his 1877 atlas. Thayer's map of Colorado used Arapaho in 1873. Since then it has remained on the peaks, sometimes spelled differently, and now used in the plural. Unsolved is the problem of who named the Arapaho Peaks and when.

Arch Rocks   FOREST CANYON
Below the Pool on the Fern Lake Trail are these arching rocks, probably named by the guests of nearby hotels, such as Fern Lake Lodge or the Brinwood.

Arikaree Peak (13,150')   INDIAN PEAKS
The Arikaree tribe now lives in North Dakota near Fort Berthold. The name means "horn," used because Arikaree men wound their hair around two pieces of bone on either side of their heads. The U.S. Board of Geographic Names gave official sanction to Arikaree Peak in October 1914, when it was suggested by the Colorado Geographic Board at the request of Ellsworth Bethel. However, the name had been used for some time before this in a collective sense. Before each of the summits in the snowy range north of the Arapahos was given a distinctive name, Coloradans referred to them all as the Arikarees. (Some old-timers still do.)

Arrowhead   GLACIER GORGE
This and Spearhead, on the opposite side of Glacier Gorge, were named at the same time by the Colorado Geographic Board, approved by Washington in 1916. The shape of the arrowhead on this mountain is especially obvious on a contour map.

Arrowhead Lake   FOREST CANYON
This, the largest of the Gorge Lakes, looks from Trail Ridge Road as if it might slope downhill; seen from the cliffs of Mount Ida its shape resembles a large arrowhead. The name was suggested by Dr. W. J. Workman of Fern Lake Lodge or by Julian Hayden. (See Gorge Lakes.)

The shape of the arrowhead would have been considerably altered if the sixty-foot dam started by Henry Heinricy of Loveland had raised the level of the lake fifteen feet, as he hoped. Heinricy planned a fishing resort at this out-of-the-way lake and was ready to file on water rights when the establishment of Rocky Mountain National Park in 1915 ended his venture.

Aspen Brook   Estes Park
The aspen tree's Latin name *Populus tremuloides* means a poplar that trembles. The leaves shake in the slightest breeze because their flat stems are set at right angles to the leaves. Nicknamed "popples" by Wisconsin lumbermen, westerners call them quaking aspens, or simply quakers.

Aspens tend to sprout following a fire, hurrying to cover the unsightly burn. (See Butterfly Burn.) On poor soil they grow scrubby and deformed and their boles are yellowish; on good soil they grow tall and straight. Their trunks, covered with white powder, have almost as many modulations of white as Chinese porcelain. Aspen groves arrange themselves on open hillsides in patterns. In winter they look like smoke against the snow. When the miniature leaves first show in the spring, the effect is yellow-green; all summer they provide a fresh contrast to the dark conifers, then blaze into gold in the fall. Botanists still puzzle as to why most aspen leaves turn yellow, others rose or red.

On white aspen trunks animals record that they have passed this way. Look for scratches left by bears who sharpen their claws on aspen trunks higher than you think they possibly could be—even a small bear can stretch and climb. Aspen boles that are black toward the bottom, like those in Horseshoe Park, show that wintering elk have nibbled the bark. Wherever aspens grow near streams, beavers leave signs. They leave pointed stumps where they have felled aspens with their sharp incisors, and paths through the forest where they have dragged logs to the water to use for food or dams or houses.

Audubon, Mount (13,223')   Indian Peaks
John James Audubon (1780-1851) painted pictures of hundreds of birds and of many wild animals. His prints still rank high as nature portraits, and are priced even higher as collectors' items. Audubon was born in Haiti, lived in France, Kentucky, Louisiana, England, New York City, and is buried in that town's Trinity Churchyard.

Although Audubon never came to Colorado, two of his admirers did. Dr. C. C. Parry, botanist, and Dr. J. W. Velie, zoologist, arrived in Denver on June 2, 1864, were shocked at the devastation of the Cherry Creek flood, then proceeded to the mountains of the northern Front Range to botanize. (In August they joined William Byers in an attempt to climb Longs Peak.) Camping a few days west of the present town of Ward, Parry reported that they observed a "smooth rounded peak" which they climbed despite deep snow, "supposing it was Mount Edmonds." (See Arapaho Peaks.) "At the suggestion of my companion, Dr. J. W. Velie, we concluded to affix to this well-marked elevation the name of the distinguished naturalist, Audubon."

In 1914, Ellsworth Bethel must have been torn between his admiration for Audubon and his systematic scheme to label with Indian names all the peaks between the Arapahos and Longs. The naturalist won out.

Bethel recommended the retention of Audubon, named fifty years before, even though it did stand right in the middle of the Indian Peaks.

Azure Lake   FOREST CANYON
Named by Dr. W. J. Workman in color contrast to Inkwell Lake just below it. (See Gorge Lakes.)

Baker Gulch, Pass; Baker Mountain (12,397')   NEVER SUMMER
Two distinctive peaks finish off the southern end of the Never Summer Mountains—Bowen and Baker. Grand Lake people link their names together—Bowen 'n Baker—just as mountain climbers say Grazentorreys for two peaks near Georgetown.

John R. Baker, from Indiana, grizzled mountain man, trapper, explorer, adventuresome climber, was the first person to reach the top of Baker Mountain, probably in the summer of 1875 when he and the charming twenty-two-year-old Kentuckian, Charles Royer, found a mine on its slope and filed a claim. The September before, Baker had been elected sheriff of newly organized Grand County. Its only precinct stretched from the Front Range to the Utah line. The election at Hot Sulphur Springs drew twenty-five votes from perhaps ninety adult males entitled to vote.

Later, Baker with a partner named Bartholomew bought the meadowland east of Baker Gulch from a Mr. Hartzell, a sawmill operator. They called it Green Mountain Ranch, a name still in use in 1972 when the Carl Nelsons, owners since 1934, held out for more than a million dollars for the property. In January 1972 the National Park paid them the million, and William Mekeel, the Park's lawyer, paid them an extra dollar (his own) artfully framed.

In 1878, Mary Jane Young, known as "a little dancing gypsy," brought her two children to visit Grandpa Baker. She homesteaded the choicest land on Grand Lake, later called Craigs Point. In 1881, her neighbors held a house-raising party for the widow-woman. In one day they erected Fair View Hotel for her. A bronze marker now stands near the site of this hostelry because here, on July 4, 1883, four men killed each other in a political squabble.

South of Baker Mountain is Baker Gulch, notable as the upper terminal of the Grand Ditch, and for its snowslides. In 1881 three men met the white death in Baker Gulch; a fourth lay beneath the snow for twenty-four hours before he was rescued alive. On December 14 of the next winter,

Jules Harmon (he of the exquisite handwriting as county clerk), manager of the Hidden Treasure Mine, died under the snow, aged thirty.

Battle Mountain (12,044')   GLACIER GORGE
The keen eye of naturalist Enos Mills noted the effects of wind and snow and fire on this mountain, and named it after the battles of nature. For the same reason, he named nearby Storm Peak. Abner Sprague stated that the fire on Battle Mountain, the effects of which are still obvious today, occurred before he came to the area in 1875.

Bear Lake   GLACIER GORGE
Horace Ferguson, early rancher, saw a bear at this lake and, because very few bears frequent the area, he named the lake after the bear. No grizzly bears live in Rocky Mountain National Park now, so Ferguson's bear probably was a black bear, a deceptive name because black bears may be colored cinnamon brown or blonde. When down on all fours these bears stand about three feet high, may weigh up to five hundred pounds. They live on their fat in the winter, hibernating lightly. The cubs are tiny, weighing less than a pound at birth. Twin cubs playing in the springtime are charming to watch, but the mother bears guarding them are unpredictable and can be vicious.

Beaver Creek—NEVER SUMMER; **Beaver Brook, Meadows, Point**—
ESTES PARK; **Beaver Mountain** (10,491')—FOREST CANYON
Beavers do not live on mountains, so this mountain indubitably derives its name by association with Beaver Brook. The same hill was once called Brinwood Mountain, named for Brinton Woodward, chancellor of the University of Kansas in 1893, who owned land at its base.
The beaver is the largest rodent in the Park. He works at night, and may sometimes be seen in the twilight hours. The sound of his flat tail hitting the water as he dives is unmistakable. Evidence of his presence is in every aspen grove near water, where one may see pointed aspen stumps, felled aspen trees, trails where he dragged logs to water, dammed-up streams, and beaver huts in the ponds made by his dams.

Bench Lake   GLACIER GORGE
This early named lake lies on a bench, or shelf, on the side of a mountain. Such lakes on shelves left by glaciers are known to geologists as hanging lakes.

Bench Lake   GRAND LAKE
Located about five and a half miles up the North Inlet Trail from Grand Lake, then about one mile north of the North Inlet Trail at an altitude of about 10,200 feet.

Bennett Creek   NEVER SUMMER

Joe Bennett grazed cattle in this territory, trailing them up Long Draw from the Poudre.

Bierstadt Lake, Moraine   ESTES PARK, GLACIER GORGE

Bierstadt was suggested as a name for this moraine by the Colorado Geographic Board in 1914, officially accepted in 1961; but Bierstadt Lake was named fifty years before.

The Earl of Dunraven was never content with the small or second-rate. He wanted all of Estes Park as his hunting preserve, and he wanted the hotel he built for his friends to have the best possible view of Longs Peak. To pick the site he imported one of America's top artists, Albert Bierstadt (1830-1902), renowned for his romantic interpretations of western scenery covering square yards of canvas. Bierstadt made periodic trips west for inspiration, his first in 1858 with surveyors in Wyoming. In December 1876, Lord Dunraven brought him to Estes Park, and the artist returned the next summer. The Earl's number one factotum, Theodore Whyte, drove Bierstadt around the park behind a matched four-in-hand, and named a lake admired by the artist for the artist. Abner Sprague gave Whyte the credit for thus naming Bierstadt Lake.

Though Bierstadt admired the lake that bears his name, it was not here that he chose the perfect site for Lord Dunraven's hotel. For this he merely corroborated the taste of Joel Estes and Griff Evans, recommending the hotel be built a little south of their cabins. Back in Philadelphia, Bierstadt executed a large oil painting of Longs Peak, for which the Earl is said to have paid $15,000. Shipped to Ireland, the canvas hung in Dunraven Castle to remind the Earl of the rugged American pioneers who thwarted his plans for an American hunting preserve. (See Mount Dunraven.)

When the Denver Public Library moved into its new building in 1956, Roger Mead, contractor for the structure, presented the Bierstadt painting of Longs Peak to the library. With a simpler frame replacing the carved gilt original, Bierstadt's magnificent canvas now hangs in the Western History Room of the library, from whose northern windows Longs Peak itself is visible.

Big Meadows   GRAND LAKE

Early literature of the Park describes the western descent from Flattop to Grand Lake via the Big Meadows. The 1914 Arapaho name was Tonahutu—meaning Big Meadows.

Big Owl Road   WILD BASIN

Charles Edwin Hewes published a verse in 1922 telling of the "Big Owl of Big Owl Hill." As an introduction to the poem he wrote:

The Big Owl of Big Owl Hill is a subject both interesting and romantic to the dwellers of the Vale of Elkanah. It was discovered, as the poem describes, in 1907, by the Poet himself, on the afternoon of an early fall day as he was locating his homestead in the south end of the Vale; which tract, however, did not include the Big Owl's domain, but which locality was subsequently patented as a homestead by Miss Katherine Garetson.

It is believed at this writing, 1921, there are at least two pairs of these birds in the Vale, their species being the western horned owl, large magnificent nocturnal fowl whose low soft notes are the invariable accompaniment of every quiet evening.

Big Thompson River—ESTES PARK, FOREST CANYON, MUMMY RANGE
The 1914 Arapahos called this the "Pipe River," because they sat on its shore to carve pipes out of stone they probably had brought with them from some other place.

Many theories surround the name Thompson, the one provable fact being that it dates back to the 1830s when fur traders left written records using the name. The most likely tale seems to be that the river was named for Philip Thompson who was trading mules at Fort Vasquez in the 1830s. He was, however, more intimately connected with Browns Hole, in the northwest corner of the state.

Another story, quite elaborate, tells that a man named Thompson was killed by Indians on this river. He was a big man with a small brother—hence Big and Little Thompson. Another theory is that the name honors David Thompson of the Northwest Fur Company, though he probably never came this far south.

Bighorn Creek—ESTES PARK, MUMMY RANGE; **Bighorn Lake**—NEVER SUMMER

Bighorn Flats   FOREST CANYON, GRAND LAKE
This great expanse of high country north of Flattop Mountain offers good grazing to bighorn sheep. The flats are part of a geological peneplain. (See Flattop Mountain.) When Indians wanted to cross from Bear Lake to the Kawuneeche Valley, they climbed to the divide, then angled northwest across these Bighorn Flats. The trail they made is now crossed by a ditch built to collect water from this rolling plain. It empties into Spruce Canyon. Henry J. Heinricy of Loveland constructed this ditch in 1902 with $2,000 he secured from Greeley men when Loveland men were not interested. Later the city of Loveland bought the ditch and its water rights for more than $2,000.

Bighorn Mountain (11,463')   MUMMY RANGE
Sprague states that Pieter Hondius named this mountain. (See Hondius Park.) It may have been called Dome Rock earlier. Bighorn

sheep, sometimes called Rocky Mountain sheep, are the world's most skillful mountaineers. The lambs start rock climbing before they are a week old. The rams grow powerful curved horns with which they battle for their harems. Racing at each other, they leap into the air for the final impact, which sometimes can be heard a mile away. Listen for it in November during the mating season. This splendid creature, chosen for the symbol of the Colorado Mountain Club in 1912, has recently become the official state animal of Colorado.

Abner Sprague wrote that bighorns were decimated by scabies about 1878. Recently bands of bighorns have been observed in the Park area. (See Rams Horn Mountain.)

Black Canyon, Black Canyon Creek　　　　MUMMY RANGE

Black this canyon looks with its steep sides and thick timber. The name was probably used even before the MacGregor family settled there. Later F. V. Hayden noted that "from a black gorge, Black Canyon Creek brings water," the present water supply of the village of Estes Park.

Black Lake　　　　GLACIER GORGE

The Glacier Gorge Lakes (not to be confused with the Gorge Lakes) bear the names of colors—Black, Blue, and Green. They appear as early as Enos Mills's 1905 map.

Black Pool　　　　FOREST CANYON

Blue Lake—GLACIER GORGE; **Blue Lake**—INDIAN PEAKS

Bluebird Lake　　　　WILD BASIN

Two kinds of bluebirds summer in the Park region, the western bluebird and the mountain bluebird. The western bluebird usually nests in holes in dead ponderosa pines. Like its eastern cousin, it has a reddish breast and blue wings, but it also has red on its back; sometimes it is called the chestnut-backed bluebird.

The mountain bluebird nests in the lower meadows of the Park and in burned areas near timberline. After the young leave home, usually in early August, the birds migrate vertically to meadows above timberline where they flash their true blue for a few weeks, then descend to the plains to migrate horizontally south.

In 1908 William Cooper named various lakes after birds. He wrote, "I found ouzel already named and it occurred to me that it would be appropriate to give names of Alpine birds to the others of the headwaters of Ouzel Creek." Walking upstream from Ouzel Lake, already named by Enos Mills, Cooper named the next lake Ptarmigan, the small pond higher up he called Bluebird, and the highest Pipit Lake. On their 1915 map the U.S. geological surveyors changed Ptarmigan to Bluebird, ignored the pond, and retained Pipit; in 1961 they named Lark Pond.

Bluebird Lake had a name before Cooper went to Wild Basin-Arbuckle Reservoir #2. Frank P. Arbuckle was a Denver man, prominent in business and in the Democratic Party, who also owned a ranch six or seven miles above Lyons on the North St. Vrain River. (His death in New York in 1896 made the front page of the *New York Times* not only because of his importance but because of the unanswered question—was he murdered?) At his death his widow, Emma, ran a resort on the St. Vrain ranch until 1903 when, according to the *Lyons Recorder,* William A. Welch became the new owner of the "Arbuckle summer resort, known as the Dale St. Vrain."

In 1902 Mrs. Arbuckle, searching for water after a dry summer, her twenty-four-year-old son, Frank, and the caretaker of her ranch, Jabez Billings, filed on five reservoirs in Wild Basin and started to build dams on two of them. Within two years they sold out to a group of Longmont businessmen organized as the Arbuckle Reservoir Company. In 1933 the Reservoir Company sold its rights in these reservoirs and in another Wild Basin reservoir (Sandbeach Lake) to the city of Longmont for $92,000. To this day Longmont city officials refer to Bluebird, Pear, and Sandbeach as the "three Arbuckles."

Of the original five Arbuckle filings, Pear Reservoir and Bluebird Lake are the only two on which dams were built in 1902. Between 1912 and 1919 the Arbuckle Reservoir Company constructed a larger dam on Bluebird Lake. Rolley Neely, one of the rodmen on the survey, recalled details of that late summer job. The men packed in with two mules, their bread on the lead mule; arrived in camp they found no bread. The second mule, following closely, had eaten every bit. The rodmen threw together a raft of sorts to measure the depth of the lake. The engineer in charge declined to board but the two boys put to sea, their soundings showing a depth of fifty feet in one place. For triangulation points the party used Ouzel Lake, which they called Lily Lake; Mahana Peak; and "a mountain to the south." The country was so rough Neely wore out three pairs of shoes in eight days, and came out in a September blizzard with wet, cold feet.

The next summer, 1914, the construction of the dam started, accompanied by problems in transportation. The reinforcing steel was chained in bundles to the axle beam between two wagon wheels, one end left dragging on the ground. The driver balanced on the axle and urged four straining horses up the narrow trail. Donkeys packed sacks of cement to Bluebird Lake, but no sand was there to mix with it. Plenty of granite—mountains of granite. The contractor undertook to make sand out of granite. Three days the men worked to take a rock-crusher apart, load it on mules, drive the mules to camp, and reassemble the crusher. For power they used an old automobile engine packed in the same way. Cal Maier of Longmont, water commissioner since 1934, recalled in 1965 that "the granite was not very fine, not much cement, but for 40 years the dam held together pretty good."

Boulder Brook, Field   GLACIER GORGE

The Boulder Field, the famous hazard on Longs Peak, marks the end
of the horse trail now as it did in 1873 when Isabella Bird rode "as far as
what, rightly or wrongly, are called the 'Lava Beds,' an expanse of large
and small boulders, with snow in their crevices." William Byers called the
Boulder Field "a rocky plain tilted upward," and in the late 1880s F. H.
Chapin wrote, "On this Boulder Field, covering perhaps a hundred acres,
are strewn great slabs of granite—some as much as 20 feet in width and
30 feet in length—and between them are heaped boulders, great and
small." Whatever he calls it, the climber on the Boulder Field of Longs
Peak prays for balance as he leaps from rock to shifting rock, and is tan-
talized by water running beneath the boulders far out of reach.

Boulder-Grand Pass   GRAND LAKE, WILD BASIN

The name refers to the counties joined by the pass. Jack Moomaw
proves his theory that Indians used the pass by showing various kinds of
rocks he picked up on the pass which are not indigenous to the area. Who
else but Indians would have imported them?

Bowen Gulch; Bowen Mountain (12,154')—Two miles south of
Baker Mountain

Because a county clerk had poor handwriting this mountain is called
Bowen instead of Bourn. James H. Bourn arrived in Denver June 4, 1874,
from Missouri, with his twin sister, Mrs. James H. Crawford, and her husband. The Crawfords settled down to found the town of Steamboat
Springs, but not twenty-five-year-old Jim. He was what his brother-in-law
called "a sport." In Middle Park he hunted and fished and raced his
horses against Indian ponies, winning buckskin. He prospected. His
Wolverine Claim, discovered in 1875, lay far up Bourn Mountain. He
moved on—to New Mexico, to California, to British Columbia, and,
finally, to Northfield, Minnesota, near iron mines.

Box Canyon   NEVER SUMMER

Many canyons in the Rockies bear this name. Visitors feel that the
stream is so boxed in by cliffs that neither they nor the water will ever
find an exit.

Box Lake   WILD BASIN

Jack Moomaw called this Pit Lake, but Henry Hutcheson filed on it as
Box Lake. He planned to drain Eagle Lake by a tunnel into Box Lake, so
he could claim the water rights. A tunnel was started, dug perhaps forty
feet, but never finished.

Bridal Veil Falls (9,062')   MUMMY RANGE

Bryant, Mount (11,034')   GRAND LAKE, LAKE GRANBY
Grand Lake summer people suggested the name Mount Commodore
for this peak, but the Colorado Geographic Board preferred Mount
Bryant. The two names refer to the same man—Commodore William H.
(Harry) Bryant, a lawyer and graduate of the University of Virginia, who
lived in Denver but summered at Grand Lake. Why the nautical title, two
thousand miles from an ocean? Because Bryant was the first Commodore of the Grand Lake Yacht Club, the highest (according to the
local Chamber of Commerce) yacht club in the world. Organized in 1901,
it held its first race the next year. Harry Bryant, in a flat-bottomed scow,
raced Richard Crawford Campbell in a rowboat, both crafts being rigged
with sails.
In 1912 the Grand Lake Yacht Club built its club house on the north
shore of Grand Lake on land donated by J. N. Pettingell. (See Pettingell
Lake.) Sir Thomas Lipton gave a $1,500 silver loving cup, which is still
passed around to the winner of the yacht races held during the August
Regatta Week. The modern skipper must cope not only with the vagaries
of mountain breezes but with the hazards of high-powered motor boats, a
contingency undreamed of by Commodore Harry Bryant in his flatbot-
tomed scow. Mrs. Bryant was the daughter of Governor Routt, and Mrs.
Routt was the sister-in-law of Bayard Craig. So one family of summer cottagers has three names on the map—Mount Bryant, Routt National Forest, and Mount Craig.

Buchanan Creek, Pass   INDIAN PEAKS
The name of the pass is usually credited to James Buchanan, who
defeated Fremont to become the pre-Civil War President of the United
States. If this is true (but we have found no documentation to prove it) the
name is more relevant than most political names on western maps
because Buchanan was the president who signed the bill creating Colo-
rado Territory on February 28, 1861. Yet early maps of Colorado, even
Hayden's 1877 atlas, do not name this pass at all.
On March 27, 1881, banker Buckingham of Boulder incorporated the
Boulder, Left Hand, and Middle Park Railroad, sending his surveyor to
the top of Buchanan Pass. (One wonders what that surveyor's name was.
Perhaps Buchanan?) Some sort of trail went over the pass long before the
Colorado State Legislature in 1895 appropriated $10,000 to build a road.
Four years later, having spent $8,900, the state surveyor reported the
route impractical. Then who built the road shown on Nell's maps of Colo-
rado (1899 to 1907), up the Middle St. Vrain and down to the Grand River?
Today only a zigzag trail surmounts the pass, but a road of sorts runs up
the Middle St. Vrain along the floor of the valley called the Vale of
Enchantment by the Stapps of Stapps Lake Lodge, before lumbermen covered it with slash.

Buck Creek—ESTES PARK; **Buck Gulch, Lake—**WILD BASIN
   The historian would like to attribute this name to one of the earliest residents of the Estes area, Hank Farrar, called Buck by Milton Estes, Buckskin by Enos Mills, but doubtless Buck Creek, Gulch, and Lake were named for the male deer. When a buck comes to a lake to drink, the sight of him lifting his antlered head from the water is reason enough to name a lake for him.

Bulwark Ridge (10,890')   MUMMY RANGE
   Ellsworth Bethel found that "Signal, Lookout, and an unnamed peak appear as one long mountain with a palisade aspect, and hence they are sometimes known as the 'Palisades.'" Our Bulwark Ridge?

Butterfly Burn   ESTES PARK
   About 1929 fire destroyed the lodgepole pines that covered this slope of Twin Sisters Peak. Ruth Ashton Nelson, Park naturalist, immediately started a year-after-year ecological study of the burn. Aspens started to grow immediately since their roots had not been killed by fire. In a few years the aspens covered an area shaped like a butterfly, green in summer, yellow in autumn—the Butterfly Burn.

Cabin Creek   WILD BASIN
   According to Joe Mills, who must have heard the tale from Elkanah Lamb, Kit Carson spent a winter (probably in the 1840s) on the eastern slope of Longs Peak, and in the spring bargained with Indians to help him carry out his furs. Parson Lamb pointed out the remains of an old cabin at the foot of Cabin Rock as the Kit Carson cabin. This impressed young Joe Mills, and for his own cabin he selected a location near Cabin Rock. In 1926 Joe Mills recorded in his book, *A Mountain Boyhood,* that "the walls, the hearth, and part of the stone chimney still mark the site of that stone cabin" built by Kit Carson. In 1966 a pile of rocks remains. Cabin Creek is named on the 1882 Township Survey, and subsequent maps; Cabin Rock is located on the 1911 Cooper-Babcock map.

Cache la Poudre River   MUMMY RANGE, NEVER SUMMER
   This name is one of the few of French origin in Colorado, stemming from the French-speaking Creoles of St. Louis. In 1836 fur trappers, caught in an early fall snowstorm, dug a hole beside a stream, not far from present Bellvue, in which they deposited some of their supplies, including

black powder. Carefully they restored the surface of the ground above their cache to its natural look, even burning wood over it—an old Indian trick. The next spring, happily, they found their cache intact. They referred to the river thereafter as the hiding place of the gun powder— "La Cache la Poudre."

Ever since then, innumerable changes have been rung on the spelling and the pronunciation of the name of the river. The most ingenious of many spellings was by L. J. Eastin in his *Emigrant's Guide to Pike's Peak,* published in Leavenworth, Kansas, March 1, 1859. He wrote "Cochela Padre." To the Coloradan, the pronunciation of this name presents no problem. Just call it the "Pooder."

Cairns, Mount   GRAND LAKE

James Cairns came from Canada in 1881 to establish the first store in the village of Grand Lake. When Cairns was the oldest living inhabitant, Abner Sprague named a collection of mountains between the North and East inlets for him—Cairns Mountains. Maps from 1905 used this label, in the plural, until the U.S. Geological Survey in 1915 changed the name to Mount Cairns and confined it to the mountain marked by cliffs rising above the north bank of the East Inlet.

Calypso Cascades   WILD BASIN

In Greek mythology, Calypso was a sea nymph whose charms detained Ulysses on her island for seven years. *Calypso bulbosa* is the Latin name for the charming fairy slipper, one of the twenty-two orchids that have been identified in Colorado. Because he was a botanist, young William Cooper knew and used the name when he surveyed Wild Basin in 1908. He gave the name to the Calypso Cascades on the Cony Creek Trail that runs through a series of large patches of fairy slippers. Usually, the flower-lover is lucky if he sees more than three or four blossoms in one spot.

Cameron Pass   NEVER SUMMER

This pass was named for a peripatetic gentleman of early Colorado, General Robert A. Cameron (1828-1894). "I went to Indiana," he wrote, "when it was a wilderness, and to Chicago when it was a mud hole, and now I want to go to Colorado." This he did in 1870, as vice-president and superintendent of the Union Colony (present Greeley), in charge of greeting and locating colonists. In 1872 he organized an agricultural colony at Fort Collins; and then he became the vice-president of Fountain Colony, now Colorado Springs, where Camerons Cone bears his name. From there he moved to Canon City as warden of Colorado State Penitentiary.

Cameron explored the headwaters of the Poudre River in 1870. The pass was named for him by Union Pacific Railroad surveyors. It first saw use in 1881 as the route of a toll road to Teller City in North Park.

Forty-five years later the automobile road across Cameron Pass was dedicated. Years ago, near the top of the pass, each summer Sunday, services were held in a church with the sky for a roof.

Campers Creek   WILD BASIN

Caribou Lake; Caribou Pass (11,851')   INDIAN PEAKS

Caribou is the name for northern reindeer, but that does not mean that Colorado was ever host to these animals. It was host to a man who had probably seen caribou herds in the North Country. The story is that George Lytle, one of the men who filed on the Caribou Lode in August 1869, said the Middle Boulder Creek country reminded him of the Cariboo Mountains in Alberta Province, Canada, and why not name the mine Cariboo?

It was a lucky name. The Caribou Mine produced silver by the ton. In 1873, when General U. S. Grant visited Central City, he walked from his carriage to the Teller House on a sidewalk paved (for the occasion) with silver bricks from the Caribou Mine. In 1872 a Dutch syndicate (the town of Nederland commemorates their nationality) bought the Caribou for three million dollars and made an enormous profit.

But the Caribou Mine and Caribou town are far to the east of Caribou Lake and Caribou Pass. True, but a trail leads from the town across the Continental Divide and down to Middle Park, called the Caribou Trail. It crosses Arapaho Pass, which sometimes was called Caribou Pass. The 1958 Geological Survey map of the Monarch Lake quad specifies a point as Caribou Pass about a mile and a half northwest of Arapaho Pass, and not on the Continental Divide. (See Arapaho Pass.)

What about the spelling—Cariboo or Caribou? This was settled on June 27, 1871, as reported in the *Central City Register*. The U.S. Post Office Department decided to spell the name Caribou for two reasons: (1) Caribou was the accepted French spelling of the Indian name of the animal, Cariboo being a corruption; (2) Caribou would make a distinction "between two or three Cariboos up north."

Cascade Creek—INDIAN PEAKS, MUMMY RANGE; Cascade Falls— GRAND LAKE; Cascade Lake—ESTES PARK, MUMMY RANGE

Castle Lake, Lakes   WILD BASIN

The rocks on an island in Castle Lake looked like a castle to Ranger Jack Moomaw, who named the small lake; Castle Lakes, less than a mile to the south, are really just ponds.

Castle Rock—FOREST CANYON; Castle Mountain (8,834')—ESTES PARK

Chaos Canyon, Chaos Canyon Cascades   GLACIER GORGE

Located on the east side of the Continental Divide between Hallett Peak and Otis Peak. Sometimes mistaken for the Andrews Glacier area,

Chaos Canyon contains much more difficult terrain due to glacial debris. Though sometimes this canyon is called Otis Gorge, Abner Sprague thought Chaos appropriate because of the jumble of boulders. Chaos Canyon Cascades are located below Lake Haiyaha on Chaos Creek.

Chaos Creek   GLACIER GORGE

Chapin Creek, Pass; Mount Chapin (12,454')   MUMMY RANGE
This mountain is named on Mills's map of 1905. At least three stories tell why the mountain is named Chapin. Dr. Homer James, son of the founders of Elkhorn Lodge, gallantly said he named it for his wife, Jennie Chapin, whom he married in 1905. She and Elizabeth Foote were partners in a small general store in Estes Village.
But his sister, Eleanor Estes James Hondius, heard her mother say:

Mr. Chapin, for whom Mount Chapin was named, was a guest one summer, and occupied one of the little bedrooms. He always kept his window open, and every day a hen would come in through the window and lay an egg on his bed. In those days, eggs were hauled in each week by wagon from the valley; when they arrived, half were broken, and the other half should have been. So Mother kept a few hens at the ranch.
She didn't want Mr. Chapin to know about the hen laying an egg on his bed each day, so she would listen carefully for the hen's cackle, then hastily remove from Mr. Chapin's bed the egg and any feathers the hen might have lost. Each morning Mr. Chapin had a fresh egg for breakfast without ever suspecting where the egg had been laid.

The third and most probable candidate for Mount Chapin stayed at the Highlands, H. W. Ferguson's hotel, in the fall of 1886 and for two succeeding summers. (Perhaps he stayed at the Elkhorn Lodge some other summer, and is the same Chapin as mentioned in Mrs. James's story.) Frederick Hastings Chapin of Hartford, Connecticut, came, with his wife, to climb the Rockies with other members of the Appalachian Mountain Club. W. L. Hallett, a cattleman who had a cottage on Marys Lake near the Highlands, acted as their guide. In 1887 Chapin named Hallett Peak; in 1888, so the story goes, Hallett named Mount Chapin.
Chapin wrote up his Colorado climbs for the magazine of the Appalachian Mountain Club. Collected and enlarged, these were published in book form by the club in 1889, with the title *Mountaineering in Colorado: The Peaks about Estes Park.*

Chasm Falls   MUMMY RANGE
Originally called Horseshoe Falls, these falls on Fall River were renamed by the father of Minnie March Service to avoid confusion with the Horseshoe Falls on Roaring River. The water of Chasm Falls drops

twenty-five feet into a whirlpool where revolving stones are gradually enlarging a pot hole in the canyon floor.

Chasm Lake   GLACIER GORGE, WILD BASIN
Elkanah Lamb thought Chasm Lake occupied the crater of a volcano. "No doubt," he wrote, "this lake occupies the opening caused by internal forces—throwing up and bursting through." Actually the lake lies in a glacial cirque. With the east face of Longs Peak as a background, the name Chasm is appropriate and seems to have been used in pioneer times. Perhaps in 1873 it bore another name—Gold Lake. That year Captain Edward Berthoud, Colorado's engineer after whom Berthoud Pass was named, wrote this tale:

> One lake near Long's Peak is Gold Lake, which is noted, not only for its clear cold water, but is fabled by the Indians and old trappers as the resort of some *lusus naturae,* which the following legend illustrates:
> In Gold Lake, Indian tradition recites that there dwells, in its deep cold waters, an animal but rarely seen. It is described by them as biformal in shape, having a human head, arms and body to the waist, while the rest is the body of a horse. Rarely seen, it approaches the shore only in the evening. The resemblance of this animal is ludicrously like the classical Centaur of the Greeks. . . . Is this an evidence of Indo-Greek tradition revived by a lousy Arapahoe near Long's Peak? or is it tradition repeating itself? We pause!

Chasm View   GLACIER GORGE, WILD BASIN
From this point the climber on the Cable Route can look down, down, down the East Face of Longs Peak to Chasm Lake—definitely a chasm view.

Chickadee Pond   WILD BASIN
This is one of the bird names given to lakes in Wild Basin by W. S. Cooper. The mountain chickadee lives in the northern Rockies all the way to timberline, winter and summer. It is a little thing, grayish, with a black bib and cap, and a white stripe running above each eye. It is friendly, especially around cabins, where it will perch its featherweight on a patient hand offering doughnut crumbs. Along trails and in the forests it chirps its friendly call—chick-a-dee-dee.

Chickaree Lake   GRAND LAKE
Chickarees are the common, chattering tree squirrels of the mountains, sometimes called pine or Fremont squirrels. They are gray with rusty yellow on their back. Small, alert, agile, they run up and down tree trunks in the spruce and fir forests, leap from tree to tree, and chatter incessantly in winter as well as summer. They eat seeds from the cones of

evergreen trees, piling up debris sometimes to a depth of a foot or more. The tuft-ear or Abert's squirrel lives lower than the chickarees in ponderosa pine country.

Squirrels carry their bushy tails high over their backs. This habit was observed by the Greeks; the word squirrel comes, by a circuitous route, from two Greek words that mean shaded rear-end. The way most Americans pronounce the word squirrel is so difficult to imitate that suspected spies are sometimes asked to pronounce it to prove their nationality.

Chiefs Head Peak (13,579')   GLACIER GORGE, WILD BASIN

This name was well established before Cooper used it on his 1911 map, although on the 1910 Burlington map it appears as Mount Barrett. In 1915 Bethel complained that he could not find out who Barrett was, and wanted to call it Comanche Peak. The U.S. Board on Geographic Names refused this request, probably for two reasons: (1) Comanche had already been used for a peak by the 1876 King Survey, northwest of Hagues Peak; (2) they preferred the already established local name, Chiefs Head. The 1914 Arapahos called it Head Mountain since they saw in it the profile of the head of an Indian, complete with war bonnet, just as we see it today. The war bonnet lies to the south, the face has a long forehead, a distinct nose and chin, and even an eye when the snow stays late into the summer. Some imaginative people can see the outline of the chief's body stretching north.

Chipmunk Lake   MUMMY RANGE

The stone walls provided as guard rails by the park service at parking areas on Trail Ridge Road, like Many Parks Curve and Farview Curve, serve as dining tables for little animals and birds who demand handouts from human visitors. Chipmunks and ground squirrels stuff their expandable cheeks with peanuts or bread and whisk off to eat or store them. To tell which is a chipmunk, which a ground squirrel is easy. Chipmunks have stripes on their cheeks, and down the middle and sides of their backs; ground squirrels are larger and have stripes only on their sides. Also chipmunks scurry a bit faster than the larger ground squirrels.

The word chipmunk comes from two Ojibway Indian words meaning headfirst and mouth, the idea being that these little creatures—about six inches long with a five-inch tail—lead with their mouths, which they certainly do when a handout is possible. Chipmunks build long tunnels below the frost line and live in rooms enlarged in the tunnels. One is a bedroom furnished with a grass mattress, others are pantries. Their worst enemy is the weasel, who can insinuate his body into their holes.

Chiquita Creek, Lake; Chiquita Mountain (13,069')—MUMMY RANGE

In 1902 a book was published called *Chiquita, an American Novel: The*

Romance of a Ute Chief's Daughter. It was written by Merrill Tileston (see Mount Tileston), and published by Merrill in Chicago.

The novel reads no better today than in July 1902, when Ellis Meredith, literary reporter for the *Rocky Mountain News,* reviewed it. She headed her article, "This is the place for the Scalping Knife." She even punned on the "B-Uteful Chiquita."

The story tells that Jack, a stalwart American, camped in the White River country of the Utes. Chief Yamanatz had a beautiful daughter, Chiquita, who longed to be educated so that she could help her tribe. When Jack mentioned that a college education cost money, Yamanatz took him to the California desert where they scooped up enough gold from the floor of the Blazing Eye Mine to send Chiquita to an eastern woman's college. She prepared to help her people by studying French, Spanish, German, Russian, Greek, Latin, elocution, and music. Jack married a white girl; Chiquita, home with her tribe, died young. Included in the book are accounts of the Meeker Massacre, a climb of Longs Peak, and a poem commemorating the death of the eccentric New Englander Carrie J. Welton, the first woman to die on Longs Peak.

Enos Mills may have been responsible for naming the mountain after the book. (Maybe he liked the author.) It appears on Mills's 1905 map, which is based on information furnished by Abner Sprague; but Sprague disclaimed naming it.

The mountain might have been named, not for the novel, but for Chipeta, wife of Chief Ouray of the Utes. Her name had variant spellings, such as the Spanish diminutive Chiquita, and Sabeta, a peak in the San Juan Mountains which Henry Gannett stated was named for Ouray's wife.

Cirque Lake   MUMMY RANGE
When glacial ice pulls away from a mountain, it may pull rocks with it, leaving steep walls in the form of an amphitheater, usually with a lake at the bottom. This recess is called a cirque. The Park contains many cirque lakes. The two most noted being Chasm Lake and Iceberg Lake.

Cirrus, Mount (12,797')   NEVER SUMMER
Meteorologically speaking, cirrus is the name for the highest clouds, isolated, feathery, and rather filmy. Four of the peaks in the Never Summer Mountains are named for cloud forms. This pleasant invention was the brain child of James Grafton Rogers who named Mounts Cirrus, Cumulus, and Nimbus in 1914; in August 1921 Roger Toll added Mount Stratus. (See Mount Howard.)

Cleaver, The   GRAND LAKE, WILD BASIN
This marks the termination of the distinctive, slender, granite ridge extending from Isolation Peak. It was named because of its shape by

Phillip Ritterbush and his committee of five of the Park staff who made up names for the 1961 Geological Survey map.

Colorado River   GRAND LAKE, LAKE GRANBY, NEVER SUMMER
   El Rio Colorado—the Ruddy River. Anyone who sees the liquid mud of the Colorado River in Arizona in flood times knows why the Spaniards called it that, although today, thanks to modern dams behind which the river dumps its silt, the water runs clear most of the time. The river had other names. In 1776 Father Escalante spoke of El Rio San Rafael, a name retained on the San Rafael Swell in Utah. To Fremont in 1843 it was the Grand River, but ten years later the Gunnison-Beckwith report called the present Gunnison River the Grand, and said it "joins the Nah-un-kah-rea, or Blue River of the Indians and mountain men, which rises in Middle Park, and is erroneously called Grand River on some of the most correct maps."
   By the 1860s, on most maps, the river names had sorted themselves out. A stream rising above Breckenridge was the Blue. The water that rises in the inverted "U" made by the Continental Divide in the northwestern corner of the Rocky Mountain National Park, and leaves the state of Colorado below Grand Junction, was definitely the Grand River. Hence Grand Lake, and Grand Junction where the Gunnison River makes a junction with the Grand. Below Moab, Utah, as geography students learned by rote, the Grand and Green formed the Colorado.
   So matters stood until Edward F. Taylor (1858-1941) arrived in Glenwood Springs in 1887. From that time, first as state senator, then as powerful U.S. congressman, he campaigned to change the name of the Grand River to the Colorado River. But he reckoned without his neighbor states. Arizona felt it was bad enough to explain that the Grand Canyon of the Colorado River was in Arizona, not Colorado, but to change the name of the upper river to Colorado was too much! Utah rose to defend its Green River—it was longer than the Grand. This was true. Colorado replied, equally truthfully, that the Colorado branch produced more water. In 1921 the Utah Legislature introduced a bill to change the name of the Green River to Colorado, but failed to vote on the measure in that session. The astute politician, Ed Taylor, knowing that the Utah Legislature did not meet again for two years, encouraged the Colorado State Legislature on March 24, 1921, to pass a bill renaming the Grand River. Seething neighbor states asked the U.S. Board on Geographic Names for a decision. The board declined. The matter went to Congress. Here Utah did not complain, probably because of some political move of Ed Taylor. On July 25, 1921, President Harding signed the bill into law, presenting the pen with which he signed it to Representative Taylor of Colorado. The name became officially the Colorado River from La Poudre Pass to the Gulf of California.

Columbine Bay, Creek—GRAND LAKE, LAKE GRANBY; **Columbine Falls**—GLACIER GORGE; **Columbine Lake**—GRAND LAKE; **Columbine Lake**—INDIAN PEAKS

The type specimen of the Colorado columbine was found in 1820 by Dr. Edwin James, Colorado's first botanist and climber, south of Elephant Rock near Palmer Lake. This was about the first of July, the height of the columbine season for the eight-thousand-foot altitude. From the foothills to alpine meadows, from June to September, one can follow columbines in the Rockies. It is as ubiquitous as it is lovely. It was made the official state flower of Colorado in 1899. DO NOT PICK!

The word columbine comes from the Latin word for dove, but its scientific name—*aquilegea coerulea*—comes from a larger bird. Aquilegea is akin to "eagle," because the flower has spurs like an eagle's talons. *Coerulea* means cerulean blue—azure—like the Colorado blue sky at its deepest. When Dr. Edwin James saw blue flowers above timberline on Pikes Peak in 1820 he wondered if their proximity to the sky had any relation to their color. The Colorado columbine ranges in color from lavender through the blues to all white, but is never yellow or red like the garden varieties. True, July on the Western Slope produces a red columbine, but it lacks the petal skirts of the blue variety.

In the Rocky Mountain National Park columbines have left their names on bays, creeks, falls, lakes, but not on a mountain. This seems a pity because the rare dwarf columbine, intense blue, sometimes rewards the exhausted climber on the very summit rocks.

Comanche Peak (12,702')　　　　　　　　　　　　MUMMY RANGE

This peak was named on King's atlas of 1876. There must be a story behind the name, else why would a mountain here be named for a tribe of Plains Indians who lived mostly below the Arkansas River? Their savage treatment of Texans earned them an evil reputation. (See also Mahana Peak.)

Coney Creek, Lake, Upper Coney Lake　　　　　　INDIAN PEAKS

The dictionary accepts two spellings for the name of this little animal—cony and coney—as does the U.S. Geological Survey. Perhaps to distinguish the two creeks, it labels the one that runs into the Middle St. Vrain as Coney Creek; the one that runs into the North St. Vrain as Cony Creek. (See Cony Creek.)

Continental Divide

All visitors to the early West endeavored to explain the Continental Divide. "Water-parting," a succinct and accurate term, was seldom used; the explanation in nine out of ten books of travel went into poetic detail thus: If two drops of water fall within an inch of each other on either side of the line that marks the division of the drainage systems of the Americas, one drop ends in the Atlantic Ocean, one in the Pacific. "So close in infancy, so far separated at their watery grave," added Crofutt in his 1881 *Grip-Sack Guide to Colorado*. It was a relief in the 1930s when Thomas Hornsby Ferril produced another version in his poem "Old Men on the Blue":

> *Up where the Mississippi River ends*
> *And the bodies of the frozen dragonflies*
> *Begin to float to the Gulf of California.*

Geological forces did not leave a simple straight line on the map of the Americas to divide the waters of the Atlantic Ocean from the Pacific; the Continental Divide is erratic. Look at what it does in the northwestern part of the Rocky Mountain National Park, where it makes an inverted U-turn around the little creeks that flow into the North Fork of the Colorado River. Then it twists generally southeastward, at Sawtooth Mountain reaching its most easterly point in North America. Farther south it makes a right-angle turn, so that between South Arapaho Peak and Mount Neva it runs due west.

Moreover, geological forces put only two of Colorado's fifty-three, fourteen-thousand-foot peaks along the Hump, a colloquial term for the Continental Divide; these two, Grays and Torreys peaks, stand squarely on it. You don't believe that Longs Peak is not on the divide? Trace the water that flows from it. It is all collected by the Big Thompson or the St. Vrain en route to the Atlantic Ocean by way of the South Platte, the Missouri, the Mississippi, and the Gulf of Mexico.

Cony Creek—WILD BASIN; **Cony Lakes**—WILD BASIN, INDIAN PEAKS;
Cony Pass—GRAND LAKE, WILD BASIN

A cony is a small animal of great personality and many names, including two spellings—cony and coney. Another name—pika (pronounced pie′·ka)—comes from the Mongols of the Ural Mountains. The cony's high-pitched squeak earns him the name of Eek, and Joe Mills called him Little Chief Hare.

"If you pick a cony up by his tail his eyes will fall out," mountain guides have been known to tell children. The cony is quite safe from this fate, however, not only because he has no tail but because he moves much too fast for a child to catch; so fast that he can usually dodge the talons of swooping hawks by disappearing under rocks. He has more trouble eluding vicious weasels, especially the white and hungry weasels of winter. The cony lives in rockpiles, usually above timberline, but the rugged climate does not force him to hibernate. As summer draws to a close, he frenetically collects grasses to cure and store beneath the rocks for his winter haystacks. Mountain climbers like to watch these characters though they have difficulty seeing them because conies are the color of rocks—in fact they never would see them if the conies were not so vociferous. (See also Coney Creek.)

Cooper Peak (12,296')   INDIAN PEAKS
On the 1958 Isolation Peak quad map this peak appears as Copper Peak, but on the 1961 map of the Rocky Mountain National Park this name is spelled Cooper—a typographical error to be corrected on the next edition, an embarrassed Geological Survey man of Denver stated. That will make eight Colorado mountains called Copper. The name on this mountain reflects abortive attempts to make copper mining pay in such mines as the Copper King and the Fourth of July. But the name Cooper has significance in this country, too. William S. Cooper named what we know as Ogalalla Peak for his father. So now we have by chance and temporarily a Cooper Peak just south of one also temporarily so named. (See Wild Basin.)

Copeland Falls, Lake, Moraine   WILD BASIN
For a man who has left his name on these features as well as on a mountain, little is known about John B. Copeland. A man of that name pioneered in Central City in the 1860s and was still there in the 1870s. Starting in 1889, "Old Man Copeland," as Lon C. Allen of Longmont remembers him, homesteaded 320 acres near Copeland Lake. He proved up on the homestead March 4, 1896.

On February 2, 1900, the *Denver Times* reported that the Colorado State Game and Fish Department had brought suit against John B. Copeland for "keeping fish in his lake without first securing a license." The license cost $10 for two years; the fine for violation was $10 to $500. How the pioneer must have sputtered that in the old days he could have kept his own fish in his own lake without asking anybody's permission, much less pay $10 for a license, and he would not have had to buy a fishing license to catch his own fish from his own lake for his own dinner, either. Something, perhaps the sputtering, softened the heart of the Game and Fish Department. They agreed to withdraw the case "if Copeland will pay costs and take out a license. It is the intention of the officers to prosecute future cases to the end, however."

The lake into which Copeland dumped the fish that got him into trouble was a small lake in a moraine, fed by springs. Copeland dug a ditch from the North St. Vrain Creek to his lake, enlarging the pond by an earthen dam. He still owned the land in 1903 when William H. Davis of Denver filed with the State Engineer's Office his intention to build a million-dollar Copeland Park Reservoir. Other than surveying it and entering it on the records nothing came of this scheme.

In 1902 and 1903 the *State Business Directory* lists "Copeland Park, J. B. Copeland, Mgr." Does this mean that Copeland was running a resort? By 1910, Copeland or somebody else had built Copeland Lake

Lodge, because the 1910 Burlington map shows it plainly on the exact spot where a lodge was built in 1914. What happened to the earlier lodge, and what happened to John B. Copeland?

In the late fall of 1913, Burns Will, together with Walter McCaslin and an auto dealer in Longmont named Wylie, formed a company to start Copeland Lake Lodge. They opened for business in the spring of 1914 in a building east of Copeland Lake, beside the road. Two other Longmont men, Walter Coulehan and Frank Richart, were concerned in the venture, either then or a couple of years later, when the company dissolved. Burns Will and his wife built another hotel south of Allenspark.

In 1913 the city of Longmont bought 129 acres surrounding Copeland Lake and filed on a reservoir. No million-dollar scheme this time—the dam was expected to cost only $63,000 and be only forty-three feet high. The dam was built, the water right secured, and Longmont uses the water. Copeland Dam washed out in 1934, but Longmont replaced it with another earthen dam. Today the North St. Vrain flows from Copeland Lake down to Button Rock Reservoir. This Longmont project of the late 1960s drowned twenty-five cottages (the "Faculty Ranch") and a prolific stretch of fishing stream, beloved for almost forty years by professors of the University of Colorado. From Button Rock the water flows to a diversion dam six miles above Lyons, thence by conduit to Longmont.

Copeland Mountain (13,176')   WILD BASIN

Copeland Mountain is a sturdy mountain quite capable of withstanding assaults from factions that have tried to change its name. Bethel reported that an earlier name for Copeland had been Rosa, after either Monte Rosa, the high mountain in the Alps, or a girl. The Stapp family of Stapps Lake Lodge knew it as Mount Mack, after an early rancher; the 1882 township map locates Mack's Ranch. Enos Mills wanted to call it Mount Tyndall. (See Tyndall Glacier.)

The heaviest campaign to change the name of Copeland Mountain was conducted by admirers of Clarence King (1842-1901), who had many admirers. King was head of the 40th Parallel Survey, debunker of the Great Diamond Hoax, first director of the U.S. Geological Survey, a gifted writer, and a charming man. Also, he actually had been in Estes Park. On August 5, 1871, he headed for the uplands west of Greeley "in a light 4-wheeled buggy over a track hardly fit for a commissariat mule," wrote his biographer Wilkins. In Estes Park King lodged with Griff Evans, where he met Bostonian Henry Adams. They began a lifelong friendship by climbing Longs Peak the next day.

The war for changing Copeland Mountain's name to Mount Clarence King was triggered by William S. Cooper, who wrote the name on his map of 1911. He argued with the U.S. Board on Geographic Names for years, backed by people like Ellsworth Bethel, who wrote the Washington bureau that "Copeland, pioneer of Allenspark, was probably a worthy man, but it is one of the unfortunate names in the Allenspark region." The board continued to refuse to sanction the change. One of the reasons was that features in other states bore King's name; another was that they approved of local names. All this time the local people, headed by Burns Will, ignored the furor over changing the name. Copeland Mountain it was to them, Copeland Mountain it is today.

Copper Peak—See Cooper Peak.

Corral Creek, Park   NEVER SUMMER
Remnants of the fence of a corral may still be seen in this park. Perhaps beaver trappers built it to keep their horses from wandering where Indians could steal them, but definitely lumbermen used it for their horses. These men cut railroad ties and floated them down the Poudre to the plains. Cowboys and sheepherders were grateful for the old corral when they grazed their cattle in this park.

Cow Creek   MUMMY RANGE
This predates 1882, because the township map of that year notes the Cow Creek Stock Ranch.

Coyote Park   INDIAN PEAKS
Ancient Indians of Mexico called this animal *coyotl;* modern Americans pronounce coyote with either two or three syllables. From the prairies almost up to timberline, the coyote yelps, wails, bays the moon from hunger or loneliness, or calls to his mate. Sometimes mistaken for a small wolf—even at times called a prairie wolf—he looks much like a dog, with a yellowish gray coat and bushy tail. He is cunning, adaptable, and prolific, so that, although man continuously wages war on him (outside the National Park) the coyote survives and multiplies. He eats everything—rodents, vermin, carrion, an occasional sheep. He hunts down jackrabbits and the swift antelope by chasing them in relay teams. Indians endowed coyotes with supernatural powers, admiring them for their tricky wisdom; mountain men regarded them with superstition; modern ranchers consider them an annoyance. The coyote, always present, inevitably leaves his name on the land.

Cracktop   FOREST CANYON, GLACIER GORGE
In the early 1950s, Cheley Camp counselors named this mountain for the crack in its crest, easily seen from Trail Ridge Road.

Crags, The   ESTES PARK
The name was already established before the Cooper map of 1911.

Craig, Mount (12,007')   GRAND LAKE
This rounded mountain stands squarely in the middle of most photographs of Grand Lake; the 1914 Arapahos called it Middle Mountain. It
had other names. In 1874, W. H. Jackson, photographer of the West, called
it Round Mountain. H. H. Bancroft's *History of Colorado* (1890) speaks of
"Grand Lake in the immediate shadow of Round Top," and to some Grand
Lake people this mass at the head of East Inlet will always be Roundtop, to
balance Flattop at the head of North Inlet. Other old-timers call it Baldy, or
Old Baldy, because its pate is treeless, and others call it Mount Wescott,
thinking it absurd that it does not memorialize Judge Joseph L. Wescott
who looked across the lake from his cabin to the mountain for forty-seven
years—1867 to 1914. Bert A. Goodman, a forest service man, reported the
year Judge Wescott died that "Reverand Craig had named the mountain
after himself. I believe that it should be called Mount Wescott because that
was its original name and is most favored by the natives."
These many names persist in spite of the official name given by Grand
Lake villagers. A Denver magazine, *The Colorado Graphic* for August 18,
1888, reported that "Reverand Bayard Craig of this city feels altitudinous
since the admiring citizens of Grand Lake have named a mountain for
him. Mount Craig sounds well."
William Bayard Craig, Canadian-born graduate of Yale Divinity
School, came west in 1882 at the age of thirty-six. Since his sister-in-law
was Mrs. Governor John L. Routt of Denver, he had good connections. He
was pastor of Central Christian Church in Denver both before and after
1894-1902 when he served as chancellor of Drake University. Though he
visited Grand Lake only a few summers, he is remembered as a man of
forceful character. He dealt in real estate around Grand Lake; Craigs Point
north of the outlet of the lake was once his property; and he sold the Bar-
bee-Warren cabin to Dean H. Martyn Hart of St. John's Cathedral, Denver, also a man of character. The town of Craig also bears his name,
courtesy of his influential friend, railroader David Moffat.

Crater, The; Crater Gulch—See Specimen Mountain.

Crater Lake   INDIAN PEAKS
At the base of the spectacular spire of Lone Eagle Peak lies Crater
Lake, not in a volcanic crater but in a glacially formed basin. The Colorado
Geographic Board was pained by this scientific inaccuracy; they recom-
mended the name be changed to Hyslop Lake, a name used by old-timers.

Crystal Lake, Little Crystal Lake   MUMMY RANGE

Cub Lake   FOREST CANYON
Abner Sprague named this lake, not because he had seen a bear cub
there, but because it was little, just a cub of a lake.

Cumulus, Mount (12,725')   NEVER SUMMER
This is one of the peaks of the Never Summer Mountains that James
Grafton Rogers named for cloud forms. The dictionary defines a cumulus
cloud as "a massive cloud form having a flat base and rounded outlines
often piled up like a mountain. It commonly appears in the early afternoon
on warm days, and may afford rain or thunder gusts." Cumulus clouds piled
high in the east are often the most spectacular part of a summer sunset.

Cutthroat Trout Bay   LAKE GRANBY
Native trout, commonly called "cutthroat" because of the blood-red
markings on the lower jaw, were the only trout the first white men found
in Colorado. The committee of local men who named the various features
of Lake Granby after kinds of trout—Kamloop Cove, Rainbow Bay,
Lochleven Cove—wisely added the word Trout to Cutthroat Trout Bay;
Cutthroat Bay might not entice fishermen.

Dark Mountain (10,859')   MUMMY RANGE
The staff of the Rocky Mountain National Park proposed this name in
1942 because the mountain is covered with dark conifers and is near
Black Canyon.

Deer Island   LAKE GRANBY

Deer Ridge; Deer Mountain (9,937')   ESTES PARK
When Chapin used the name Deer Mountain in 1886 it was probably
already an old name. In 1913 the ladies of Estes Park, organized in 1912
as the Estes Park Women's Club, raised enough money by bake sales and
dances to pay for building a trail to the summit of Deer Mountain. From
behind the Elkhorn Lodge it followed the ridge to the top. The local newspaper reported Mesdames Stead, Hayden, and Hondius inspected the
trail but "had to walk much because of fences."
The kind of deer in the Park is the mule deer. He has big ears like a
mule, a small rump patch, and his white tail waves a black tip. The fawns,
often twins, wear spots for camouflage. Deer are curious and may stand
watching a passerby as long as the passerby quietly watches them. Usually anyone on a trip into the Park who really looks for deer will see them.

Desolation Peaks (12,949')   MUMMY RANGE
Climbers gave this anthropomorphic name to these rocky summits,
according to the National Park Service who recommended the name
in 1961.

Devils Ladder   Estes Park

A local name for the very steep, rocky portion of trail just west of the East Portal of the Alva B. Adams Tunnel.

Devils Gulch—Northeast of Estes Park

The Devils Gulch Road belies its name as it gently rises northeast of Estes Park to an elevation of 7,980 feet. Then it sinks 600 feet in about a mile to the floor of West Creek, a branch of the North Fork of the Big Thompson. Perhaps it earned its satanic reputation from the way the clouds boil up from it, like smoke spewing out of Hell, long after the sun has burned off the clouds on the higher slopes. Hayden labeled this Devils Cañon in his 1877 atlas, and indicates no trail dropping down it. Eventually a trail was built, and then a wagon road which was used by early automobiles but with difficulty. George Dennis, who homesteaded at the foot of Devils Gulch, was the road overseer for the North Fork of the Big Thompson. In his Model-T Ford he took an hour to drive to the top of Devils Gulch, a ten-minute drive today (but the road still involves a precipitous hairpin turn).

Hayden's designation of Devils Cañon probably changed to Devils Gulch by popular western usage; not *gorge,* which word is western but derives from an Old French word meaning *whirlpool,* nor *gully* which is cousin to *gullet,* also French, but *gulch,* a purely western word. *Webster's Dictionary* gives it no lineage, suggests it perhaps imitates the sound of gushing water, and ends the discussion with "Orig. Western U.S."

In contrast to Devils Gulch, quiet Glen Haven lies near its foot, a community originally sponsored by the Presbyterian Assembly Association.

Dickinson, Mount (11,831')   Mummy Range

A rancher named Dickerson lived near this mountain; the mountain was not named for him, local opinion to the contrary, but for a visiting lady. Enos Mills suggested the name Dickinson to the Colorado Geographic Board about 1914. The lady so honored was the first woman on record to climb Longs Peak. The date—September 1873.

Miss Anna Dickinson was thirty-one years old, attractive, dynamic, with a flexible voice, artfully controlled with which she thrilled audiences as a lady lecturer. When just out of her teens, Anna lectured, by invitation, the senators of the United States, inspiring them to finish the Civil War. She was for the Union, against slavery, and for woman suffrage. Between engagements as a lecturer, she went on the stage as a tragedienne.

Miss Dickinson had many beaux; the one she was interested in was Whitlaw Reid, in 1872 the editor-in-chief of Greeley's *New York Tribune.* Another beau was Ralph Meeker, son of Nathan Meeker who founded the Union Colony at Greeley, Colorado. Ralph worried when in 1873 Anna had a fit of depression. He persuaded her that the Colorado climate would invigorate her. Correctly chaperoned by her clergyman brother, Anna

came west. Ralph was right; she was invigorated sufficiently to ride burros up Pikes, Grays, and Lincoln peaks. For Mount Elbert she borrowed
a government mule and guide from a survey party. Presumably she was
the first woman to gain the top of this, at present the highest mountain in
Colorado. (In 1873 the honor of being the highest vacillated between
Mount Lincoln and Sierra Blanca.)

By September 1873 Miss Anna thought climbing was over for the season, but in Estes Park she met F. V. Hayden and James Gardiner, surveyors. She noted that Hayden's eyes were blue and he had soft brown hair;
Gardiner's eyes were amber and his hair was gold. Doubtless the gentle-
men noted Miss Dickinson's small but shapely appearance. What Gardiner later wrote about Miss Anna, however, referred not to her charms
but to her political influence, she being "in" with the powerful *New York
Tribune*. Gardiner needed her influence. The surveyors of the West each
winter had to wheedle appropriations out of Congress for the next summer campaigns, and Gardiner wrote that Miss Dickinson was "no mean
power to enlist in a cause." His method of enlisting her support was to ask
her to climb Longs Peak with the survey party.

This, the largest group up to that time to attempt the ascent of Longs
Peak, included Anna, Hayden and Gardiner, and Anna's brother, the Reverend Mr. John Dickinson; her admirer, Ralph Meeker; William Byers,
the mountain-climbing editor of the *Rocky Mountain News;* and seven others. Longs was one peak to whose top Anna could not ride a burro, but she
got there with the aid of a lemon. ("Never climb without a lemon," was her
advice to mountaineers.) She carried to the summit a yard-long, spring
tape measure, a puzzling piece of mountaineering equipment. On its
metal case she scratched her name and left it on the peak. Abner Sprague
saw this on the summit of Longs Peak in July of 1874, but on his next visit
the metal case and records of other climbs, including those of the 1868
Powell first ascent, had disappeared except for pieces of a photograph of
Powell which had been riddled with bullets.

After the climb, camping below timberline, the Hayden party sat by
the fire, kept blazing "with heaps of whole trunks of dead trees," and
talked "of all things that touch the brain and soul," Anna wrote. From this
discussion came decisions to name two mountains near Longs Peak: one,
Mount Meeker for Nathan Meeker of the Union Colony; the other, Mount
Lady Washington.

Anna's record of being the first woman to climb Longs Peak was a nar-
rowly won distinction, since her party met, at the foot of the mountain,
three women in another group about to ascend. They may not have made
the summit, but the next month dumpy Isabella Bird of the magic pen
climbed to the top. She started out in boots loaned her by Griff Evans, her
host, but discarded them in favor of a pair of small overshoes she found in
the boulders of the "Lava Beds," presumably left by Miss Dickinson.

In July of 1874, the next year, the *Rocky Mountain News* reported that Longs Peak climbers "near the tip-top . . . found a cloak folded in the crevice, just where the redoubtable Anna Dickinson had left it, forgetfully, last September when she climbed to that dizzy pinnacle. The garment was forwarded."

Dorothy, Lake (12,061')   INDIAN PEAKS
Henry Lehman had a granddaughter named Dorothy, and she is the only Dorothy that has been mentioned as a possible explanation of the name of this lake. The Lehman Ranch was on the South Fork of the Colorado River below Monarch Lake, and the Lehmans rode over Arapaho Pass whenever they came to Denver. On the east side of the pass the trail skirted Lake Dorothy.

Doughnut Lake   FOREST CANYON
Dr. Workman or Julian Hayden, on the fishing trip which resulted in naming the Gorge Lakes, thought of doughnuts because the lake is small and round and has an island in the middle. This may be the lake the Colorado Mountain Club intended to call Terra Tomah Lake. (See Gorge Lakes and Terra Tomah Mountain.)

Dove, The   GLACIER GORGE, WILD BASIN
Paul Nesbit, whose love affair with Longs Peak resulted in a pamphlet telling all about it, reports that the Dove is the obvious name for the snowbank lying above the Keyhole which resembles "a white bird flying downward with wings outstretched, that is, until the right wing melts away in late summer."

Dragons Egg Rock   WILD BASIN
Named about 1921 by Ranger Jack C. Moomaw.

Dream Lake   GLACIER GORGE
Dream Lake was once known as Emerald Lake, and Dr. Workman of Fern Lake Lodge called it Lake Ursula, not for a girl but for *ursus,* the Latin word for bear, because it was near Bear Lake. George Barnard named this Dream Lake during the Colorado Mountain Club's second annual outing in 1913. Barnard was chairman of four of the first five outings of the club, generously making it possible for others to share his ability to penetrate into high country, especially of the northern Front Range. He led the 1913 outing to Bear Lake, the 1914 outing from Grand Lake to Fall River, and the 1916 outing to Wild Basin. (The Colorado Mountain Club returned to Wild Basin in 1919 and to Shipler Park, with Roger Toll as leader, in 1921.) On these trips and many others, by himself or with Jim Rogers, Barnard worked for the Colorado Geographic Board in its search for suitable names for the Rocky Mountain National Park terrain.

George Cooper Barnard (1876-1947) was born in Michigan, lived in California, and came to Denver in 1897. He worked for the Colorado & Southern Railroad until 1910; then, as contractor, built many Park Hill homes. In 1922 he entered the real estate and insurance business. His remarkable ability to interest young people in mountains has inspired succeeding generations to do likewise.

Dry Gulch ESTES PARK

Dunraven, Mount (12,571') MUMMY RANGE

The Irish Earl of Dunraven's name was Windham Thomas Wyndham-Quinn (1841-1926). His titles included Fourth Earl of Dunraven and Viscount Mount Earl and Adair. Too long a name for one mountain, the Colorado Geographic Board stretched it across Dunraven Peaks. Afterwards, someone confined the Earl's name to the west summit, leaving the east summit unnamed. For this peak, Bethel once suggested Laramie, for the mountain scout, mistakenly thinking it a variation of Larimer, Denver's first real estate promoter. Then Bethel remembered Anna Dickinson, whom he considered the most charming woman he had ever heard speak. On the present map, the west summit is Mount Dunraven, the east summit has no name, and Dickinson perches on the eastern end of the ridge, perhaps honor enough for a woman?

Besides being titled, the Irishman was a millionaire and a sportsman. In 1867, the Earl of Dunraven was a war correspondent in Abyssinia. H. M. Stanley (who later found Dr. Livingstone in darkest Africa) was also there as a reporter. One account states that the Earl and Stanley tented together. Perhaps Stanley told Dunraven about hunting in Colorado; Stanley had been in Colorado the year before. In fact, he borrowed $50 to build a raft so he could float down the Platte River to get out of Colorado.

In the winter of 1872, Lord Dunraven and two titled friends arrived in little Denver, hired a hunting guide, and, two days after Christmas, descended on Griff Evans in Estes Park. Griff put them up in one of his well-ventilated log cabins and Mrs. Evans fed them.

The hunting was superb. The next winter the Earl of Dunraven returned and by 1874 decided he would acquire the whole of Estes Park for his private hunting preserve. The Earl hired Theodore Whyte as resident manager, and acquired perhaps fifteen thousand acres of land, some by purchase, but most by cheating on the homestead laws. His Lordship announced in the *Rocky Mountain News* that admission to Estes Park, his game preserve, was by invitation only. But keeping people out of the area was impossible, as the Earl noted in his memoirs:

> After a time people began to wander in. . . . It became evident that we were not to be left monarchs of all we surveyed. Folks were drifting in prospecting, fossicking, preempting, making claims; so we prepared for

civilization. Made a better road, bought a sawmill at San Francisco, hauled the machinery in, felled trees, and built a wooden hotel, and did pretty well with a Chinese cook who could make venision and anything else out of bogged cow beef.

This hotel, usually called the English Hotel, operated from 1877 until it burned in 1911. The summer it opened a reporter wrote an article thanking "the noble earl" for building the hotel and for fencing thousands of acres of land "lest objectionable parties interfere with the freedom and comfort of the guests at the hotel."

South of the present Lake Estes, Dunraven's agent, Theodore Whyte, built not only the hotel but also ranch houses, stables, and a home which still stands. On George's 1913 map of Colorado this community had a name—Mountearl. Remember the Irishman's full title that included Viscount Mount Earl? Here Whyte ran what western cattlemen would call "a big spread," meaning a large cattle ranch; and he did his best to protect the Earl's claims, some spurious, to almost all of Estes Park. Whyte irritated the settlers by fencing land claimed by others, by running his cattle on other people's territory, and by threatening the neighbors in a high-handed way. Eventually, the Americans went to court. They proved that Dunraven had acquired twenty-one parcels of land from five or six men, none of whom had lived on the land or made improvements as specified in the homestead laws.

This troubled the Earl in Ireland. He wrote:

People came in disputing claims, kicking up rows; exorbitant land taxes got into arrears; we were in constant litigation. The show could not be managed from home, and we were in danger of being frozen out. So we sold what we could get and cleared out, and I have never been there since.

The absentee landlord disposed of his Estes Park holdings—about six thousand acres, in 1907. B. D. Sanborn and F. O. Stanley bought the land.

Dunraven's name remains in Estes Park though he was there less than a dozen visits, but his manager's name, Theodore Whyte, who lived in the Park at least twenty years, is not memorialized. Once there was a lake named Whyte's Lake; Bierstadt painted a picture of it. Perhaps it was the lake, made by damming Fish Creek, that stood in front of the English Hotel. W. H. Jackson took pictures of it. When the dam was allowed to break, the lake disappeared.

Theodore Whyte was not only the local representative of the Earl of Dunraven and his whipping boy, but he put his heart and money (his own and his wife's) into trying to make a success of ranching. He raised alfalfa and pedigreed oats to feed his pedigreed Herefords and imported horses, never letting his stock graze on unfenced land, a point of disagreement with his American neighbors. He not only irritated the settlers by trying to protect what he considered land belonging to the Earl, but continually amused them with his British ways. He hunted the fox in pink coat with cries of "yoicks" to encourage his imported hounds, and jumped gates and fences. To supervise the estate, he drove a four-in-hand, and always returned home in time for tea.

Theodore Whyte grew up in Devon, then came to the Canadian Northwest where he trapped for three years with the Indians for the Hudson Bay Company. When he was twenty-six, in 1872, he came to Colorado. As the Earl of Dunraven's agent, he lived in the white house that still stands in Estes Park, which his second wife, Lady Maude Ogilvy, made attractive with embroidered hangings and English silver. After his bankruptcy in 1896 he returned to England to manage an estate. In 1950 two of his daughters were living together in Scotland.

Dunraven, Lake   MUMMY RANGE

Let's look for Irish nobility on the way to Lake Dunraven. We can use the road up Dunraven Glade, through private property opened to the public in 1970. About two miles from the North Fork we look for the site of Lord Dunraven's hunting lodge (and buried cask of whiskey). Mason Knapp of Glen Haven saw its ruins on his honeymoon in 1895, ruins left over from 1874 when the Earl built a supply cabin for hunting parties. A mile further up we reach Trail's End Camp, the eighty acres bought by Frank Cheley in 1941. Where the riding ring is now, the Knapps, in 1897, ran a sawmill. Walking the Dunraven Trail, we presently see the ruins of the Deserted Village. Labeled Dunraven Park on the 1907 quad map, it was called Dunraven Meadows by the Earl's hunting parties who tented hereabouts. Here the Simonds brothers had a sawmill which they sold to Fred H. Sprague in 1909, who ran a resort here until an outbreak of dysentery closed it. In 1914 Norman Fuller bought the place, spent that one summer here, then deserted it. From Lost Lake, where the trail stops, a steep scramble ends at Lake Dunraven on the slope of Mount Dunraven. By the time we get there, we are tired of the Earl's name. Could it be that Americans are impressed with Irish titles?

Dutch Creek   NEVER SUMMER

Little and Big Dutch creeks remind us of eight Germans who formed a clique in Lulu City, as did groups of Irishmen and Swedes. Each nationality had a nickname, the Germans being known as Dutch. One night the Dutchmen, home from a spree at Grand Lake, started a free-for-all in Lulu. When the smoke cleared away, the townspeople found much damage, including a broken arm on a respectable woman. Blaming the Dutchmen, the majority of citizens ordered them out of town. The Germans climbed to the west, settling two miles above Hichens's claims on Big

Dutch Creek. The villagers still held their grudge, expressing it by climbing to a point above Dutchtown in order to shoot down on the Germans. Finally a border line was agreed on—a small ridge between Hitchens Gulch and the North Fork. The story, as told by Lloyd Redburn of Grand Lake, concludes that Dutchtown lasted longer than Lulu City.

Eagle Cliff Mountain (8,906')   ESTES PARK
The golden eagle, dark, with a seven-foot wing spread, is occasionally seen in the Park. The bald eagle, America's emblem, rarely visits the Park, and then only in winter.

Eagle Lake   WILD BASIN
This is overshadowed by the Eagles Beak. (See also Box Lake.)

Eagles Beak   WILD BASIN
Ranger Naturalist Ferrel Atkins, who is studying the historic sites in Rocky Mountain National Park, has a record showing that this rock was once known as Pipit Rock. It does not stand near Pipit Lake, but is certainly more the size of an eagle than of a pipit. The Cheley Camp boys and girls have called it Eagles Beak since the early 1950s.

East Face   GLACIER GORGE, WILD BASIN
The East Face of Longs Peak drops vertically 1,630 feet. A Princeton professor, J. W. Alexander, made the first ascent on September 7, 1922, by way of Lambs Slide to South Broadway and then up the Notch Couloir. The next day, Alexander with Jack Moomaw, who had been unable to accompany him the day before, climbed the East Face again by way of what has since been known as Alexanders Chimney. On September 10, six members of the Colorado Mountain Club (including one woman), after eleven hours, reached the top in time to see "the purple shadow of Longs Peak on the pink haze of the eastern plains." The group included Dudley Smith, who had long studied the route from his cabin in Estes Park.

The smoothest part of the face, high and to the north, is known as the Diamond because of its shape. Two California climbers, laden with jangling hardware, made the first ascent of the Diamond in August 1960, spending fifty-two hours on the job.

The names of various features on or near Longs Peak are on the Geological Survey map of Glacier Gorge, found at the end of this book. Names of routes and ledges on the East Face are identified in Paul Nesbit's pamphlet *Longs Peak: Its Story and a Climbing Guide.* These include

Alexanders Chimney, Fields Chimney, Stettners Ledges, Kieners Route, all named for men who pioneered the routes, and the narrow ledge dubbed Broadway by climbers grateful to reach its comparative safety.

A word of warning—the East Face is for technical climbers only. They must register with the Park authorities before attempting the climb, and report back after the climb. This seems reasonable since the Park rangers must rescue those in trouble on the East Face.

East Inlet   GRAND LAKE

Two creeks feed Grand Lake—East and North inlets. They have no other names, but are known only as inlets from their beginnings on the Continental Divide to their ends in the lake.

Echo Creek   GRAND LAKE

Elephant Island   GRAND LAKE, LAKE GRANBY

The Lake Granby businessmen who named this island must have had a reason for the name. It may be that at high water the island is only as big as an elephant; or that at low water it looks like an elephant; or that on it grow little red elephants. These flowers always amuse the young in heart, whether in Greenland or Colorado, because each blossom on its upright stem comes equipped with an elephant trunk.

Elk Tooth (12,848')   WILD BASIN

On the southern rim of Wild Basin stands Ogalalla Peak with its great arm stretching eastward. On this arm the most prominent rock was called Elktooth in location claims for mines and in an early survey for a reservoir. W. S. Cooper in his 1911 map of Wild Basin labeled this Mount Caroline after his mother. In 1965 Dr. Cooper remarked that he was happy the name had not survived, since the highest point his mother ever reached was the top of Oldman Mountain—8,310 feet above sea level, on the usual stroll from Elkhorn Lodge.

When the Colorado Geographic Board was trying to connect ridges with their parent mountains—like Paiute, Paiute Horn—they called the point Ogalalla Horn, but the U.S. Board on Geographic Names decided in favor of the original name, but spelled it in two words, Elk Tooth.

This is the only geographic feature in the Park region that bears the name of elk; sheep aplenty—Sheep Rock, Sheep Mountain, Bighorn Flats, Rams Horn Mountain—but this is the lone elk. Abner Sprague stated that when he came to the region in 1875 he saw elk by the thousands. From the west, they crossed the divide about Christmas time and descended into the meadowlands, there to be met by hunters with repeating rifles and four-horse teams. Hauled to Denver, the carcasses sold for three or four cents a pound. Each year thereafter fewer and fewer elk appeared. After 1880 the butchers conducted their slaughter in North Park. In the 1880s and 1890s when men were naming so many geographical features in the National Park region, they did not see elk around, so used the name but once.

In 1913 Estes Park people raised enough money to bring elk back. Men of the forest service and biological service loaded twenty-nine elk into two railroad cars at Cinnabar, Montana, transferred them at Lyons to Stanley Steamers, and pastured them temporarily east of the Stanley Hotel. In 1915, twenty-four more arrived and were released directly into Little Horseshoe Park, which they quickly claimed as their own. Today progeny of these elk gather in the fall, bugling their challenges across the meadows.

The elk is a member of the deer family, kin to the English red deer sometimes called elk, the variety hunted by Robin Hood in Sherwood Forest. To distinguish between the two, our elk is called the American elk, or wapiti. This is an Algonquian word, accented on the first syllable by naturalists, on the second by Colorado miners who dug flakes of pure gold out of the Wapiti Mine near Breckenridge.

Embryo Lake   GLACIER GORGE
William Hickox, a fine photographer from Rochester, New York, spent three summers in Estes Park. He prized his picture of this little lake, and, deciding it needed a caption, called it Embryo Lake.

Emerald Lake   GLACIER GORGE
Superintendant Roger Toll wrote that Emerald Lake is about twenty feet lower than any surface outlet, so water drains through the moraine deposit.

Emerald Mountain (9,237')   ESTES PARK
Early delegates to the Y.M.C.A. camp called this Green Mountain. Abner Sprague said in 1923 that he had long preferred Emerald Mountain. The Park rangers, wishing to avoid commonplace names, adopted Emerald for the hill.

Emmaline Lake   MUMMY RANGE
Emmaline Lake was named by Frank R. Koenig for his mother. (See Hazeline Lake and Ramsey Peak.)

Enentah, Mount (10,781')   GRAND LAKE
The 1914 Arapahos called this *Enetah-notaiyah* (man-mountain) because near its summit a fringe of pine trees made it look like a man's head. The Colorado Geographic Board decided on the spelling Enetah (accent on the second syllable), but a second "n" slipped into print.

Estes Cone (11,006')   ESTES PARK, GLACIER GORGE
The 1914 Arapahos knew this and the Wind River Cliffs as the Three Buttes. The name Estes Cone predates Hayden's 1877 atlas. Geologically, a cone is an isolated remnant of erosion, conspicuous despite its relatively low height.

Estes, Lake

This lake was made and named when the Colorado-Big Thompson Project brought water through the Alva B. Adams Tunnel to fill it.

Estes Park

The word park used in connection with today's national parks means a tract of land kept in its natural state, but to early Colorado travelers it meant a high valley surrounded by mountain ranges, and without exception their books devoted paragraphs to the explanation of North, Middle, and South parks (spelled parcs by the French). Smaller tracts of land surrounded by mountains were also called parks, like Estes Park, though the 1914 Arapahos expressed the same idea by calling it the "Circle."

Estes Park was named for Joel Estes (1806-1875), a Missourian, who had tried his luck in California, returned from its mines with a sizable stake, farmed in Missouri, and had then come west with the Colorado gold rush. He went into the cattle business near Fort Lupton on the South Platte River. About the middle of October 1859, he and one of his sons, Marion, Milton, or Joel, Jr.—in later years each claimed the honor—followed the Little Thompson River into the hills looking for a place to graze cattle. In 1929 Milton wrote:

> I shall never forget my first sight of the Park. . . . We stood on the mountain looking down . . . where the Park spread out before us. No words can describe our surprise, wonder and joy at beholding such an unexpected sight. It looked like a low valley with a silver streak or thread winding its way through the tall grass, down through the valley and disappearing around a hill among the pine trees. This silver thread was Big Thompson Creek. It was a grand sight and a great surprise. . . . In 1860, the year after the discovery of "The Park," as we called it from the day we came in there, we built two houses and corrals for the stock. (Their first cabin was where Fish Creek enters the Big Thompson.) We then returned home and drove the cattle from the Platte River ranch to the Park. Father said it would not take much, if any time, to herd the cattle, if we fenced the trail at a place before it entered the Park. . . . By 1863 father and I had made sufficient preparations to move our families to the Park.

Of Joel Estes's thirteen children, three sons and a daughter were still living at home. Milton's family consisted of his wife and two babies. Milton's memoirs tell of wholesale hunting and fishing, and trips to Denver every two or three months to sell wild meat and hides. "The women of our families, my mother, sister, and wife, cheerfully shared with us the rugged life of the pioneer. With dutch-ovens, iron kettles hanging over open fire places; they cooked food that could not be surpassed."

Visitors to the Park agreed with Milton's opinion of the food. In April 1864, John T. Prewitt ate a beaver-tail supper at the Estes home. "That

Mrs. Lady was a mighty fine cook," he wrote, and boarded with her three days. He found Joel Estes, whose slight speech impediment added charm to his vivid way of expressing his thoughts, as interesting as he found hunting above timberline on Longs Peak.

William Byers, editor of the *Rocky Mountain News,* named Estes Park in an article he published on September 22, 1864, about a month after he, George Nichols, Dr. C. C. Parry, and Professor Velie had failed to climb Longs Peak. He stayed two nights with the Estes family and named the park for them. His diary, which is disappointingly succinct, records his trip. He left Denver August 16, 1864, spent the night in Boulder with the Nichols family, and camped the next night:

> . . . six miles in the mountains at the upper crossing of the St. Vrain Creek. Long's Peak covered with new snow this afternoon. Aug. 18. Reached Estes Park and stayed for the night at Mr. Estes. A rough wagon road but can easily be made good. Left wagon 5 miles back. Aug. 19. Moved up to timberline on the north side of Long's Peak and in the evening climbed to the foot of the Peak. . . . Aug. 20. Ascended the east peak (Mount Meeker) and found the west, or loftiest, was inaccessible. Returned to Estes in the evening. Fine day. Aug. 21. Returned to Mr. Franklin's at foot of mountains. Pleasant day. Expenses: Bill at Estes $2.20.

Mrs. Estes and her daughter-in-law were lonesome despite running a boarding house for occasional droppers-in, and Joel disliked the deep snow of the winter of 1865-66. On April 15, 1866, he left the park and moved his family to New Mexico. Today a bronze plaque on a granite boulder marks the spot where the Estes family lived, east of Lake Estes near a ragged pine tree.

How much Estes received for the sale of his holdings in the park seems to be a matter of opinion. Milton Estes wrote, "Father sold the Park, with all his right, title and interest in the same, and in consideration of one yoke of oxen. Michael Hollenbeck and a man whose real name we never knew, but who went by the name of 'Buck,' made the purchase."

In June 1904 Mr. Hollenbeck of Highlandlake recalled for the *Lyons Recorder* that Estes traded his interest in Estes Park to him for one three-year-old steer. "Estes took the steer and moved out," said Hollenbeck. Enos Mills wrote:

> The Estes abdicated their scenic throne for one of the following considerations: Fifty dollars, a yearling steer, or yoke of oxen. It is impossible to say which one of these is correct, but had Michael Hollenbeck given them all these he had become a monarch dirt cheap.
>
> In a few months a Mr. Jacobs gave $250 for the claim, but in a short time it was acquired by a regular Robinson Crusoe of a character called Buckskin. (A trapper named Hank Farrar.) Late in 1867 the Estes claim

came under the control of Griff Evans, and in due course lost its identity by becoming some of the acres of the Earl of Dunraven. . . . Griff Evans founded the first permanent settlement by coming to stay—and by staying for nearly a score of years.

Though nothing is named for Griffith Evans in the Estes Park region, his name and hospitality are spread across the pages of almost every account written by visitors to the area in the 1810s and early 1880s. Isabella Bird noted the Evans family as "jovial, hearty Welsh people from Llanberis, who laugh with loud, cheery British laughs, sing in parts down to the youngest child, are free hearted and hospitable, and pile the pitch pine logs half way up the great rude chimney."

Griff Evans worked hard for this reputation. How he got to Estes Park was told in the *Lyons Recorder* for December 22, 1921, by Captain George W. Brown, an early rancher near Longmont. He remembered that Mrs. Griff Evans came to tell him of the splendid opportunity they had to go to Estes Park and acquire the ranch of Jacobs, but they had no way of getting there. Captain Brown, because he had never been to Estes, offered to take them. The Evans furnishings were not a heavy load—"a broken cook stove, two chairs past using, a table with one leaf gone, and a few pieces of bedding." After the wagon turned over a few times on the rough road, the furnishings were less useful. Before he left the Evans family at the Jacobs's cabin, Captain Brown divided his bullets and powder with Evans, his flour and potatoes with Mrs. Evans. Until Griff Evans acquired a horse, he carried saddles of venison on his shoulders to the John Reece place on the South St. Vrain to trade for supplies. But sometime before 1873, Griff Evans had prospered enough ("Evans makes no end of money by taking people in at $8 a week," noted Isabella Bird) to bring up a chamber organ.

Griff Evans sold his property to the Earl of Dunraven on November 7, 1878, for $500. When he left the park, with a reputed $18,000 in his pocket, he lived in the large red sandstone house that still stands near the entrance to the North St. Vrain Canyon just west of Lyons.

Eugenia Mine   Glacier Gorge

On Battle Mountain, a short walk from the Longs Peak Trail, tumbled-down buildings mark the site of a mine dug into the mountain about one thousand feet. Not old for a Colorado mine, the Eugenia lode was recorded in September 1905—which probably means it was not named for the Empress of France, since by that time the Napoleonic fever had cooled. The company was incorporated by Carl P. Norwall and Edward A. Cudahy of Chicago. (Is this one of the meat-packing Cudahys of that city?)

Carl P. Norwall lived near the tunnel of the Eugenia Mine, not in a mine shack but in a comfortable home. He had two daughters and one piano, three reasons why young guides from Longs Peak Inn and Hewes-Kirkwood Lodge spent many pleasant evenings at the Norwalls.

One of these young men was Harold Dunning, a professional guide on Longs Peak in 1911-1912, from whom the information about the Eugenia Mine came. Born in Gandy, Logan County, Nebraska, on May 28, 1891, Harold Dunning died in 1973. He first saw Estes Park when he was five years old. He ran a shoe store in Loveland for over fifty years, and every Friday for twenty-five years, summer and winter, drove an itinerant grocery van from Loveland to Raymond and Allenspark. With an avid interest in history, he collected historical objects for the Loveland Historical Museum, and a vast store of historical data, which he published in a Loveland newspaper column, later in book form. His writings are a rich mine, producing more worth in authentic information than the Eugenia Mine ever produced in metal.

Fair Glacier   INDIAN PEAKS
Fred Fair, Boulder County surveyor and mountaineer, went into the Crater Lake country west of Pawnee Pass and discovered this small glacier in 1908. Junius Henderson of the Science Department of the University of Colorado named it Fair Glacier, and named the glacier on the east of the divide after Fred's wife, Isabelle. (See Arapaho Glacier; Lone Eagle Peak.)

Fairchild Mountain (13,502')   MUMMY RANGE
Lucius Fairchild (1831-1896), son of the first mayor of Madison, Wisconsin, was three times governor of his state, and the Fairchild home was the social center of Madison. In 1878 President Rutherford B. Hayes sent Fairchild to Paris, in 1880 made him minister to Spain. He was a militant veteran of the Civil War, saying, when President Cleveland, Democrat, ordered the Confederate flags returned to the southern states, "May God palsy the hand that wrote that order." In 1886, Fairchild, as commander-in-chief of the Grand Army of the Republic, traveled with thousands of other veterans to the G.A.R. convention in California. He and his daughter were headlined in the Denver papers when they stopped there and rode the narrow gauge train to Colorado's greatest tourist attraction, the Georgetown Loop.
Some of Fairchild's admirers, climbing in Estes Park, named Fairchild Mountain, one of the few purely political names in the area. Chapin mentioned Fairchild Mountain in 1888; in 1908 Ellsworth Bethel recommended to the U.S. Board of Geographic Names that the name be retained.

Falcon Lake WILD BASIN

Falcons are small hawks, measuring from nine to twenty inches, with pointed wings. Of the four varieties found in the Park, the prairie falcon, pigeon hawk, and peregrine falcon are less common than the sparrow hawk, which nests along the lower borders of the Park and in late summer seeks food at the elevation of Falcon Lake and above timberline.

Fall Creek; Fall Mountain (12,258') MUMMY RANGE

Fall Creek rises on Fall Mountain and runs north to the Poudre. The creek was probably named first, and then, by association, the mountain. This is a common pattern in mountain nomenclature.

Fall River ESTES PARK, MUMMY RANGE

Arapaho Indians called Fall River Trail the Dog's Trail, because snow enabled their dogs to pull travois. This makes sense; the trail notoriously holds snow until late summer.

Road building on both sides of the divide was simultaneous. On the east—Fall River. In September 1913, "Tom Tynan's boys," convicts from the Colorado Penitentiary, moved into cabins at the foot of Fall River to start building a road. In two years thirty-eight men had completed it to the top of the switchbacks.

Two Colorado governors promised that Colorado would finish the road through to Grand Lake if Congress would create the Rocky Mountain National Park, a bribe that provoked the ire of one congressman who resented this effort "to take over a beautiful natural tract for the benefit of automobilists." The promise was not kept quickly. A new survey took from 1917 to 1918; a contractor, J. N. Jacobson, finished the road from the switchbacks to Milner Pass in September 1920.

On the western side, Dick McQueary, Grand County contractor, and Franklin I. Huntington, lanky surveyor, plotted a road from Poudre Lakes to the North Fork of the Grand River in one day in 1912. In 1915, the Grand County Commissioners hired McQueary to complete the half-made road from Grand Lake through the bogs to Squeaky Bob's resort. Next year the U.S. Geological Survey made a precise survey up to Milner Pass. The state paid McQueary $49,000 to build the 5½ miles with nine switchbacks. The grading was done from August 1917 to June 1918, the road finished by the summer of 1920. Although rebuilt twice, 1932 and 1942, the route remains essentially the same.

The official opening day, September 14, 1920, saw Dick McQueary driving from Grand Lake to Estes Park, and L. C. Way, superintendent of the National Park, driving not only to Grand Lake but to Berthoud Pass, Denver, and back to Estes, the first use of this scenic loop.

With the road open, maintenance, especially on the Fall River side, remained. On July 23, 1923, a cloudburst eradicated five miles of road, stranding one bus and five passenger cars. Every spring the big drift at the top had to be hand shoveled. Three snowslides could be depended on to run after the road was open for the summer. In June 1929, Old Faithful ran each day between 2 and 3 PM for thirteen consecutive days. The grade, too, was steep; many a Model-T backed up because its reverse had more power than its low gear, and on the second switchback, reached by a 12-percent grade, drivers backed and filled to make the turn.

After Trail Ridge Road opened in 1932, traffic on the Fall River Road was confined to cars going up only. In 1952 the Park closed the road above Chasm Falls. On July 1, 1968, it re-opened for up-traffic only.

Fall River Pass (11,796')   MUMMY RANGE
There sits Fall River Pass at 11,796 feet. Four miles down the road, over 1,000 feet lower in altitude, is Milner Pass. Fall River Pass does not span the Continental Divide, Milner Pass does. What does Fall River Pass cross? The divide between the waters of Fall River which flows east and the Poudre which flows north, and they both reach the South Platte River.

Fan Falls   WILD BASIN
Named by Ranger Jack Moomaw.

Fan Lake   MUMMY RANGE
Fan Lake, formed by the Fall River flood of 1982, lies west of the alluvial fan in Horseshoe Park. Even though this lake may once have been considered to be a transient feature, the name "Fan Lake" is in fairly wide usage, including by the fish resource management.

Farview Curve   NEVER SUMMER
The view extends from the Never Summer Mountains and their Grand Ditch, down the Colorado River toward Grand Lake and Middle Park.

Fay Lakes   MUMMY RANGE
C. E. Fay of Tufts College climbed in this area with Chapin in 1888. Fay was later the first president of the American Alpine Club.

Fern Creek   FOREST CANYON
Who named Fern Creek? Here are the choices:
1. Abner Sprague said he named Fern Creek because the trees in the canyon through which it runs sway in the wind like giant ferns.
2. Dr. Workman and Mr. Turck of Denver discovered Fern Creek and named it for the bracken that grows along its lower reaches. Then they discovered Fern Lake, thinking it was the source of the creek.
3. A younger daughter of Dr. W. J. Workman said he may have named it for one of the earlier of his four wives; she was not sure, however, that one of his wives had been named Fern. Since Dr. Workman's

first child was born in 1873 and his last in 1918, the younger daughter may be forgiven for not knowing definitely the name of the earlier wife. Just for the record, here are the names of the wives: Katherine J. Elbert, 1872; Emma Wells Howard, 1881; Julie (Lulu) Ripley Oliphant, 1888; Florence J. Mount, 1915.

Fern Falls   FOREST CANYON
Dr. Workman called these Lulu, the nickname of his third wife.

Fern Lake   FOREST CANYON
Dr. William J. Workman came to Denver from his home in Ashland, Kansas, about 1900. In the winter he practiced his profession, living at 1057 Race Street, Denver; but he managed to spend at least five months a year in Estes Park, fishing. He built Fern Lake Lodge in 1910 and sold it five years later so he could devote his whole time to fishing, which he did skillfully despite a withered arm. When someone asked him if he had climbed Longs Peak he looked surprised and said, "Hell, no! There are no fish up there!"

Whether or not he named the lake, Dr. Workman's lodge (enlarged by subsequent owners) made the area one of the best-known beauty spots in northern Colorado. At the end of a five-mile trail, Dr. Workman built a series of cabins and a central building that housed a living room, dining room, and kitchen. The living room floor was made of cross sections of logs, sawed smooth and laid flat, with pounded dirt between. The dining room demonstrated the doctor's inventiveness by its large Lazy Susan table. Here he entertained his guests by spinning fish stories. The kitchen was well supplied by packhorses from the end of the road in Moraine Park. After 1915 various people ran the lodge—Cliff Higby, Frank W. Byerly, Mrs. Edna Bishop, her son James. After 1939 meals and lodging were no longer furnished, but light refreshments for tired walkers were available until 1950. The lease expired in 1958 and the Rocky Mountain National Park took back the land.

In February 1916, the Estes Park Outdoor Club took the directors of the Colorado Mountain Club to a "snow frolic" at Fern Lake Lodge, owned at that time by Clifford Higby. The next year and each winter thereafter until 1934, the lodge was opened for about two weeks for the winter outing of the Colorado Mountain Club. Supplies were laid down in the fall, with fresh food carried in by the lodge owners. Ranger Jack Moomaw, one of the sturdiest of skiers, brought in cases of eggs, and added a modern touch in 1925 by packing in a radio. The outings lasted sometimes for ten days, with capacity crowds of forty-five. A history of the art of skiing in Colorado could be written by observations of the skiers on the Fern Lake Trail. In 1917 they wore snowshoes, dragging their skis behind them. Gradually they learned to walk uphill on skis bound with rope to prevent backward slips. Then came Lieutenant Albizzi from Italy, the first controlled skier the club knew. After help from him (lessons $1.00), skiers could turn corners on the down trail without falling. The highlight of every outing, whether one skied well or not, was the moonlight trip to Odessa Lake.

Fifth Lake   GRAND LAKE
The highest of the five lakes on the East Inlet of Grand Lake. In September 1913 the poet, C. E. Hewes, called this Amethyst Pool.

Finch Lake (9,912')   WILD BASIN
Spruce and fir trees around this lake house the Cassin's finch, with its rosy red head, breast, and back. It is the only finch in the forested parts of the Park.
A related bird, the brown-capped rosy finch, nests in cliffs above timberline, where his rosy wings flash against the snowbanks as he snatches insects. This finch, indigenous to Colorado and New Mexico, winters in the foothills on the edge of the plains. Ornithologists have been known to come to Colorado just to see this rosy native.

Finger, The   ESTES PARK
This free-standing spire is also known as Fish Creek Pinnacle.

Fish Bay   LAKE GRANBY

Fish Creek   ESTES PARK
Fish Creek now runs into Lake Estes, but in the days of the English Hotel it was dammed to make a lake near that resort. When the Estes family settled near Fish Creek in 1863, their second location, Joel Estes, Jr., became the fisherman of the family. His older brother, Milton, wrote that it was the duty of this youngster

> to drive up the cows, look after the horses and catch the fish the family used. . . . The largest trout that any of the family caught weighed three and one-half pounds. . . . We fished with grasshoppers or with artificial flies, which we made; and we would change the flies, until we found the color that suited the fish. . . . We kept the fly on top of the water and kept it moving, and the fish would jump after the fly. . . . It was a regular Paradise for the fisherman in those days in the Park.

Flat Top Mountain (11,355')   NEVER SUMMER
To distinguish this mountain from the better publicized Flattop between Bear Lake and Grand Lake, the authorized spelling is in two words.

Flatiron Mountain (12,335')   MUMMY RANGE
Frank R. Koenig, looking at this mountain from the north, thought it resembled his wife's flatiron.

Flattop Mountain (12,324')   GLACIER GORGE, GRAND LAKE

The park service maintains a trail from Bear Lake to the top of Flattop Mountain. Then the trail branches. The longer branch first swings north across the Bighorn Flats, then descends by Tonahutu Creek to the North Fork of the Colorado River. Indians used this trail; the 1914 Arapahos called it the Big Trail. The shorter branch, made by white men in 1901, descends the North Inlet to Grand Lake.

When W. L. Hallett guided Chapin to Flattop Mountain in 1887, they called it Table Top Mountain. It stands on the plateau that gently rolls along the 12,000-foot level west of the Continental Divide from Bighorn Flats south to Andrews Glacier. It has given its name—Flattop Peneplain—to a vast geological feature of the northern Colorado Rockies.

Peneplain is a hybrid word geologists manufactured by adding the English word *plain* to the Latin word for *almost.* Geologists explain the Flattop Peneplain by telling of two sets of mountains—maybe more—that rose and were washed away before the present Rockies were formed. Each was flattened to almost a level plain just above sea level. Following the creation of the present Flattop Peneplain near sea level, great forces within the Earth's crust irresistibly lifted the whole plateau to its present position, over two miles above sea level. The plain originally included Trail Ridge and continued to the north; traces of it can be found as far south and west as Berthoud Pass. In the Park region, Trail Ridge and Bighorn Flats once had no Forest Canyon between them; Mounts Ida, Julian, Terra Tomah, and perhaps Stones Peak, were all one mound. Then the glaciers and streams started to cut back, back, back from the east to carve the spectacular scenery motorists on Trail Ridge Road admire across Forest Canyon.

Flint Pass   MUMMY RANGE

Because he found chips of flint on this pass, indicating that Indians had made arrowheads here, Roger W. Toll named it in 1927.

Forest Canyon   FOREST CANYON

First known as Willow Canyon, Forest Canyon earns its name from the heavy stands of conifers along the slopes of the upper Big Thompson River valley. Abner Sprague thought he named this canyon, but so did the fishing party who named the Gorge Lakes.

Forest Canyon Overlook   FOREST CANYON

For a good look at Forest Canyon, park your car and walk to this lookout point. The dark green forest is deep below you, at the foot of the great peaks that form the Continental Divide opposite the overlook. To help you identify the mountains, the park service has drawn an outline of the view with each peak named.

Forest Canyon Pass   NEVER SUMMER

Forest Lake   FOREST CANYON

Fourth Lake   GRAND LAKE
The Fourth and Fifth lakes on the East Inlet of Grand Lake deserve names, not numbers.

Fox Creek—MUMMY RANGE; **Fox Creek**—WILD BASIN
Theodore Whyte, the Earl of Dunraven's resident manager, hunted the red fox behind imported Irish hounds. The few foxes these hounds pointed for their pink-coated masters could not have affected the fox population of the Park as much as the trap lines set out by men who made their living selling fur; fox pelts were especially valuable. In the fifty years since the National Park banned hunting and trapping, the fox population has increased so that one is occasionally seen today.
The red fox is smaller than a coyote, some say not as cunning. It runs chiefly at night. Usually its coat is reddish gold, but crossbreeding produces heather mixtures, with various colors in one litter.

Fox Park   INDIAN PEAKS
This valley at the western foot of Buchanan Pass was known to local people as Paradise Park. The 1958 Isolation Peak quad labels it Fox Park.

Frigid Lake   WILD BASIN
A record in the file of the Rocky Mountain National Park states that Roger Toll named this in 1924 because he found ice on it in mid-August. Another note states that the lake may have been previously called Isolation Lake. Perhaps from this name Colonel Allen S. Peck derived the name for Isolation Peak.

Frozen Lake   GLACIER GORGE, WILD BASIN
Roger W. Toll in 1922 observed three small ice fields, not *glaciers,* above this lake. The lake is frozen most of the year.

Gable, The   FOREST CANYON
A gable, according to the dictionary, is the vertical triangular portion of the end of a building. The rock called the Gable that stands above Fern Lake is somewhat triangular and certainly vertical and has snow cornices in the winter.

Gabletop Mountain (11,939') FOREST CANYON
This mountain extends back from the Gable. South of it two other tops decorate the skyline—Knobtop and Notchtop.

Gash, The GLACIER GORGE, GRAND LAKE

Gaskil (Site) (i.e., Gaskill) NEVER SUMMER
Captain L. D. C. Gaskill (spelled with two ls) was the manager of the Wolverine Mine in Bowen Gulch, and his is the name commonly used for the town at the foot of the gulch, although the 1884 *Colorado Business Directory* gives Auburn as an alternative name. Gaskill was headquarters for the Wolverine Mine, the most important mine not only in Bowen Gulch but probably in the North Fork region. Nothing is left of Gaskill's buildings, not even of its Rogerson Hotel. Today a large and symmetrical blue spruce grows out of a hole in the ground to mark the cellar of a saloon, once lined with cobblestones.

Gem Lake ESTES PARK, MUMMY RANGE
Gem Lake, one of the few lakes in the Park not formed by glacial action, has neither inlet nor outlet. Its waters come from Heaven or seepage, and flow nowhere. Israel Rowe, the bear hunter who first visited Rowe Glacier, discovered Gem Lake.

George, Mount (12,876') INDIAN PEAKS
Russell D. George (1886-1955) deserved to have a mountain bear his name. He was Professor of Geology at the University of Colorado from 1903 to 1934. As Colorado state geologist from 1907 for about twenty years, his word became law on matters geological. In 1913 he published a topographical and a geological map of the state. His interest in oil shale dated back to 1917; in 1966 some of his prophecies on the importance of that source of oil are materializing. Dr. George, as state geologist, was a member unofficial of the Colorado Geographic Board.
We have no documentary proof that Mount George on the current U.S. Geological Survey map was named for Dr. George. Even his associate professor, P. D. Worcester, had never heard that it was. But Dr. George's climbing friends, from time to time, called three different mountains for him. Two of these, Apache Peak and Mount George, switched places every now and then, the U.S. Forest Service and the Geological Survey disagreeing on their locations. This so confused the Boulder Group of the Colorado Mountain Club that when they announced a climb of what they thought was Mount George they would add "or Apache Peak," and vice versa. To add to the confusion, Boulder climbers at one time routinely called the prominence northeast of Isabelle Glacier (now officially Shoshoni Peak) Mount George, or simply, the George.

Gianttrack Mountain (9,091')   ESTES PARK

In the manuscript of the 1914 Arapaho trip, Oliver Toll wrote that Tom Crispin, the interpreter, recounted a legend of enormously large human footprints about two feet in length on Sheep Mountain. "But," Tom remarked, "the Indians did not trouble to follow up their discovery." From this, the mountain was called the "Giant's Tracks." Sheep Mountain was the white settlers' name for a long ridge until the Colorado Geographic Board decided to christen each of its three summits: Lily Mountain on the south, Rams Horn Mountain in the middle (a less cliched name than Sheep), and, remembering the Indians, Gianttrack on the north.

Legends have a way of changing. The two-foot-long giant tracks the Indians saw have now petrified into two water-filled potholes, each big enough to hold a Volkswagen, not on Gianttrack but on Lily.

Glacier Basin   ESTES PARK

When in 1877 Frank G. Bartholf, owner of much land along the Big Thompson River, admired and playfully claimed this basin as his own, Sprague named it Bartholf Park. The two men were still friends in 1904 when Bartholf was the president and Sprague the engineer of a proposed electric railroad, the Loveland and Estes Park Railroad Company. The line did not materialize, but the name Bartholf remained on the park until the U.S. Board on Geographic Names changed it, for the 1961 map, to Glacier Basin "to agree with common usage." The original name is still retained by geologists who call the ancient glacier that formed the basin Bartholf Glacier.

Glacier Creek, Falls, Gorge, Ridge; Glacier Knobs (10,225')—
GLACIER GORGE

Many features of the Park bear the word glacier. This is appropriate; glaciers carved the Park. Geologists theorize that about a million years ago the climate of the northern part of the Earth grew cold, and snow fell, packed, and turned to ice. As the Earth warmed after the Ice Age, or Pleistocene Era, heavy ice moved down the valleys, scooping them into U-shapes. Ice plucked rock from mountain walls leaving cirques. Ice pulverized stones as it moved, so that water flowing from glaciers looked like milk, and high country lakes looked like cream-of-turquoise soup. Remnants of this tremendous force remain in the Park—moraines, cirques, and lake basins; living glaciers still grind rocks.

Glass Lake (i.e., Lake of Glass)   GLACIER GORGE

Everybody but the U.S. Board on Geographic Names calls this Lake of Glass. Abner Sprague heard with his own ears Robert Sterling Yard name it so, when Sprague was guiding that national park official around the area. Local residents correct you if you speak of Glass Lake —"Oh, you mean

Lake of Glass," they say. The Park trail signs direct you to the Lake of Glass.

The U.S. Board on Geographic Names may have invoked their rule for simplification when they approved Glass Lake in 1932; perhaps they will reconsider according to their system of abiding by well-established local names, and will give official sanction to Lake of Glass.

Gore Range Overlook   MUMMY RANGE

The blue mountains far to the south of this parking place on the Trail Ridge Road form part of the southern rim of Middle Park. They bear the name of an Irish baronet who predated the Earl of Dunraven by some twenty years. Sir St. George Gore hunted in the West, starting in 1855, mostly on the upper Missouri. Many tales are told of him. His equipment included what today we call a camper—a bedroom built into a wagon. Each day his valet supervised a bucket brigade who filled his portable bathtub. When the Irish sportsman felt too lazy to mount a horse but wanted to shoot, he sent his retinue, numbering about forty, to act as beaters; they herded the game toward his tent door where he could shoot without rising. In the evening, so runs the tale, he read Shakespeare aloud to Jim Bridger, mountain man and guide.

Historians can prove that Bridger guided Gore, but have not yet documented the tale that the first road into the Gore Range was made for his wagons, nor that the Irish lord slaughtered game to such an extent that the animal population in the Gore Range has never returned to normal.

The two highest peaks in the Gore Range are named Powell and Eagles Nest. Major John Wesley Powell climbed Mount Powell after he had made the first ascent of Longs Peak. In the can in which they left their names on Mount Powell, his college boy companion also left a biscuit. The one-armed Major had made the biscuit, and the boy was sure it was hard enough to last for eternity.

In 1976, the U.S. Congress set aside over 133,000 acres in the Gore Range as the Eagles Nest Wilderness. Nothing emphasizes the unspoiled nature of this area so much as the popular designation of the mountain peaks as Peak A, Peak B, Peak C, et cetera.

Gorge Lakes   FOREST CANYON

The gorge in which these lakes lie has no name; it should not be confused with Glacier Gorge. Credit for naming most of the Gorge Lakes goes to a fishing party. Perhaps Al and Julian Hayden organized this group of five fishermen. They had previously investigated Hayden Gorge with Abner Sprague, the time he named Hayden Spire and Mount Julian. Ed Andrews, of Andrews Glacier, was with them, and their engineering partner Bob Larimer of Chicago, and, of course, the dedicated fisherman of Fern Lake Lodge, Dr. Workman. When they found no fish in the high lakes, they spent the day climbing and naming lakes. Julian Hayden named Arrowhead and Doughnut lakes for their shape. Dr. Workman was so struck with the contrasting color of the lake above Inkwell that he forgot his compulsion to name lakes for girls and called it Azure Lake. These names have remained on the map, but two other names given by Dr. Workman on this trip have been changed—Glacier Lake to Highest Lake; Primrose Lake to Little Rock Lake. The other Gorge Lakes are Forest Lake, Love Lake, and Rock Lake. A collective name sometimes used for the Gorge Lakes is Paternoster Lakes, because they resemble beads strung on a string.

Gourd Lake   INDIAN PEAKS

Grace Falls   FOREST CANYON, GLACIER GORGE
Grace Workman (Mrs. H. C. Hansen) was one of Dr. Workman's daughters by his second wife.

Granby, Lake (8,280') (spillway elevation)   LAKE GRANBY
As part of the Colorado-Big Thompson Project, the water level of this reservoir goes up and down—up when rain falls or snow melts, down when farmers or cities need water. The name comes from the nearby town of Granby named in 1905 for Granby Hillyer, lawyer from Lamar (later Denver), a friend of David Moffat who was building his broad-gauged railroad across Middle Park.
The skyline of the Indian Peaks seen from the western shore of Lake Granby is almost identical with the view of the same skyline seen from the plains near Longmont (in reverse, of course). From the west, youngsters personify the outline of the Indian Peaks, calling it the Old Man of the Mountains, or Old Abe Lincoln. Mount Toll is the rugged head of the figure stretched along the skyline to the south. The Old Man even has toes, formed by rocks that look like Lone Eagle Peak but are not.

Grand Bay   LAKE GRANBY

Grand Ditch   NEVER SUMMER
The Grand Ditch collects water from the Never Summer Mountains and carries it across the Continental Divide to Long Draw Reservoir. Although technically the name is Grand River Ditch, the 1961 map uses Grand Ditch. This may be because the U.S. Board on Geographic Names tends to simplify names, or because the Grand River has been changed to the Colorado River, or because of the need to distinguish this ditch from the enormous canal near Grand Junction known as the Grand River Ditch. Every name connected with the Grand Ditch since its inception in 1890 has been changed. The Never Summer Mountains were known as Rabbit Ears or the southern part of the Medicine Bow Mountains. The pass over which the ditch crosses the divide was Mountain Meadow Pass, now La

Poudre Pass. Even the name of the Poudre River has variations, as in the report in the *Denver Republican* for October 10, 1897, which states that A. G. Allen had spent the summer constructing "a large high-line feeder for the North Fork Ditch across the divide to the Cachula Poudre."

Various companies have been connected with the Grand Ditch. The company that now owns and operates it is the Water Supply and Storage Company, a non-profit farmers' cooperative with headquarters at Fort Collins, with the enviable record of financing its extensive operations without one cent of government aid.

Irrigation ditches seldom are built all at once and, no exception, the Grand Ditch inched piecemeal along the Never Summer Mountains until on September 1, 1890, the first segment started carrying water across the divide. In 1894 three more miles were built, in 1897 another few miles. Then the ditch head rested at Opposition Creek in Hells Hip Pocket. On August 3, 1906, the District Court at Hot Sulphur Springs awarded the ditch company Priority #83. Total length of canal—eleven miles; total number of headgates—twelve.

This setup satisfied the irrigation company until it decided it needed a reservoir on Long Draw, northeast of La Poudre Pass, but the land belonged to the Rocky Mountain National Park. Congress whittled enough land from the Park holdings for the Long Draw Reservoir in 1923. In the season of 1930, the reservoir opened.

It could hold about six thousand acre feet of water, more than the company could collect. The Grand Ditch had to be lengthened. This took another act of Congress because, in 1929, the Park had acquired the Never Summer Mountains, from which the ditch gets its water. With permission of Congress, the company built three additional miles of ditch at the reputed cost of less than $500 for machine labor, as against $375,000 for hand labor on the first eleven miles. In 1932 the ditch was completed to its end in upper Baker Gulch.

View the Grand Ditch today from Trail Ridge Road. Its scar on the side of the Never Summers looks like a lateral incision, and although it is seventy-five years old, the wound is still raw. The fourteen-mile ditch starts in Bakers Gulch and runs north to La Poudre Pass at an exact slant designed to keep the channel reasonably clean but not to wash out the banks (which it does in wet years). On the eastern side of the pass the water flows into Long Draw Reservoir where it rests until late summer when the farmers around Fort Collins need it for the last irrigation of their sugar beets. Ditches like the Grand Ditch have turned what Major Long called the Great American Desert into the Sugar Bowl of America.

What stories the men who built the Grand Ditch could have told! John McNabb, for instance. He helped build almost every ditch that carried water into the Poudre—constructed the Michigan Ditch, rebuilt the road and bridges after Chambers Lake Dam broke, helped build the town of

Walden in North Park, and as a tie-cutter won fame as the best ax-man on the Poudre, in all "a man to match the mountains," as his friend Norman Fry called him.

McNabb supervised the construction of many miles of the Grand Ditch. His men lived in two ditch-camps, one for Swedes, one for Chinese, the same nationalities, perhaps some of the same men, who, along with the Irish, built the western railroads. The coolies worked on the Grand Ditch in the summer of 1899. They were brought up from the plains by way of the Poudre, over the divide and down to the ditch-camp, great quantities of rice being shipped to them by burro-back over the same route. With shovels and wheelbarrows, about thirty Chinese worked all summer moving rock and earth at a daily wage of seventeen cents up to almost a dollar, depending on which report one reads.

For the Orientals the company built a large dining room and cabins. Whether or not they lived in the cabins is a matter of opinion. Some people claim that small groups of Chinese dug holes in the side of the hill, erected frame entrances, and lived in these caves. The holes are still there, both above and below the Grand Ditch, quite close to the present ditch-camp, now a backcountry campground.

Others, including John Holzwarth, say the caves were for storing supplies. They were definitely used for that purpose when Holzwarth was a youth, some years after the departure of the Chinese. He remembers supplies being stored in the caves in the fall before the snow fell to be used in the spring by maintenance men on the ditch, where work began long before the snows melted enough for supplies to be brought in. One of John Holzwarth's winter chores was to ride up periodically from his father's ranch on the North Fork to check the temperature of the caves. One time it had fallen to 28 degrees, and he found 3,300 pounds of frozen potatoes! He also had to turn the eggs in five cases, a quarter of a turn each trip. He remarked that by spring the eggs were pretty stout. Somewhere by the ditch-camp, he added, rests a ton of sledge hammers, a lost cache.

Grand Lake (8,367') Grand Lake

> *"White man, pause and gaze around,*
> *For we tread now on hallowed ground!"*
> *So said a chief to me one day,*
> *As along the shore we wound our way.*
> *"Tell me chieftain," then I said,*
> *"About this fight so fierce and red;*
> *For I have often heard before*
> *Of a desperate fight in the days of yore."*

So begins Judge Wescott's saga of "The Legend of Grand Lake," commemorating a fight between a Cheyenne-Arapaho band and Ute Indians.

To protect them from the enemy, the Utes put their women and children on rafts and sent them to the middle of Grand Lake. One of the sudden storms for which Grand Lake is notorious drowned them all. Most of the Ute men were killed in battle. Thereafter Indians avoided this lake, calling it Spirit Lake because it is haunted by the souls of the dead. If you do not believe this tale, get up early some summer morning as the sun reaches the eastern shore of the lake. You will see spirit-like vapors rise into the air.

So runs the legend according to Judge Wescott. The 1914 Arapahos remembered only a minor battle, when they surprised some Utes on Sage Brush Flats, drove them to the ridge by the lake, then up the slopes of Shadow Mountain. They remembered nothing about a raft. The Ute fatalities were one man, one woman, and a baby.

On one point the two versions agree—the Arapaho names for Grand Lake included Spirit Lake, but their explanation of the name differs from Judge Wescott's version. The 1914 Arapahos said this:

> Once the lake had nearly frozen over, so that only a little patch of water was left in the center of the lake. In the snow on the ice the Indians found many buffalo tracks. The tracks of one especially large buffalo seemed to come from the center of the lake and return there. The Indians concluded, therefore, that some enormous supernatural buffalo must live in the lake, from which they called it "Spirit Lake."

Grand Lake is the largest natural lake in Colorado, about two miles long. The name comes, of course, from the earlier name of the Colorado River. It has had other names. In 1863 an Irish writer M.O'C. Morris, used Still-Water Lake. In 1901 the commanding officer at Fort Duchesne, Utah, consulted the interpreter for the Northern Utes who said that the Ute name for Grand Lake was *Ungarpakareter,* meaning Red Lake. Phiminister Proctor, the artist who made the statues of the Indian and the Cowboy in Denver's Civic Center, spent much time at Grand Lake from 1875 to 1885. He remembered still another Indian name—"Meteor Lake, because of the number of meteors visible at certain times of year. The fool whites changed the name to Grand Lake."

Granite Pass   Glacier Gorge

Green Knoll—Never Summer; **Green Lakes**—Indian Peaks; **Green Mountain** (10,313')—Grand Lake; **Green Ridge** (8,970')—Grand Lake, Lake Granby

Green Lake—Glacier Gore; **Green Lakes**—Lake Granby
As a guide on Longs Peak, Paul Nesbit used to sit with his customers above Glacier Gorge and point out the three upper lakes; to Paul,

geographically minded, they resembled the maps of Iceland, Italy, and South America. The lowest was South America, and for a time that name was in general use, but maps before and after have called it Green Lake.

Grouse Creek—Lake Granby; **Grouse Creek**—Mummy Range
The two creeks that bear this name are on opposite corners of the Park region—northeast and southwest—but both are in the nine-thousand-foot altitude range. They run in country thick with conifers, just the place for dusky grouse to live. To avoid this duplication of names, one Grouse Creek might be changed to Fool Hen Creek, the name hunters call dusky grouse. The birds deserve the name; when they are disturbed on the ground, they noisily fly to the limbs of trees where they watch the hunters take aim and fire. If the first shots go wild, the fool hens remain sitting while the hunter fires again.

Another popular name for dusky grouse is blue grouse, a name that dates back to August 26, 1776, when Padre Escalante was startled by one in present Montrose County, Colorado.

Teenagers looking for new dance movements and drum rhythms should rise before dawn to see the courting dance of grouse. During their strutting the dusky grouse males inflate purplish sacs in their throats, then let the air out in a series of mellow pops.

Gull Island   Grand Lake, Lake Granby
Several species of gulls nest around Great Salt Lake and the marshes of the Great Plains, and then sail the skies of the West. The one most likely to be seen around Lake Granby is the ring-billed gull that nests near Salt Lake. Its bill looks as if someone had snapped a rubber band around it.

Over mountain valleys on the eastern slope of the Park the Franklin's gull may be seen. They nest in the marshes of the Great Plains. In late July hundreds of these graceful birds soar over the irrigated farmlands of northern Colorado and spill upland into the Estes Park region, feeding on schools of sawflies and other airborne insects. These plains birds winging over Glacier Basin seem incongruous.

Hague Creek   Mummy Range

Hagues Peak (13,560')   Mummy Range
The Hague brothers, James and Arnold, were Bostonians, grandsons of a sea captain, graduates of Yale University and scientific schools in

Germany. They worked for Clarence King, also a Yale graduate, on the Survey of the 40th Parallel. The Hagues were his kind of men—quiet, scholarly, thorough. James Hague was one of the men who exposed the Great Diamond Hoax, and his report on the mining industry (Vol. II of the 40th Parallel reports) told all that in 1870 was known about western mining.

His younger brother Arnold (1840-1917), slight in build, not overly strong, was more intimately connected with the Estes Park region than was James. Arnold climbed Longs Peak with Clarence King and brainy Henry Adams in 1871, the year smoke from forest fires prevented topographical work. He may have used the top of Hagues Peak as a triangulation point, giving his fellow workers an obvious reason for naming it. Arnold Hague and S. F. Emmons wrote *Descriptive Geology,* the monumental opus published by the survey in 1877. After 1883, Arnold Hague concentrated on the geology of Yellowstone, and wrote a number of treatises on its rocks and geysers.

Haiyaha, Lake GLACIER GORGE

This was one of the Indian words suggested by Harriet Vaille, chairman of the Nomenclature Committee of the Colorado Mountain Club. The lake was called Rainbow on Nell's map, but J. G. Rogers noted, "Rainbow Lake name disappeared. Lake Haiyaha was approved." The name, meaning rock, was adopted because, as Emch wrote, "the bottom of the valley is filled with an indescribable mass of huge boulders."

Half Mountain (11,482') GLACIER GORGE

After glaciers finished slicing the rock on this mountain, only half a mountain was left.

Hallett Creek—GRAND LAKE; **Hallett Peak** (12,713')—GLACIER GORGE, GRAND LAKE

"The first difficulty which presents itself to the mountaineer in Colorado," wrote Frederick Chapin of the Appalachian Mountain Club, "is a lack of guides." The club members easily hired guides in the Swiss Alps, but in Estes Park in 1887 Chapin wrote:

> The hunters object to climbing or walking; and although very familiar with the country, hunting as they do all around the peaks, it is rarely that they climb to the mountain tops. One of their number, a dweller in an upper park, told me he did not "see anything in the high mountains, and did not know about the scenery." "Yes," said a listener, "he don't know about anything but 'bar.'"
>
> But our little company at Ferguson's was well provided with a leader in the person of a gentleman who has a cottage near this ranch, who spends all the summer months in the mountains and knows thoroughly every trail and stream for many miles around. To him I am indebted for all that I saw

of the Front Range, excepting my ascent of Long's Peak or of some of the lower elevations. (Parson Lamb or his son Carlyle guided Chapin up Longs Peak.)

The sharpest peak in the Front Range, as seen from the valley of the Big Thompson Creek, which runs through Estes Park, is a mountain near the centre of the range, to the left of Table Top Mountain (Flattop). It rises from the large snowfield which hangs like a true glacier (Tyndall Glacier) to a steep ridge connecting the peak with Table Mountain. . . . When our acknowledged leader proposed taking our little company, consisting of a member of the Appalachian Mountain Club, the surgeon, and myself, over the mill trail to the Continental Divide, I had no doubt that my plans would succeed.

The day fixed upon was late August. We were to have been off at six o'clock, but it was half past six before we left the ranch. We intended to take a barometer, but our leader dropped it on the porch as we were packing, and it fell three thousand feet. We rode off, however, in good spirits, thinking ourselves fortunate in getting started even so early, for the horses had to be "rounded up" for us; and Tom, the mule, galloped all over the hillside before he was captured.

Chapin explained why he rode as far as possible up any mountain: he carried his photographic equipment, including bulky plates. "The ideal way to climb mountains is to have nothing whatever to carry—no camera, no theodolite, no rifle—nothing to load one down except perhaps a cracker and a bottle of cold tea." On this climb Chapin saw mountain sheep but had a bad case of buck fever when he tried to shoot them with his camera.

The horsemen followed a trail, and then cairns, until they reached Flattop. Here the leader waited with the horses while Chapin and Dr. Otis climbed the sharp peak to the south. They found

a cairn on the summit, probably piled up years ago by some indefatigable member of the Survey party. . . . We scanned the depths of the gorges below, and all the rock-strewn waste of Table Mountain, hoping to have one more glimpse of the big-horn. . . . A wilder scene . . . they cannot find, nor better hiding-places, nor a more awful series of cliffs to wander among than the ravines of Mount Hallett.

Thus, simply, Chapin announced the christening of the mountain for their leader, William L. Hallett. That this photogenic peak in the Rocky Mountain National Park should be so named is appropriate, not only because Hallett was a summer resident of Estes Park from 1878, but because he was one of the first Colorado men to climb mountains for the sake of mountain climbing.

William L. Hallett and his mother came to Colorado in 1878 from Springfield, Massachusetts. They almost immediately went to Estes Park, staying first at the English Hotel, then with the Fergusons. Hallett went back to New York for his bride in 1879, and his idea of a honeymoon was a horseback trip from Estes Park to Grand Lake with Abner Sprague as guide. On three acres given them by Ferguson, in 1881 the Halletts built Edgemont, the frame house with the Victorian flavor that still stands near Marys Lake, and there his two daughters and four sons spent sun-drenched summers. In the winter they lived in Denver at 1200 Vine Street. (This is not the family of Judge Moses Hallett and his son Lucius who lived at 900 Logan, nor the Sam Halletts of Aspen and 847 Pearl Street, Denver.)

The mines of Leadville and Aspen, the Gunnison country, and the San Juan were clamoring for trained engineers in the late 1870s, but William L. Hallett, a recent graduate of the Massachusetts Institute of Technology, went into the cattle business. In Colorado Springs in 1882 he helped organize the Powder River Live Stock Company. In the fall of 1886, twenty-four thousand head of cattle bearing their "21" brand grazed in Wyoming. After that incredible winter, the company gathered only eight thousand head. Despite the $400,000 loss, the company stayed in business, but dissolved in 1893.

William L. Hallett had his own ranch west of Loveland, Colorado. He pushed his cattle to the high country of Estes Park for summer grazing. Unlike most cattlemen, he was interested in mountains not simply as feeding lots but as unexplored territory. His most publicized adventure was his fall into a crevice on a snowbank which turned out to be a crevasse in a glacier. (See Rowe Glacier.)

Hallett's friendship with Chapin and other dedicated mountaineers doubtless influenced him and eighteen young men of Denver to form in 1896 the first climbing club in Colorado, the Rocky Mountain Club. Hallett was vice-president and chairman of explorations. The club evidently considered him their star climber because they picked him to go with Italian climbers on the first ascent of Mount St. Elias in Alaska, but, at the last minute, the Italians decided not to include any Americans. When the Rocky Mountain Club sent an expedition to climb the Grand Teton in Wyoming, Hallett was to be their leader. Members of the club collected $150 to pay his expenses, but, again at the last minute, he was unable to leave his job with the Arkansas Smelter at Leadville. Substituting as leader, Frank Spalding, later Episcopal Bishop of Utah, planted the flag of the Rocky Mountain Club on top of the Grand Teton on August 16, 1898. After his adventures in cattle raising, William L. Hallett returned to his engineering profession, as smelter manager, then as an employee of the Denver Water Board. Three of his sons, graduates of the Colorado School of Mines, became practicing engineers. William L. Hallett died in 1941, at the age of ninety.

Hallowell Park—See Hollowell Park.

Hanging Valley FOREST CANYON

During the Ice Age a huge glacier over one thousand feet deep filled the valley of Horseshoe Park. Smaller masses of ice in the tributary valleys did not cut as deep as the principal glacier. When the ice melted, it left these side valleys hanging about one thousand feet above the glacial floor. Their streams have since cut their way downward, frequently forming sheer falls like Thousand Falls and Horseshoe Falls.

Harbison Meadow GRAND LAKE

Harry Harbison built the Harbison Ditch to bring water to his Columbine Lake where he homesteaded. His two-story building still stands in Grand Lake village. He kept a store on the first floor, let the villagers dance to the tunes of three fiddlers on the second.

Another Harbison family settled on the North Fork of the Colorado. The two daughters, Annie and Kitty, took up homesteads, including the present Harbison Meadows. The homestead law stipulated residence on the land a certain number of nights a year. Each sister had a cabin in which she slept, the cabins being about ten yards apart on either side of the boundary line of their homesteads. The Harbison women were famed for their fried chicken dinners which summer residents of Grand Lake enjoyed on Sunday outings. The sisters had a brother named Robert who was not noted for his industry, but he did manage to deliver the milk from the Harbison dairy herd. This involved not only driving to the village but also rowing across the lake to summer homes on the southeastern shore.

The Harbisons were kindly people. When Henry Schnoor, who lived on the Green Mountain Ranch, was left with the rearing of his two baby girls, the Harbisons took the children. Schnoor was not a widower—his wife simply walked away from what she considered the God-forsaken country of the North Fork.

Harvey Island (8,321') LAKE GRANBY

The waters of Lake Granby now cover the Jim Harvey Ranch, except for the hill called Harvey Island. The Circle H brand no longer sizzles the hide of Jim Harvey's cattle, but marks a restaurant on the shores of the lake. Harvey's daughter and son-in-law, the Frank Nortons, have turned from ranching to boating at the Norton Marina.

Hayden Creek, Gorge, Lake, Spire FOREST CANYON

Sprague named these features in 1911 after two tenderfeet, Al and Julian Hayden. (See Mount Julian.) In 1886 Chapin noted the spire was "one sharp rock-peak [that] deserves attention of mountaineers." The sign at Forest Canyon Lookout labels it Hayden Prong; and Walter Fricke states that, because of difficulty of access, only five ascents were made between 1923 and 1964.

Haynach Lakes   FOREST CANYON, GRAND LAKE
The 1914 Arapahos used the word *haa´·nach* to mean snow water. This name the Colorado Geographic Board modified for these lakes. John Holzwarth speaks for a number of North Fork residents when he says, "They are always the Murphy Lakes to me," but he does not add any information about Murphy.

Hazeline Lake   MUMMY RANGE
About 1913, Frank R. Koenig married Hazel Ramsey, daughter of Hugh Ramsey of Pingree Park. (See Ramsey Peak.) Abner Sprague guided them on their honeymoon to this lake, which the young husband named for his wife, adding the *line* to rhyme with Emmaline Lake, which he had named for his mother.

Helene, Lake   FOREST CANYON, GLACIER GORGE
Dr. Workman of Fern Lake Lodge was pestered by two girls who insisted he name lakes in their honor. To satisfy two at once he called this Lake Helmary. Later this pleasantry was superseded when Dr. Workman wished to honor Helene, daughter of a Denver lawyer, George Stidger, a summer cottager. (See also Two Rivers Lake.)

Hell Canyon   INDIAN PEAKS
Surveyors for the Union Pacific Railroad in 1882 almost lost their lives before they were able to struggle out of this canyon during a storm. The name expresses their feelings about the canyon. (See Pawnee Pass and Mount Irving Hale.)

Hells Hip Pocket   NEVER SUMMER
Here the Grand Ditch runs in a flume under the big rocks of precipitous Opposition Creek. The hellish name is credited to Squeak Wheeler, he of the graphic vocabulary acquired during his services with the Rough Riders of the Spanish-American War.

Hiamovi Mountain (12,395')   INDIAN PEAKS
An undocumented source gives Hiamovi as derived from an Indian word meaning God. Was this the meaning Ellsworth Bethel had in mind when he proposed this name for the mountain that stands between Paradise Park and Hells Canyon? Or was it named for a Cheyenne named Hiamovi (High Chief) who helped Natalie Curtis collect songs, legends, and pictures for her book, published by Harper in 1908, called *The Indians' Book?* Hiamovi painted many of the illustrations and contributed an account of Cheyenne life before the white men came West.

Hidden Cove   GRAND LAKE, LAKE GRANBY

Hidden River   FOREST CANYON

Chapin in 1886, descending from the snowbank on Stones Peak, probably by Hidden River, wrote: "This unnamed and unexplored canyon rivals in the steepness of its walls many of the famous gorges of Colorado."

Hidden Valley, Hidden Valley Creek—FOREST CANYON, MUMMY RANGE

When the southern lateral moraine of the now-melted Fall River Glacier dammed Hidden Valley it forced the waters of Hidden Valley Creek to flow, not due north as its natural instincts would have led it, but due east along the south side of the moraine. Here beaver dams near the present road gave it the name of Beaver Dam Creek at one time. After about a mile the creek found a low place in the moraine, and cascaded down four hundred feet to the bed of Horseshoe Park. This plunge from a platform gave it the name of Bench Creek at one time.

Anyone looking up the southern slopes of Horseshoe Park sees what appears to be an unbroken forest of trees to timberline. Hidden Valley is indeed hidden from this viewpoint. Now that it holds a road, a ski lodge, and tows, it is not exactly a Hidden Valley.

Highest Lake   FOREST CANYON, GRAND LAKE

Dr. Workman called one of the Gorge Lakes, Glacier Lake; this twenty-acre lake is probably the one since it lies at the foot of a permanent snowfield, under the crest of the Continental Divide at an elevation of about 12,500 feet. It is the highest not only of the nine named Gorge Lakes, but, next to the lake at Rowe Glacier, the highest in the Park.

Hitchings Gulch (i.e., Hichings)   NEVER SUMMER

A prospector named Hichens (misspelled Hitchings on the 1961 map) located a vein here in the early 1890s. Over it he erected a shaft house and built a few other buildings, and here he lived and worked for years. When he was an old man, still coming to Grand Lake for supplies, he used to ask people what he should say when he met his three dogs in Heaven. "Each of them thought he was my best friend."

Hollowell Park   ESTES PARK

George C. Hollowell's name was on this park as early as 1892 when the township map recorded it. Dan Griffith of Estes Park village remembered that Hollowell brought cattle from Loveland for summer grazing. He lived in a shack, known to cattlemen as a summer cabin, in the park that bears his name.

Hollowell Park was previously spelled "Hallowell." According to the Hollowell family, the spelling error was made in reading the original homestead land records. Since it was unclear whether the letter after the "H" was an "a" or an "o," the most common spelling was used. Family members still live in Loveland, Colorado, and they have requested that the National Park Service use he correct spelling, which is "Hollowell."

Hondius Park ESTES PARK, MUMMY RANGE

Pieter Hondius came from Holland to Estes Park for his health, and bought two thousand acres of land on Beaver Creek including Hupp's homestead. In 1914 the Arapaho Indians, camping on Beaver Creek, told of a big spring high on Deer Mountain near which stood a huge tree. Hondius knew the spring—he piped its waters to the cabins at Elkhorn Lodge—but not the tree. His belief in the stories told by the Indians was strengthened when he later found the rotting trunk of an enormous tree near the spring.

Hondius married Ella James, daughter of the owners of Elkhorn Lodge. She managed the lodge in the summers while Pieter, retreating from asthma, spent many summers at Lawn Lake: an employee brought him supplies once a week. In the winters Mr. and Mrs. Hondius and their son sought warmer climates. In 1934 Pieter Hondius died at Palm Springs. The next year Mrs. Hondius built a $7,000 addition to the Estes Park Library in memory of her husband.

Horse Creek WILD BASIN

Horseshoe Falls, Park MUMMY RANGE

The flat valley of Horseshoe Park is the bed of a former glacial lake impounded by a terminal moraine. The name might come from the innumerable horseshoe bends Fall River makes as it meanders through the valley; or it might come from the shape of the valley, with the curved top of the horseshoe at the west end near Endovalley Campground, or from a lake shaped like a horseshoe.

Willard H. Ashton acquired land in Horseshoe Park in 1907. On June 4, 1908, the *Mountaineer,* an Estes Park newspaper that lived about four months, reported this about Ashton's new hotel:

> Frank Lloyd Wright, the famous architect of Chicago, drew the plans and has produced a building which seems a part of the beautiful landscape, rather than a mar upon it, as is so often the case with summer hotels.

Ashton ran Horseshoe Inn until 1915; the new owners sold it to the National Park in 1931, which razed the buildings. The bears which regularly tipped over the garbage cans outside the inn's kitchen door were forced to look elsewhere for their dinner. Now Horseshoe Park has returned to nature, except for the Endovalley Campground and the large parking lot designed for people who come to hear the elk bugle in the fall. (See Little Horseshoe Park.)

Horsetooth Peak (10,344')   WILD BASIN
The 1910 Burlington Railroad map labeled this Chisel Top; the 1911
Cooper-Babcock map called it Horsetooth Mountain; the 1961 Rocky
Mountain National Park map changed it to Horsetooth Peak.

Hourglass Lake   FOREST CANYON, GRAND LAKE

Howard Mountain (12,810')   NEVER SUMMER
We thought this an earthbound name for a mountain that stands high
among the Cloud Peaks of the Never Summer Mountains, until we found
that Luke Howard, early English meteorologist, was the first man to clas-
sify cloud forms. In 1803 he identified cirrus, cumulus, nimbus, and stratus clouds. Who but the erudite James Grafton Rogers of the Colorado
Geographic Board, namer of the Cloud Peaks, would have named the highest after the man who christened cloud forms? This theory was exploded
in a letter from Jim Rogers himself in 1965. "Your charming suggestion
about Dr. Howard," he wrote, "has no footing in my memory." Then he
cited a map published by Clason before 1913, before the birth of the Colorado Geographic Board, on which Mount Howard was printed.
    Who then was Howard? Rogers had a penciled note (when he penciled
notes he distrusted the information) on his card for Mount Howard stating, "Shep Husted says Sour Howard was a prospector living on Cinder
Creek." (Where was Cinder Creek?) Three Howard families now live in
North Park; perhaps they know the history of the name of Mount Howard.
    The *Rocky Mountain News* for July 15, 1880, refers to a Howard on the
North Fork of the Colorado River—J. E. Howard (was his nickname
Sour?). He and W. B. Baker (not the Baker of Baker Mountain) planned
to spend the winter of 1879-80 at their mining claim near Lulu City. They
managed to stay until February 20. Equipped with snowshoes, one blan-
ket each, and "what chuck they could carry," they started for Estes Park,
twenty-five miles away. Five days later they dragged into the village.
    The article reported the exact location of Lulu City in relation to Lead
Mountain, Howard Mountain, and Mount Shipler. The article also cited
Sheep Mountain near Lulu City, and one wonders whether this was an
early name for Specimen Mountain which sheep so often frequent.

Hunters Creek   WILD BASIN
Where the trail to Sandbeach Lake crosses this creek, in 1908 Dean
Babcock noted a carving on a wooden plank. It showed a party of white
men hunting. He named the creek for the hunters.

Husted, Lake   MUMMY RANGE
Shepherd Husted came to Estes Park in 1898, passed the forest service
examination in 1905, and served as ranger for two years before he became
a professional guide and wrangler in the Estes Park region. He was one of

the best. Through study and association with scientists he became an expert naturalist. As guide for the 1914 Arapaho Indians, his knowledge of every gulch and hill helped clarify their remarks, and his ability to fraternize with the jolly Arapaho, Sherman Sage, resulted in additional information. Husted's friendship as well as his skillful guide services were appreciated by such visitors to the Park as Chief Justice Charles Evans Hughes, Edna Ferber, Otis Skinner, and the Doctors Mayo.

Hutcheson Lakes   WILD BASIN
Henry Hutcheson was the contractor for at least three Wild Basin reservoirs—Bluebird, Pear, and Sandbeach. Originally from Michigan, Hutcheson arrived in Lyons in 1890 where he made his home until his death in 1941. He owned mining claims on upper Cony Creek, which probably led to the decision in 1950-1954 by the U.S. Board on Geographic Names to name four lakes—two in the Rocky Mountain National Park, two in Roosevelt National Forest—Hutcheson Lakes.

Not Hutcheson, but Hutchins, had been the name suggested for these lakes by the Park personnel. In the early 1920s Charles Bowman Hutchins, known to many as the "Bird Man," lectured on birds and other natural history subjects, not only in northern Colorado but over the United States. He was a nature guide at Grand Lake, a militant bird-lover, an artist, and a musician of sorts, holding school children under the spell of his whistled bird calls and instant chalk sketches. Could it be that some member of the Park staff thought the Bird Man's name would rest appropriately among the bird lakes of Wild Basin?

Still another name had been proposed for these lakes. The Right Reverend Robert H. Mize, Episcopal bishop of Kansas, from Salina, summered at Allens Park and tried earnestly but in vain to have the lakes officially called the Lakes of the Archangels.

Ice Field Pass   MUMMY RANGE
Roger Toll, superintendent of the Park, named this in 1924.

Iceberg Lake   MUMMY RANGE
A broad parking place on Trail Ridge Road encourages travelers to leave their cars and peer down at this lake. Many walk down to examine at close range the blocks of ice that never melt completely. The reddish brown cliff behind the lake is hardened lava, the result of the same volcanic action that created Specimen Mountain.

Iceberg Pass (11,827')   MUMMY RANGE
Roger Toll named this in 1924.

Icy Brook   GLACIER GORGE
Icy Brook starts above Sky Pond which was named by an easterner,
Robert Sterling Yard. One suspects he also named Icy Brook, because a
westerner would call it creek, and probably pronounce it "crick."

Ida, Mount   FOREST CANYON
This name and that of Mount Alice are examples of how frustrating it
can be to *cherchez la femme* while searching for name sources. Both ladies
have been impossible to trace. "Name approved at request of Dr. W. S.
Cooper, botanist. Ida not known." So reads a card in Rogers's place name
file. Mount Ida first appeared on a 1915 map, long before Trail Ridge Road
opened up the view of Mount Ida across Forest Canyon.

Possible, but certainly not probable, candidates for the honor are Ida
Webster, the first wife of Theodore Whyte, Dunraven's manager; and Ida
Lamb, a daughter of Elkanah Lamb. She died before he came to Colorado,
making this an even more tenuous theory than that he named Mount
Alice for his childhood sweetheart. This Mount Ida, about 12,840 feet
high, on the divide, is not to be confused with a point on the slope of
Mount Bross near Hot Sulphur Springs named for Ida Ganson, daughter
of a hotel keeper. Probably the first white girl-child to live in Grand
County, she had the distinction, even at the age of ten, of being an intelligent collector of insects.

Perhaps Mount Ida is named for Mount Ida in Crete, birthplace of
Zeus. Was this Colorado mountain named by someone with a classical
education like the school teacher who named Mount Olympus far to the
east of Mount Ida?

Or could Judge Wescott of Grand Lake have named the mountain from
his reading in mythology? From his cabin on the southwestern shore of
Grand Lake he must have constantly noted the sloping ridge and abrupt
drop-off of this mountain to the north, so often sprinkled with snow after
autumn showers. The cottagers who followed Judge Wescott on that side
of the lake usually called it Specimen Mountain. This bothered Charles
Hanington, knowledgeable climber that he was, but without benefit of
maps, he erroneously concluded it was Shipler Mountain.

Indigo Pond   WILD BASIN
Named by Jack Moomaw in 1921.

Inkwell Lake   FOREST CANYON
The fishermen who went to the Gorge Lakes about 1901 all noted the
reflection in this lake of the great black wall behind it. To describe this
effect, Al Hayden thought up the name Inkwell.

Inn Brook   ESTES PARK, GLACIER GORGE
This creek, originating at the Eugenia Mine, runs by the Swiss Village which stands on the site of Enos Mills's famous Longs Peak Inn. Presumably the creek was named because it ran by the inn, therefore named after Enos Mills had acquired Longs Peak House and changed the name to Longs Peak Inn. Enos Mills himself called the stream Evergreen Brook, and some records say it was called Sarah, or Sophia Brook, but Inn Brook is the name that survives.

Inspiration Point   LAKE GRANBY

Irene Lake   FOREST CANYON, GLACIER GORGE
The three lakes at the foot of Sprague Glacier were called Rainbow Lakes. On the 1961 map, one is Rainbow Lake, one has no name, and one, a dot of a lake, is called Irene. Since this is a recent decision, surely someone knows who this Irene is.

Irene, Lake   NEVER SUMMER
Squeaky Bob named this for an eastern girl who stayed at his ranch. One of his neighbors remarked that since Bob stocked the lake he had a right to name it.

Iron Mountain (12,265')   NEVER SUMMER
This mineralized mountain in the Never Summer Range makes compasses go wild.

Ironclads, The   WILD BASIN
These rocks rise like fortress walls, appearing to have little vegetation, and when walked on, the jumbled mass of stone rings like metal.

Irving Hale Creek; Irving Hale, Mount (11,754')—INDIAN PEAKS, LAKE GRANBY
The name of Hale, father and son, weaves in and out of Colorado history. The father, Horace, supervised the schools of Central City in the 1860s. In 1882 he produced $2,000 out of his own pocket to save the original Central City Opera House Association. Hale became the second president of the University of Colorado, and the Hale Science Building on the Boulder campus bears his name.
The son, Irving, in 1878 decided to take the competitive examination for West Point. Needing money and time to study, he thought of an ingenious plan. He bought a covered wagon and a team of mules wise enough to pull the wagon while he studied. All summer long, back and forth over Berthoud Pass between Central City and Grand Lake, the mules pulled the wagon loaded with freight, the student, and his books. On his last trip, when a forest fire prevented access to Berthoud Pass,

Irving drove over Rollins Pass which had been practically abandoned as a wagon road. Although he had no time to study on that trip, he passed the exams for the U.S. Military Academy and graduated at the head of his class.

Because of his brilliant leadership in commanding the Colorado troops in the Philippines during the Spanish-American War, General Irving Hale came home a hero. A bronze bas-relief of him is now at the head of the south steps of the Colorado Capitol, and Hale Boulevard in Denver commemorates him.

When General Hale was an old man, felled by a stroke, Ellsworth Bethel proposed that a mountain should be named in his honor. Harriet Vaille, in a letter dated June 1, 1915, thanked R. B. Marshall of the Geological Survey for making an exception to the rule that mountains should not bear the names of living persons. She said that General Hale, told of this honor, was, in spite of his loss of the full power of speech, able to convey his special delight at the proximity of his peak to Hell Canyon.

Isabelle Glacier   INDIAN PEAKS
Isabelle was the wife of Fred Fair of Boulder. Her glacier clings to the northeastern cliffs of Apache Peak just over the divide from his Fair Glacier. Both were named by Junius Henderson of the science faculty of the University of Colorado.

Isabelle, Lake   INDIAN PEAKS
Hazel Schmoll of Ward remembers when this was called Timberline Lake. It now takes its name from Isabelle Glacier which sends water to it from the ultimate head of South St. Vrain Creek.

Island Lake   INDIAN PEAKS
At least four islands lie in this timber-surrounded lake.

Isolation Peak (13,118')   GRAND LAKE, WILD BASIN
This summit on the Continental Divide is definitely isolated; even the trails from East Inlet and Wild Basin do not attempt to climb its formidable cliffs. This may have been the mountain Ellsworth Bethel wanted to call Sioux Peak, a name not countenanced by the U.S. Board on Geographic Names. In the *Estes Park Trail,* in 1925, Roger Toll called this mountain Clarence King, a name proposed in 1911 for Copeland Mountain. The mountain remained nameless until 1942 when Colonel Allen S. Peck, supervisor of the Arapaho National Forest, proposed Isolation Peak to the board of the Colorado Mountain Club. The staff of the Rocky Mountain National Park approved the name, preferring it to the proposed Jewell Peak, after Edward S. Jewell of the Omaha Walking Club. (See Jewel Lake.)

Jackstraw Mountain (11,704') NEVER SUMMER

The child's game of jackstraws consists of tossing many slivers of wood in a heap, then delicately trying to remove one without disturbing the others. This mountain looks like a giant game of jackstraws, with dead trees standing upright or crazily jumbled as they were left by a fire in 1872. The mountain had no name, needed none because it was so seldom seen until 1920 when the automobile road going west from Poudre Lakes afforded a good view of it. Roger Toll named it in 1924.

Whenever a forest fire started in the early West, it usually burned until rain or snow put it out, like the one in 1871 in North Park; Hague reported that this fire kept the King Survey men from doing any topographical work until an October snow brought on sparkling weather. Fires were, and are, often started by lightning. The earliest recorded fire set by a careless white camper was in 1820, when Dr. Edwin James returned after a two-day climb of Pikes Peak to find his food and extra clothing burned at his campsite. Indians deliberately set fires in the mountains as well as on the prairies to drive out game or to frighten white settlers. In 1875 Colorow, the obese Ute, never docile under white rule, set fires designed to burn the settlers' homes on the eastern slope of the northern Front Range. The story is that the wind changed, blowing the fire to the timbered hills in Middle Park where the Utes lived.

One has but to read accounts of early visitors to Denver who could not see the mountains for days at a time because of forest fire smoke (not city smaze) to be grateful for modern fire-fighting methods.

Jacob Spring ESTES PARK

This spring was not named for Jacob's Well in the Bible, nor for a "Mr. Jacobs" who, according to Enos Mills, paid Michael Hollenbeck $250 for the Joel Estes claims in the 1860s, but for Art Jacob who has lived on Fish Creek near the spring since about 1936. He and his brother Ralph, a more recent resident, are expert lumbermen. The Jacob property was homesteaded by Nettie Spalding McFadden at the turn of the century—President McKinley signed the deed—then bought by Will Porter of Denver who sold to Art Jacob. About 1958, when the U.S. surveyors were mapping the area, Art Jacob saved them time by leading them directly to the corner posts of properties on Fish Creek, and the survey men named the spring for him.

Jewel Lake GLACIER GORGE:

On July 14, 1923, the Omaha Walking Club requested that Washington name this lake in honor of Edwin S. Jewell, organizer of their club and a member of the Prairie Club of Chicago. When Washington asked Roger Toll, he approved, providing the word be spelled with one "l"—Jewel—to de-personalize it. Former names for Jewel Lake seem to have been Still Lake, Petite Lake, and Laguna Verde.

Jims Grove   GLACIER GORGE

Rocky Mountain Jim Nugent lived in Muggins Gulch from the late 1860s until his murder in 1874. He claimed to be a Canadian who had wandered the West, in Colorado since 1854. One side of his face had been clawed by a bear; the other side was handsome. He made his living hunting, fishing, and guiding. He wore his hair in sixteen long tawny curls, recited poetry of his own composition, and was a madman when he was drunk, which was often. Isabella Bird, the genteel English woman who spent the autumn of 1873 in Estes Park, fell in love with Jim in his civilized moods. She wrote her sister that he was "a man any woman could love, but no sane woman would marry." Isabella claimed that Jim's ghost, complete with sixteen curls, appeared to her in Switzerland immediately after it left his body in Colorado in 1874.

In October 1873, no premonition of tragedy marred the Indian summer idyll when Jim Nugent guided Isabella Bird to the top of Longs Peak or, as she herself wrote, dragged the lady "like a bale of goods." They spent two nights in what has since been known as Jims Grove, but Isabella called it a "Lady's Bower." They were chaperoned not only by Jim's dog, Ring, but by two young lawyers straight out of Columbia University. Isabella was more impressed with Ring's discipline than with the manners of the young men.

We know of her impressions on climbing Longs Peak because she wrote a book—the classic of Estes Park and the best publicity the area ever had. *A Lady's Life in the Rocky Mountains* was published in London in December 1879, then went into six more editions. Translated into French it was published in Paris in 1888. In America it sold eight editions up to 1912, then in 1960 the University of Oklahoma Press reprinted it, earning the gratitude of all Estes Park enthusiasts.

In October 1873, as the party on Longs Peak approached the camp spot the first night out, Miss Bird described Jims Grove:

> The pines grew smaller and more sparse as we ascended, and the last stragglers wore a tortured, warring look. The timber line was passed, but yet a little higher a slope of mountain meadow dipped to the southwest towards a bright stream trickling under ice and icicles, and there a grove of the beautiful silver spruce marked our camping ground. The trees were in miniature, but so exquisitely arranged that one might well ask what artist's hand had planted them, scattering them here, clumping them there, and training their slim spires towards heaven. . . . A group of small silver spruces away from the fire was my sleeping place . . . affording a shelter from the wind and a most agreeable privacy. . . . It was exciting to

lie there, with no better shelter than a bower of pines, on a mountain 11,000 feet high, in the very heart of the Rocky Range, under twelve degrees of frost, hearing sounds of wolves, with shivering stars looking through the fragrant canopy, with arrowy pines for bed-posts, and for a night lamp the red flames of a camp-fire.

After Jim was shot by Griff Evans in 1874, everyone in Estes Park gave different versions of the circumstances of the shooting as well as different reasons for this deed. Fundamentally it was the fault of the Earl of Dunraven. Griff Evans was the Earl's man, but Rocky Mountain Jim decidedly was not. Living in Muggins Gulch at the entrance to Estes Park, Jim could and did make trouble for British visitors intent on using the Park as their own hunting preserve. Despite two bullets festering in his brain, Jim lived from mid-June to September. From jail (the man who shot him was not jailed) Jim wrote a letter to the Fort Collins paper stating that British gold had done him in. Rocky Mountain Jim may yet take his place in history as the rugged American hero of Estes Park.

Joe Mills Mountain (11,078')   FOREST CANYON, GLACIER GORGE
Joe Mills, brother of Enos, came to Estes on a bicycle in 1898. While Joe helped his brother run Longs Peak Inn, he and Ethel, his wife, started to homestead near Cabin Rock. After the brothers parted company, Joe and Ethel ran the Crags Hotel at the south edge of Estes village. Joe was a vital force in creating Rocky Mountain National Park. After his death, his wife and the Park rangers agreed that a mountain should bear his name. Many points were considered, and in March 1949 this prominent mountain across from the Little Matterhorn was chosen to commemorate Enoch Josiah Mills.

Joe Wright Creek   NEVER SUMMER
The site of Joe Wright's homestead cabin is not far from Cameron Pass. Norman Fry, old-timer on the upper Poudre, reported that Joe Wright Creek was originally the headwaters of the Laramie River:

> Chambers Lake was supposedly at one time a canyon of the Laramie River. At some point in the past, a part of the mountain just north of the Lake slipped into the Laramie River which caused a dam and made the small Lake of Chambers. . . . The water from the lake started to flow eastward, and so the early day headwaters of the Laramie River became "Joe Wright" creek.

Julian Lake; Julian, Mount (12,928')   FOREST CANYON
Julian Hayden was born in Chicago in 1886. He first visited Estes Park in 1901. Later, as a civil engineer with a degree from the Armour Institute of Technology, he worked for B. D. Sanborn who, with F. O. Stanley,

bought the Dunraven land holdings. Julian Hayden surveyed and built the Estes Park Power Plant, and operated it for a year.

Julian, his brother Al, and Bob Larimer from Chicago hung out their engineering shingle in Estes Park village in 1906. The Haydens were also closely connected with real estate in the area, and stepped into Estes Park genealogy when Al married Louise Reed, daughter of the Reeds who ran the Brinwood Hotel and granddaughter of Horace Ferguson who homesteaded near Marys Lake. After Al's death, Louise married his brother Julian, who died in 1964.

One day the Hayden brothers and Abner Sprague made a trip to a faraway creek that runs into the Big Thompson between the Gorge Lakes and Spruce Creek. They found the canyon rough but the fishing good. Sprague noted two prominent points on the mountain that flanks the creek to the north. One he named Mount Julian and the other, the great rock that stands at the head of the creek, Hayden Spire. Perhaps the Hayden brothers reciprocated by naming Sprague Mountain which stands just south of Hayden Spire—thus commemorating a notable fishing trip to Hayden Creek.

Junco Lake   Wild Basin

This lake lies about 12,000 feet above sea level. Juncos seldom straggle above timberline, but when W. S. Cooper named this and other lakes in Wild Basin after birds he did not necessarily mean that he had seen that particular bird at that special lake.

The nesting junco of the Rocky Mountains is a gray-headed junco. About the size of a sparrow, gray with a reddish brown back, it flashes white feathers on the sides of its tail when it flies. Basically a ground-loving bird, it nests under small plants in forest glades. Bird lovers say the nests are on the east side of the plants to catch the first rays of the morning sun.

Kamloop Cove   Lake Granby

Many of the coves of Lake Granby are named for varieties of fish. The Kamloop trout gets its name from the Kamloop district of British Columbia. This trout grows extra large—a regular lunker! One of the officials of the Colorado Game and Fish Department explained that a Kamloop was a rainbow trout with an overdeveloped thyroid.

Kawuneeche Valley (Pronounced Ka·wu·nee´·che)   Grand Lake

This valley has had at least three names. Its workday name was and is the North Fork Valley. Then came the Colorado Geographic Board with its bagful of Arapaho Indian words. It recommended Haquihana Valley, meaning valley of the wolves. Haquihana was also the name of an extinct tribe who lived with the Northern Arapahos. R. B. Marshall, confident that the name would be accepted, printed it on his map published in 1915 by the Denver Chamber of Commerce as the "first and authentic map of the New Park."

But the Colorado Geographic Board changed its mind, with no explanation in the minutes, it recommended Kawuneeche "as being somewhat pronounceable." In the report of the 1914 Arapahos this word is spelled Cawoonache, and defined as meaning coyote.

Keplinger Lake   WILD BASIN
Jack Moomaw preferred Timberline Pond for this lake, but Roger Toll proposed Keplinger which was approved by the staff of the Rocky Mountain National Park in 1949. Mountain climbers agree with Toll that L. W. Keplinger should be commemorated in the Park. He was one of the college students who accompanied Major John Wesley Powell on the first ascent of Longs Peak. In fact, young Keplinger was actually the first on top at 10 AM August 23, 1868. Perhaps this was because of his eagerness, but it might have been an honor granted the youth by Major Powell because, the evening before, Keplinger had scouted the route, making a solo climb almost to the summit. (See the Notch.)

Keyboard of the Winds   GLACIER GORGE, WILD BASIN
This is a series of jagged cliffs on which the wind, howling around Longs Peak, plays mournful tunes.

Keyhole, The   GLACIER GORGE
A rock jutting from the northern ridge of Longs Peak has been called the Keyhole ever since climbers first started to ascend the peak. The hole is shaped like an oval open at the top. At the foot of the Keyhole rocks stands the Agnes Vaille Shelter House.

Kiowa Peak (13,276')   INDIAN PEAKS
The name, meaning "principal people," was suggested by Bethel in 1914. Fearless and cruel, the Kiowas were a turbulent element on the plains, fiercely defending their rights against the encroaching whites. The U.S. Government tried to confine them to Oklahoma in 1867. (See also Satanta Peak.)

Knight Ridge   LAKE GRANBY
An annual guest at the Lehman Resort on the South Fork of the Colorado River was Harry Knight of St. Louis, with his family, his children's nurses and governess, and assorted servants. Because the Lehman's was not a working ranch, the Knights repaired en masse to the Killie Ranch

(on the south slope of present Knight Ridge) to watch the de-horning and branding of the calves, offspring of the Killie's original herd of 112 Herefords. Knight became fascinated with western life. He proved up, in 1922, on 160 acres southeast of the Lehman's, and acquired most of the patented land along the South Fork, including the Killie and Lehman ranches and the meadows which he later used as a landing strip. In the 1920s a young man named Charles Augustus Lindbergh landed his plane on these meadows when he visited the Knights. Harry Knight was one of the St. Louis men who financed the"Spirit of St. Louis" and its pilot on the first air crossing of the Atlantic. (See Lone Eagle Peak.)

Knobtop Mountain (12,331')   FOREST CANYON, GLACIER GORGE
     Named by Roger Toll on September 1, 1924, to harmonize with Flattop and Notchtop.

Kokanee Cove   LAKE GRANBY
     Kokanee salmon were introduced into Colorado waters in 1951, chiefly because they thrive in reservoirs. Unlike insect-eating fish, they eat plankton—small plants and animals that float on still water. Kokanee, like their cousins the red salmon of the West Coast, usually spawn in the autumn of their fourth year, then die. Kokanee is an Alaskan Indian name meaning little redfish, and comes from the brilliant red color the fish turn when spawning. Lake fishermen catch them by trolling or using small spinners. They do not fight, but are good eating.

Krueger Rock (9,335')   ESTES PARK
     The Kruegers, who celebrated their fiftieth wedding anniversary in 1964, have long ranched in the valley of the Big Thompson. Climbers call these rocks Fish Creek or Bierstadt Pinnacles.

La Poudre Pass, La Poudre Pass Creek   NEVER SUMMER
     When the Grand Ditch first crossed the divide in the late 1880s, this pass was called Mountain Meadows Pass.

Lady Creek   NEVER SUMMER
     Archie E. Gifford of La Porte, Colorado, employee of the Grand Ditch Company, was reminded of a lady when he saw the lacy falls on this creek.

Lady Washington, Mount (13,281')   GLACIER GORGE
     Anna Dickinson is said to have climbed Mount Washington in New Hampshire twenty-six times. Perhaps the name of that peak was proposed

by her, as she sat with the Hayden Survey men by the camp fire after they had climbed Longs Peak, and the "Lady" may have been inserted by Ralph Meeker as a compliment to the fair climber. The name dates from this climb, September 1873. (See Mount Dickinson.)

Lake of Glass—See Glass Lake.

Lake of Many Winds   WILD BASIN
In 1953 when Dave Cargo and George Cowles were climbing toward Boulder-Grand Pass, near an unnamed lake downdrafts forced them to their knees, twice, then an updraft blasted Dave's hat toward Thunder Lake. Ranger Ritterbush, sympathizing, submitted the name.

Lake of the Clouds   NEVER SUMMER
This lake lies at the bottom of the cirque on Mount Cirrus, one of the peaks named for cloud formations. No date has been established for the naming of the lake, but it was after J. G. Rogers christened the Cloud Peaks.

Lambs Slide   GLACIER GORGE, WILD BASIN
Elkanah Lamb (1832-1915) spent a pleasant childhood on a farm in Indiana. After he became interested in religion, the United Brethren sent him to the St. Vrain District as a missionary to preach in the towns at the foot of the mountains. He was a powerful preacher, all six feet four of him, and a man of tremendous energy. After riding from the plains to Estes Park, thirty-five miles in one day, he was distressed and surprised when he went to the stable the next morning to find his pony dead.

Lamb was twice married, rearing both his children and step-children. For this he needed more money than the unlucrative missionfield afforded, so he homesteaded 160 acres of land east of Longs Peak. Here he installed his family in 1875. His wife ran a dairy and kept Longs Peak House, Lamb helping between sermons in the South Platte towns. Gradually he forsook his ministerial work. He and his son guided parties to the top of Longs Peak at $5 a trip. "If they would not pay for spiritual guidance," Parson Lamb wrote, "I compelled them to pay for material elevation." As guides, in 1902 they made the ascent easier for their clients by building a trail to the "Bowlderfield," which the son maintained long after their lodge was sold to Enos Mills.

Before Lamb settled for life in Estes Park he made a trip from the plains expressly to climb Longs Peak. In his memoirs he described this August 1871 climb and his descent of what became known as Lambs Slide. He tells that one by one each of the eight people who started the climb fell by the wayside:

> Brother Ross would not leave his wife, and the maternal instincts of the mother of the young lady who had fainted would not permit her to leave;

another had such a headache; another was frightened. . . . I went forward on my lonely way, . . . humorously remarking that we must climb higher than this if we ever get to heaven. Something over a thousand feet higher brought me to the summit of this historic pile of granite and quartz, a huge monster nearly three miles above sea level, ten miles around its base. The sight is magnificent. . . .

After one hour's feasting of my mental and spiritual and somewhat poetical nature on these sights and scenes, I concluded to go down the eastern face of the mountain, where man had never gone before. Some old roads, rules, grooves, and conventional codes are gray with honor, but to be tied and governed by anything because of the virtue of age is an absurdity, not to be tolerated by intelligent minds. . . .

After getting down more than a thousand feet from the summit, I began to realize the rashness of the undertaking. Having already passed dangerous points, perpendicular places, ice patches, and frowning walls, worse dangers confronted me. I concluded to go back, if possible, and go down the old way; but like thousands in life's downward trend, I soon realized the fact that I had already passed dangerous points and sloping icy places that were almost impossible to round or ascend. I then turned my course to face the music, trying to concentrate all the courage of my normal condition, both occult and physical. Regrets and repentance for rash recklessness are bitter consolations for deviations and perilous ventures, but the most unpleasant medicine must be taken by the transgressor. I hope the reader will remember this.

In my further descent, I came to a place that seemed to say, "Thus far shalt thou go, but not farther." The mountain wall was not only perpendicular, but projected with a frowning incline some degrees over my icy pathway. This miniature glacier was perhaps five rods wide, descending down to a crater lake thousands of feet below, standing at an angle of forty or fifty degrees. This projecting wall was only three or four rods in swing, then receded gradually back. Well, the inevitable in my case was to go forward. With finger holds in meager niches of the wall and my feet pressing the edge of the ice, I started across this dangerous section. Quicker than I can tell it, my hands failed to hold, my feet slipped, and down I went with almost an arrow's rapidity. An eternity of thought, of life, death, wife, and home, concentrated in my mind in those two seconds. . . .

Fortunately for me, I threw my right arm around a projecting bowlder, which stood above the icy plain some two or three feet. This sudden stopping of my acrobatic performance brought my long walking appendages around with a musical swash, turning my overcoat skirts nearly over my head, and spilling all the specimens I had gathered on the summit, which went sliding and jumping downward, seemingly glad of their release from captivity. Here I was swinging with my right arm around this bowlder, at least five feet from the body of the mountain. The conical shape of the bowlder precluded my standing upon it for a jump to safety. Getting my knife out of my pocket, I opened it with my teeth, then reached half-way to the rocks of safety and began digging a niche in the ice for a toe hold, when my knife broke in two. This left me stranded and stopped further progress in digging. My nervous system was very much unstrung by this sliding, swinging experience, but I was compelled to decide—quickly, too. So putting the tip of my left foot in the shallow niche I had cut (knowing that if my foot slipped I was a lost Lamb) then working my arm to the top of the rock, I gave a huge lunge, just managing to reach the foot of the mountain. Drawing myself out of this perilous situation, I was plainly impressed that my salvation was a divine and direct providence. I immediately fell upon my knees and thanked God for my deliverance. . . .

Then, on I went, finally coming to a perpendicular granite wall. Grooves were worn into its face by the action of water in streams and drippings for untold ages. My situation was fearful to contemplate. The mountain was perpendicular on the south over the lake; to the north, utterly inaccessible. The only alternative was to go down one of these grooves in the granite wall. Selecting one with projecting rocks sufficient for foot and hand holds, I let myself down this perilous incline. It almost makes my hair stand erect to remember this trying time of thirty-four years ago. This descent brought me to Crater Lake, nestling close to Long's Peak range. . . . Working around the lake's steep margin, I finally reached our camp, and threw myself prone upon the ground.

Lark Pond   WILD BASIN

The greatly beloved western meadowlark is a blackbird, and the lark bunting, the Colorado state bird, is a finch; the horned lark is the only native American lark. Found throughout the United States, always in open country, in Colorado it nests on the plains and on the alpine tundra, never in between. A sparrow-sized brownish ground bird, its face is patterned in black and yellow surmounted by two small feather horns. Its tinkly bubble of a song resembles not at all the music of Shelley's English skylark. Lark Pond was called Bluebird Lake on the Cooper-Babcock map of 1911.

Larkspur Creek   GLACIER GORGE

The brief course of Larkspur Creek runs entirely above 10,000 feet. There, in the short summer of the Subalpine Zone, where melting snow leaves hillsides spongy, the Barbey larkspur grows waist high and higher. Climbers push their way through its luxuriant green with the short crowded spikes of deep blue flowers, varied once in a while with a pink one.

This is one of the three varieties of larkspur that grow in Rocky Mountain National Park. An even taller variety, the mountain larkspur, blooms in August in the aspen groves of the Montane Zone. In the same zone around the Fourth of July, sometimes among ponderosa pines, sometimes among sagebrush, sometimes in spectacular fields of purplish blue on open hillsides, Nelson's larkspur blooms.

The shape of the upper sepal gives the plant its name. Long and pointed, it forms a spur like that on the foot of a bird. Larkspur is the same plant as the garden delphinium. Ranch wives have been known to buy plants of highly cultivated delphinium for their flower gardens only to have their irate husbands root out the plants as soon as the characteristic leaves show, because larkspur is poisonous to cattle. In early spring as many as one hundred head of cattle have been killed in one area in a few days by feasting on its pleasantly acid leaves. In the Park, even a rancher can enjoy the flowers unreservedly since no cattle now range there.

Lawn Lake (10,987') MUMMY RANGE

Abner Sprague accompanied some English hunters to this lake in 1871. Because the surface of the water was smooth and green while they were there, he compared it to a plot of mown lawn. Or did the Britishers tell him it looked like the green lawns of England? In the late 1880s, Hallett's less imaginative name for the lake was Forest Lake. Whatever its name, fishermen early beat a trail up the banks of Roaring River to the lake.

About 1910, Willard H. Ashton of Horseshoe Inn built a shelter cabin at Lawn Lake. He hired two college boys to stay at the cabin, do the chores, cook, and act as guides for flatlanders who wanted to climb Mummy Mountain or Hagues Peak or go over the Saddle to Rowe Glacier. The last permit secured for this shelter was dated 1920. Another shelter cabin was maintained here by the Park for a number of years, but the building was razed in 1964.

In 1911 Hugh Ramsey of Pingree Park built a dam to enlarge Lawn Lake; the water is now used on the plains by the Farmers Ditch Company. Perhaps it was Ramsey, perhaps Ashton, who enlarged the trail to a wagon road, though it really was too steep for horse-draw vehicles.

Lead Mountain (12,537') NEVER SUMMER

This name dates back at least to 1879 when prospectors around Lulu City recorded their claims as located in the Lead Mountain Mining District.

Lead ore proved a heavy nuisance to prospectors seeking metals in this district; the owners of the Wolverine Mine found that freight charges ate up their profits. Also, there are tales of pure lead. Trappers told Abner Sprague they had picked up lead nuggets on the Poudre River which they used, unworked, as bullets.

Lehman Ditch GRAND LAKE, LAKE GRANBY

The Lehman family lived on the South Fork of the Grand River. They ran a summer resort, with cottages around their large house. Mrs. Lehman was noted for her feather beds and her hospitality. When she had not given a dance for a long time, the editor of the Grand Lake paper reminded her in print that the local residents were open to an invitation. The Lehmans had four daughters and a son. The oldest girl married a man named King; their place was about a quarter of a mile from the main road between Granby and Grand Lake. When any mail was destined for Monarch Lake or the ranches on the South Fork, the stagecoach detoured to the King's place. The Lehman Ranch became part of the Knight Ranch. Before Lake Granby covered the South Fork valley, the Lehman ranch house was moved to Murray Camp, just east of the old town of Monarch. (See Lake Dorothy.)

Lily Lake   ESTES PARK

"Fittingly called the Lake of the Lilies," is what Isabella Bird wrote in 1873, and in 1888 Chapin and his botanist wife admired the water lilies blooming in Lily Lake.

The yellow pond lily is the common water lily of high mountain lakes, blooming from July to frost. The broad leaves keep the water cool enough for trout, but warn fishermen that the shallow ponds have become too deep for hipboots. Children eat water lily seeds; muskrats eat the rootstocks, as did Indians if very hungry. (See Nymph Lake.)

Lily Mountain (9,786')   ESTES PARK

Anyone interested in the evolution of geographic names should trace the name Lily on various maps of the Park area. It has been spelled Lillie, Lilly, Lilie, and Lily; and has been applied to present Twin Sisters, Gianttrack, and Lily mountains. According to Enos Mills, an engineer named Lillie settled very early in the Park. The Hayden atlases, 1877 and 1882, label Twin Sisters as Lillie's Mountain, and an 1897 map designates the same summit as Lilie's Peak. Chapin in 1888 wrote of a mountain with stupendous cliffs hanging over the valley which from the west was called Lily Mountain, from the east Twin Sisters.

Present Lily Mountain and Lily Lake are labeled Lilly on Enos Mills's 1905 map and the 1910 Burlington map. Perhaps it was W. S. Cooper's interest in botany that led him to simplify the name to Lily Mountain on his 1911 map.

The Colorado Geographic Board attacked the muddle of orthography and geography, and fastened names securely on Twin Sisters, Gianttrack, and Lily mountains, to the satisfaction of everyone except the ghost of Mr. Lillie, pioneer.

Lion Lake No. 1 and No. 2   WILD BASIN

Roger Toll considered the name of Lynes Reservoir No. 2, sometimes spelled Lyons Reservoir, and found it inappropriate. In 1923 he changed the names of these lakes to Lion.

The mountain lion, biggest of the American cats, has been seen in Wild Basin by a few people and usually from a distance. The animal may inhabit low rugged canyons, like those around Devils Gulch, and cruise into the Park during its one-hundred-mile tours in search of game.

Little Horseshoe Park   MUMMY RANGE
Here twenty-four Montana elk were let loose in 1915; here, in May 1933, tents arose for two hundred CCC men; today elk have reclaimed this Park.

Little Matterhorn   FOREST CANYON, GLACIER GORGE
This was named either by Dr. W. J. Workman of Fern Lake Lodge, or Frank Byerly, a later owner of the lodge. In 1914 Byerly took his hand-colored stereoscopic pictures of scenic beauties, like Longs Peak, Grand Lake, and the Little Matterhorn above Odessa Lake, to Washington, to show to Congress as part of the Colorado Mountain Club's campaign for the proposed Estes National Park. Arrangements for this pictorial lobbying were made by Morrison Shafroth, son of Senator John F. Shafroth of Denver and an enthusiastic member of the club.

Little Pawnee Peak—East of Pawnee Peak
The altitude of the highest point on the ridge that runs east of Pawnee Peak is 12,466 feet. In 1965, Evilio Echevarria, a mountain climber from Chile living in Boulder, proposed that this point be named Little Pawnee Peak. The name was accepted by the U.S. Board on Geographic Names too late to be printed on the Indian Peaks map in this dictionary. (See also Shoshoni Peak.)

Little Yellowstone   NEVER SUMMER
"Winnie" Winston of Kelly, Wyoming, later athletic director of the University of Illinois, was a ranger in the Park. He named this section because of the eroded yellow rocks.

Livingston Lake   NEVER SUMMER
When Julian Livingston came from his large bakery business in Chicago to summer in Estes, he built a vacation home and dammed Black Canyon Creek to make himself a fish pond now called Livingston Lake. For many summers he was an interested and generous citizen of the community. His son, Louis, also in the bakery business in Chicago, now operates a dude ranch on the Devils Gulch road.

Loch Vale and the Loch   GLACIER GORGE
In 1896, Abner Sprague, his wife, and his uncle rode over to Grand Lake and brought back Jim Cairns and a Mr. Locke, banker from Kansas City, with them. A September blizzard benighted them on a ledge above Fern Lake. Sprague remembered that the blue dye from his uncle's overalls stained the snow on the ledge. Sprague honored Mr. Locke by naming Loch Vale and the Loch after him, though he used the Scottish spelling, Loch, meaning *lake*.

Lochleven Cove   LAKE GRANBY

Brown trout, imported from Europe to America in 1883, are sometimes called Lochleven. They thrive in slightly muddy and warmish
waters, and are doing well in the impounded waters of Lake Granby.

Loft, The   GLACIER GORGE, WILD BASIN

In his book, *Mountaineering in the Rocky Mountain National Park,*
published in 1919, Roger Toll wrote about "a perfectly level platform
called the Loft, a name strongly suggested both by form and location of
the place and mode of access to it." Is this "mode of access" the narrow
passage called by Isabella Bird in 1873 the Dog Lift, below which Ring,
Jim Nugent's dog, was left "howling piteously"? In 1911, Dean Babcock
and Charley Hewes had trouble hoisting Charley's dog to the Loft.

Lone Eagle Peak (11,920')   INDIAN PEAKS

The story of Lone Eagle Peak starts with Fred Fair who lived in Boulder but preferred to spend his time in the mountains. He knew the area
around Apache Peak, on both sides of the divide, as only a surveyor (he
was official surveyor for Boulder County) and mountaineer could. In 1908
he discovered the Crater Lake country and sang its praises until his
friends called it Fred Fair's Hell Hole.

Fair spent years promoting roads (and transportation companies to
carry tourists over the roads) into the glacier country west of his home
town. (See Arapaho Glacier.) In 1923, as part of a national publicity campaign financed chiefly by the Denver & Interurban Railway, Fair
announced $1,000 would be paid to the aviator who would land his plane
on the slopes of the St. Vrain Glacier, the smoothest in the vicinity. Such a
stunt would certainly create public interest.

No aviator was tempted by this cash award until the day a barnstormer,
landing his plane near Boulder, sent word to Fred Fair that he would like to
see him. Fair went out to meet a quiet young man from Wisconsin who had
some scheme that needed financing; Slim Lindbergh said he would land his
crate on a glacier or anywhere else for $1,000. Fair looked at the crate held
together by baling wire. Thinking to himself that an accident on the glacier
would produce the wrong kind of publicity, Fair told the young flyer that the
plane would be wrecked. Slim observed that the offer said nothing about a
return trip—he was not planning to fly out. But Mr. Fair turned him down.

Four years later, in May 1927, Charles A. Lindbergh flew from New
York to Paris in a plane powered by a single engine with nine cylinders.
During his subsequent tour of America to promote aeronautics, Fred Fair
asked him if he remembered the incident of the glacier flight that was not
made. Colonel Lindbergh said he did indeed.

Whenever a national hero emerges, someone in Colorado wants to
name a mountain for him. The *Denver Post* proposed that a Colorado peak

be named after the daring aviator. Fair's mind flashed back to the glacier country. He remembered a certain sharp rock. "Towering above the ice-gouged abyss of Hell Hole stands a granite shaft that points a solitary finger skyward," wrote a reporter after he had interviewed Fair.

Organizations took up the campaign. In September 1927 Mrs. Clara De Nio of the Federated Women's Clubs of Colorado consulted Colonel Allen Peck of the U.S. Forest Service, who doubted that the peak was prominent enough. By the next August Colonel Peck, having made a trip to see it, had changed his mind. "I was astonished," he wrote, "at the impressiveness of the scenery, to put it mildly; in fact, I have seen nothing of its kind to equal it. . . . There is no question in my mind but that the peak is sufficiently impressive to justify its being named after Lindbergh and also that Lindbergh merits a peak named for him."

Early in June 1929, a promotional organization named the Colorado Association dispatched two members of the Colorado Mountain Club to see if the peak could be climbed. Carl Blaurock and William F. Ervin first scouted an eastern approach. Between Apache and Navajo peaks they were blocked by snow and night. On June 20 they tried the western approach. Walking nine miles from Monarch Lake they arrived at the foot of the peak too late for a climb that day. Finally, on Labor Day, September 2, 1929, these two climbers and Stephen H. Hart organized a first-class expedition. They even hired pack horses at Monarch Lake to carry supplies for as long a stay as was needed. Camping at Crater Lake, the following day they climbed "the granite shaft that points a solitary finger skyward." They found the ascent not difficult if the vertical face were avoided.

The committee for naming Lindbergh Peak then considered the desirability of making a view of the peak accessible to motorists by building a road either over Pawnee Pass from the east or from Monarch Lake on the west. In June 1930 the decision was that a road from Monarch Lake be built with government aid, with Fred Fair as construction engineer. The road was to be named Evangeline Road for the mother of Charles A. Lindbergh.

At that point someone thought to consult the U.S. Board on Geographic Names. The board promptly produced its rule against naming geographical features after living persons. Would the board approve a nickname? The board would. Whereupon the *Denver Post* publicized another contest. A school child won the contest with Lindy, but the name that seemed more appropriate to the committee was proposed by a veteran at Fitzsimons Hospital—Lone Eagle. Fred Fair approved and offered to persuade the club women to change. Harry Knight said that his friend Lindbergh would surely approve. Colonel Peck thought the new name would be "undoubtedly more acceptable to Colonel Lindbergh, and I think a little more appropriate because of the opportunities for symbolism in the name."

As of 1966 the road from Monarch Lake has not materialized, nor is Lone Eagle Peak visible from any present highway. Symbolically, perhaps a mountain named for the man who first dared fly across the Atlantic should remain somewhat inaccessible.

Perhaps Ronald L. Ives of the Colorado Mountain Club thought Lone Eagle Peak should have companions when, in 1932, after he climbed the mountain northwest of Crater Lake, he suggested the mountain be named Dwight Morrow Peak, for Lindbergh's father-in-law. Ives also suggested Anne Peak (Lindbergh's wife) for the 12,799-foot point between Peck and Fair glaciers. Nothing came of these suggestions and Lone Eagle Peak still stands alone in Fred Fair's Hell Hole.

Lone Pine Lake   GRAND LAKE
Charles Hewes called this Verdant Lake in September 1913, but Fred McLaren said the lake named itself for a lone pine on its lone island. Today, one dead pine is surrounded by three lodgepoles, four spruces, and five willow bushes, all fledglings.

Lonesome Lake   FOREST CANYON

Lonesome Peak (10,588')—Less than two miles south of Monarch Lake
The High Lonesome Mine is on the side of this isolated peak and the High Lonesome Trail runs beside it.

Long Draw, Long Draw Reservoir—See Grand Ditch.

Long Meadows   GRAND LAKE

Longs Peak (14,256')   GLACIER GORGE, WILD BASIN
That the highest mountain in the Estes Park region (the fifteenth highest in Colorado) should bear the oldest name seems appropriate. A hundred and fifty years is a long time in the West, and the date was 1820 when a young army officer, Stephen Harriman Long, led twenty-two men on horseback and two dogs (even the dogs rode part of the way before they died of thirst on the plains of eastern Colorado) from north to south along the foot of the Front Range of the Colorado Rockies. Dr. Edwin James, age twenty-three, was the botanist and geologist of the expedition and the first person on record to climb Pikes Peak. His journal of the Long expedition, published in 1823, became the textbook for every literate traveler who planned a journey west. On its map the plains of northeastern Colorado, now fertile under irrigation, bore the stigma of being the Great American Desert. The mountain toward the northwest was labeled Highest Peak. Naturally, this soon became known by the name of the man who led the expedition; in 1842, Fremont was pleased that fur traders were using the name Longs Peak.

Two names were used for this peak before 1820—one by Indians, one by trappers. The Indians used the two highest peaks in Rocky Mountain National Park, Longs and Meeker, for a utilitarian purpose. When the natives traveled the piedmont plains and needed a compass point, there stood the Two Guides. (The French wrote the Indian word for this as *Nesotaieux*.) French-speaking trappers, aping Indians in all things in order to survive in the Indian world, used the peaks in the same way, calling them *Les Deux Oreilles,* the Two Ears. Camping under the cottonwoods at the mouth of Cherry Creek the trappers could tell at a glance which direction was northwest, for there stood the Two Ears (though Mount Meeker almost hid Longs Peak). In 1858 William Larimer laid out the streets of downtown Denver northwest-southeast, to the confusion of subsequent inhabitants. He could have used the square top of Longs Peak for his surveying point on Seventeenth Street. "Longs Peak . . . just fills the vista of the principal business street. . . . The people look upon this glorious alpine view as one of the properties of the town." So wrote Bayard Taylor in 1866, and so it is a hundred years later. Many a harried banker, emerging from his skyscraper office onto Seventeenth Street, checks on Longs and Meeker before he goes about his business.

Lookout Mountain (10,715')   WILD BASIN
Because of intervening, lower mountains, it is hard to find an eminence from which to view the peaks that form the jagged rim of Wild Basin. W. S. Cooper used this mountain for a triangulation point when he first surveyed Wild Basin. On the Burlington map of 1910 the mountain is called Triangulation Point.

Lookout Springs   ESTES PARK

Loomis Lake   FOREST CANYON
A Dr. Loomis is reputed to have built the first cabin at Fern Lake, even before Dr. Workman built Fern Lake Lodge. Dr. Loomis found the skeleton of an especially large fish on the shores of this lake. He talked about it, and talked about it so much that the lake was named for him.

Dr. Workman preferred, as usual, to name this lake for a girl—two girls, in fact. Sally Reed (Mrs. Charles Reed of the Brinwood, mother of Mrs. Julian Hayden), and Dora Sprague Stead (Mrs. J. D. Stead of Steads Ranch) were honored. Saldora Lake was the result, but Loomis Lake is the official name.

Lost Brook—FOREST CANYON; **Lost Creek**—NEVER SUMMER

Lost Falls   MUMMY RANGE
Up to 1961, these falls on the North Fork of the Big Thompson were simply called the Falls.

Lost Lake   MUMMY RANGE
    Lee and Parker of Johnstown in 1911 raised the level of Lost Lake by a one-foot dam and dug out the bottom, so they could claim an equal amount of water from the North Fork of the Big Thompson.

Louise, Lake   MUMMY RANGE
    In 1941 E. A. Abbott of Chicago, remembered when Shep Husted, long ago, guided him on a trip above Lost Lake on the North Fork of the Big Thompson. They named a lake there after Mrs. Abbott—Lake Louise.

Love Lake   FOREST CANYON
    This miniature body of water seems to have had no official name before the 1961 map. Whether it is named for an emotion or a man named Love is not clear.
    Pettingell Lake was once unofficially named after a man called Jack Love. He was a carpenter in Grand Lake village, and sometimes worked for Fred McLaren, superintendent of the western side of the Park. Fred regularly sent him up to Pettingell Lake with fingerling trout, and Jack was so impressed with the scenery that the Park rangers jocularly called that Love's Lake, though it was never an official name.

Lulu City (site), Creek; Lulu Mountain (12,228')   NEVER SUMMER
    Miners started a town in the valley of the North Fork of the Grand River in 1879, naming it after a girl. But what girl? In the memories of old-timers two Lulus vie for this honor. The majority claim Lulu, daughter of Benjamin Franklin Burnett, one of the founders of Lulu City. Squeaky Bob Wheeler remembered her as the most beautiful girl he had ever seen, whose lips were red without benefit of lipstick. H. N. Wheeler, first super-intendent of the Colorado National Forest, and old-timers of the Poudre country claim the honor for Lulu Stewart, whose father, Samuel B. Stewart, homesteaded at Rustic on the Poudre in 1881 and carried mail to Teller City.
    The Colorado Geographic Board recorded both Lulus but declined to make a choice. They did, however, choose to change the name of Lulu Pass to Thunder Pass. Perhaps as compensation to the girl named Lulu, the forest service suggested Lulu Mountain which was accepted by the U.S. Board on Geographic Names in October 1929.

Lumpy Ridge (9,606')   ESTES PARK
    The 1914 Arapahos described the rocks that project all along this ridge with a word that translated as Little Lumps. The Colorado Geographic Board, recognizing the appropriateness of the name, retained Lumps but discarded Little. They added two other names in common use on either end of Lumpy Ridge: the rather thick Needles on the northwest, the plump Twin Owls to the southeast.

Lyric Falls   Wild Basin
    Named by Jack Moomaw, ranger.

McDonald Cove   Lake Granby
    This name commemorates one of the fishing resorts now covered by
Lake Granby. When I. L. Killie controlled about 1,200 acres on the South
Fork of the Grand River, his upper and lower ranches, which he owned,
were separated by a school section which he leased at some nominal sum
like 6¢ an acre per year. Edgar L. McDonald, a businessman from Fraser
in Middle Park, acquired the lease on part of the school lands, paying
more than Killie; and then Miss Margaret Murray, a spinster, acquired
part of the school lands to start Murray Camp at the bend of the river.
McDonald was a stockholder in the Rocky Mountain Lumber Company.
After its box factory burned in 1908, McDonald, for transportation to
Granby and to entertain his guests, equipped an automobile with metal
wheels and wooden flanges and ran this contraption on the rails of the
Rocky Mountain Railroad. (See Monarch Lake.)

McGregor Mountain (10,486')   Estes Park, Mummy Range
    Alexander Q. MacGregor, a lawyer from Milwaukee, came to Estes
Park to hunt in 1872. He was entranced not only with the scenery but with
Maria Clara Heeney, an art student from Wisconsin on a sketching tour.
Her mother, Georgiana, chaperon of the group, proved her own feeling
for the scenery by buying land in Black Canyon. To this land MacGregor
brought his bride in 1874. On June 2, 1876, she became Estes Park's first
postmistress, a job she had held unofficially when anyone brought mail
up from Longmont. Six months later Griff Evans's wife took over the job,
then the next year Theodore Whyte.
    In 1875 A. Q. MacGregor opened a toll road to Estes, but had trouble
collecting toll until he put the toll gate on the bridge over the Little
Thompson River—"Pay or swim." MacGregor, hunting with his son on
June 17, 1886, was killed by lightning on Fall River Pass. About ten years
later another son came from Denver with his wife and daughter and
worked the ranch until his death in 1950. After that, the daughter, Muriel
MacGregor, B.A., M.A., LL.B., led a lonely life coping with her land, her
Angus cattle, and vandals. She died October 22, 1970. Her will requested
that Black Canyon Ranch (valued at a million dollars) be worked as a
ranch, profits going to schools or charities.

McHenrys Notch; McHenrys Peak (13,327')   GLACIER GORGE
B. F. McHenry, who taught higher mathematics and science at Union Christian College, Merom, Indiana, spent three summers in the Estes Park region in the early 1890s, camping one summer in Wild Basin with some boys under his charge. Abner Sprague named the mountain after him, calling him "a nice old man."

On September 19, 1898, Professor McHenry wrote a description of his attempt to climb McHenrys Peak to George H. Knifton, president of the Rocky Mountain Club. The letter tells of a conditioning outing of twenty days:

> [We went] up Windy Gulch, over that magnificent Rocky Mountain walk to Specimen Mountain; thence down the worst of mountain trails to a branch of the Grand River which was full of trout easy to catch; thence to Grand Lake; thence to Flat Top Mountain, and down over Bierstadt Moraine. . . .
>
> Feeling now prepared for any adventure, we, J. B. Maple, Howard McHenry, my son, and self set out with determination to go to and climb the mountain they have dishonored by my name. We soon found out that following a trail is an easy task compared with the work of going where never a trail was cut. To get our donkey into the great gorge west of Long's Peak or into any of the many wonderful gorges leading to it; or to find a place for camping somewhere south of Flat Top; or coming in by the south of Grand View Hotel and taking advantage of their 7 miles of new trail, and so finding a camping place within less than a half day's walk (and climb) of the unexplored region, all these were undertakings we submitted to ourselves and did our best to achieve. We failed to accomplish what we set out to do, but we did not fail. We were all the while in country grand beyond description. Whoever opens up to students of nature and lovers of the grand and beautiful that "heart of the Rocky Mountains" a little south of west of Longs Peak will be a benefactor not only to that large class of the best of mankind, but through them to the race. I trust your club will succeed in doing what we have failed to do; and further, I trust that the beauty, the grandeur, the sublimity of that region will so pervade the hearts of those you send that they will not rest till they make a way by which others can go and enjoy the best the Rocky Mountains afford.

Mahana Peak (12,632') (Pronounced Ma´·ha·na)   WILD BASIN
Although Ellsworth Bethel submitted Comanche as a name for one of the Indian Peaks (probably present Chiefs Head), the U.S. Board on Geographic Names, doubtless noting that a peak thirty-five miles to the north had borne the name Comanche since the 1876 King Survey, turned down his suggestion. Bethel was irate until he (or more likely Harriet Vaille, who was a gentle person) discovered a compromise. The Taos Indians called the Comanche tribe *Mahana;* thus the Comanches took their place among the Indian tribes of the Front Range.

Many Parks Curve   ESTES PARK, FOREST CANYON

Spread out below this vantage point are several open tracts or mountain parks rimmed by tree-covered glacial moraines. Visible are Beaver Meadows, Moraine Park, Tuxedo Park, Glacier Basin (Barthoff Park), etc. The curve was named by Dorr Yeager, nature writer.

Marguerite Falls   FOREST CANYON

This is another of the female names Dr. Workman scattered over the Park. Marguerite Turck, a visitor from Denver, was of the Turck family who pioneered in Central City.

Marigold Lake, Pond   FOREST CANYON, GLACIER GORGE

The marsh marigold is not gold at all, except its center, but has white many-petaled flowers, bluish on the underside. Its leaves are dark green and rotund. It grows abundantly in wet ground, either in open places among trees or in alpine meadows. Roger Toll must have wet his boots walking through thousands of these and their usual companions, globe-flowers, before he named the lake in 1921.

Marmot Point (11,909')   MUMMY RANGE

Roger Toll named this in 1922. Woodchucks (the eastern name for marmots) love high points like this. Climbers say the marmots who inhabit the square summit of Longs Peak fare well on the lunches exhausted hikers cannot eat.

Marmots are medium-sized western woodchucks. Their nickname "whistle-pigs" describes them well, for they whistle high and shrill. They eat enough to get as fat as pigs in order to hibernate; those who live highest hibernate eight months of the year.

Marten Peak (12,041')   INDIAN PEAKS

Enos Mills showed his naturalist interest by naming geographical features for birds, like Ouzel Lake; for weather, like Storm Mountain; and for animals. Marten Peak is said to be one of his names though it stands far from his Longs Peak haunts. However, when Enos Mills was taking snow measurements he covered the whole area, and if he saw a marten or two on this peak, the sight of them is rare enough to warrant the name.

The marten lives in dense forests, spruce and pine (he is sometimes called the pine marten), and will not stay in woods that have been lumbered or burned. He is long like a weasel, has a bushy tail, is agile and vicious; a marten will kill for the sake of killing, and he has no friends. He feeds everywhere, darting under fallen trees for chickarees, snatching baby marmots from their burrows, and seizing ducks from ponds. Mice and rabbits are his staple food, and when the rabbit population is up, so is the marten.

Marys Lake (8,046')   ESTES PARK
When Mary Jane Roberts, niece of Griff Evans, told Rocky Mountain
Jim of her plan to ride by a certain lake with her fiancé on her birthday in
May 1874, Jim gallantly declared that the lake thereafter should be known
as Marys Lake. This was probably Jim's private joke, since he must have
known that the lake had been called Marys Lake since the spring of 1861,
in honor of Mary L. Fleming, bride of Milton Estes.

The Irish Lord Dunraven sainted the lake. He wrote, "The water of St.
Mary's Lake is strongly impregnated with alkali and leaves a deposit
around the edges. Sheep, deer, and cattle come for the salt."

Meadow Mountain (11,632')   WILD BASIN
W. S. Cooper submitted this name to the U.S. Board on Geographic
Names before publishing his map in 1911, saying the mountain was "a
rounded hill covered with a most beautiful alpine meadow." When he
talked of this meadow in 1965, in Mr. Cooper's memory the wildflowers
were obviously blooming again.

Medicine Bow Curve—MUMMY RANGE; **Medicine Bow Mountains**—
NEVER SUMMER
Looking northwest from the parking place on Trail Ridge Road called
Medicine Bow Curve, one sees the Medicine Bow Mountains stretching
into blue Wyoming. The name Medicine Bow was used like a blanket, cov-
ering the Never Summer Range in Colorado to the mountains south of
Douglas, Wyoming. Sections of the Medicine Bow National Forest lie
miles from the range. To clarify this mix-up, the U.S. Geological Survey
on December 3, 1961, handed down a definition. The "Medicine Bow
Mountains extend from Cameron Pass in Colorado in the south, northwest to the crossing of the Union Pacific Railroad (between Hanna and
Rawlins), and include all the highlands from Laramie River on the east to
North Park and North Platte River on the west." But the bureau defines
the Snowy Range as a "small transverse ridge that runs across the Medicine Bows." Crystalline quartzite gave the Snowy Range its name.

Colorado used to have a Snowy Range. Early Denverites spoke of the
Rockies from Evans north to James, the Indian Peaks, Longs, and the
Mummies, snowy giants all, as the Snowy Range.

No satisfactory explanation has been found for the name Medicine
Bow Mountains. It dates back to the Indians, and one explanation is that
Indians thought the range was bow-shaped. The mountains are curved on
maps, and from the air, but did they seem curved to Indians on the ground?

The more usual explanation goes back to a legend. Each year, the
story tells, friendly tribes met in these mountains to fashion bows out of
mountain mahogany and to invoke the blessings of the gods on the bows.
This was a ceremony to "make medicine."

The legend is strictly legend. No documentation has been found that any Indians held yearly ceremonials in the Medicine Bow Mountains to "make medicine." The Indians probably made bows in these mountains, but not of mountain mahogany, for the tall-growing variety *(Cercocarpus ledifolius)* does not grow in the Medicine Bow Mountains, nor have we record of any Indian bows made from it. The Indians of the Colorado-Wyoming country made their bows of the horns of mountain sheep or buffalo; or of wood—Osage orange *(Bois d'Arc)*, ash, hickory, or juniper, perhaps other wood; but none of these, except juniper, grows in the northern mountains. The Indians traded and raided in Kansas and south of the Arkansas River, and brought back not only horses and slaves but materials they could not find in their own territory, like wood for bows. So unless the legend dates from prehistoric times (as does the Indian name for Specimen Mountain) Indians could not have bows of mountain mahogany from the Medicine Bow Mountains.

The name puzzled early travelers, too. In 1856, Francis T. Bryan must have thought the spoken words had a French accent; throughout his lengthy report to Congress he spelled the name Medicine Bon—good medicine. A century ago a writer heard another name for these mountains, and was as puzzled as we are today about why they were sometimes called Medicine Bow. In 1868 W. E. Waters wrote:

> On most popular maps this spur of the Rocky Mountains is styled Meridian Ridge, or the Meridian Bow Range, but on the topographical charts of the army it is put down as I have written it, and is so called by mountaineers who are familiar with the country. Why it is designated Medicine Bow I have not yet learned.

Meeker Ridge—WILD BASIN; **Meeker, Mount** (13,911')—GLACIER GORGE, WILD BASIN

Nathan Meeker, agricultural editor of the *New York Tribune,* came west in 1869 in search of land on which to start a farming community where he could try out his theories of cooperative agriculture. With the help of William Byers, he picked the place where the Poudre empties into the South Platte River. Returning to New York, he found his boss, Horace Greeley, eager to lend to the enterprise not only the columns of his newspaper but his unblemished reputation. When Greeley became the treasurer of the Union Colony, its success was assured. Though Greeley visited the colony only once, his name was chosen for the town the colonists started.

In 1873 Anna Dickinson, lady lecturer, visited the town and was impressed. Perhaps she wondered why Meeker's name had not been used for the town; he worked very hard for a compensation of $160 a month. While she and Ralph Meeker, Nathan's son, and William Byers and the Hayden Survey men sat around the campfire after climbing Longs Peak, they may have talked of this. Why not name a mountain for Meeker? Byers may have suggested the East Peak of Longs. This would insure that Meeker's name would live in Colorado history. Six years later in 1879, Father Meeker unfortunately insured himself a more prominent niche in history by getting himself massacred by the Northern Utes on the White River Reservation.

Mertensia Falls   WILD BASIN
W. S. Cooper named these falls. Many kinds of mertensia grow in Wild Basin. Probably the variety young Cooper noticed were the tall chiming bells, sometimes called languid ladies because they droop clusters of blue and pink flowers over streams.

Michigan Lakes, River   NEVER SUMMER
At the time of the Lulu City boom, a mine and town flourished near the top of Cameron Pass. Probably a homesick miner named the mine for his home state—Michigan. The name progressed from mine to river to lake to ditch. William Rist and John McNabb, later supervisor of the Grand Ditch, built the Michigan Ditch from Lake Agnes across the divide to the Poudre drainage.

Mill Creek, Mill Creek Basin   FOREST CANYON
Horace Ferguson in 1876 defied the Earl of Dunraven's claims by homesteading near Marys Lake. When he built his Highlands Hotel, he bought lumber from a sawmill on—where else?—Mill Creek, where Hill and Beckwith had run a sawmill since 1877. They imported loggers from Wisconsin, operated a twelve-horsepower engine whose products sold for $8 to $10 per thousand board feet at the mill, $4 more in Loveland, and shipped as far as Cheyenne. In 1880 H & B moved their mill to Teller City, supplying North Park settlers until the machinery wore out. By then, Ferguson and Hallett and MacGregor all had mills in the Estes area.

Miller Creek   MUMMY RANGE
This name commemorates the first violent death in the Park area—an accident. On a hunting trip in 1871 Charles W. Denison shot Charles D. Miller who lived west of Longmont. Harold Dunning carved Miller's monument, and on October 11, 1929, set it up where Miller Creek runs into the North Fork of the Big Thompson. Here, on the exact spot of his death, Miller lies buried with, as Parson Lamb wrote, "Miller creek murmuring his last requiem."

Mills Glacier, Lake, Moraine   GLACIER GORGE
Enos Mills is fittingly commemorated by features that bear his name on two sides of Longs Peak. On the northwest, Abner Sprague named

Mills Lake after him; to the south, Mills Glacier and Mills Moraine look down to the site of Mills's hotel, famous Longs Peak Inn.

Enos Mills (1870-1922) was a Kansas farm boy who came to Estes Park when he was fifteen. He immediately started to walk alone over the northern Colorado mountains, in winter as well as summer. He learned the area in winter as a snow observer for the Colorado Department of Engineers, whose managers had recently concluded that if they knew exactly how deep the snow was in any given winter they could estimate how much water would flow in the streams that summer. In order to measure the depth of snow, Enos Mills tramped miles on snowshoes, camping where night found him. On his lonely trips, the young man observed birds, animals, trees—especially trees. In after years his most famous lecture was called "Our Friends, the Trees."

In order to make enough money to buy Longs Peak House from Elkanah Lamb, Enos Mills worked many winters in the mines of Butte, Montana. A few years after he bought the hotel it burned. He built Longs Peak Inn in 1906, demonstrating his interest in trees by using fire-killed trunks and branches as screens, spindles for staircases, and porch railings. This rustic architecture was an unfailing conversation piece, Mills always turning the conversation into a nature lesson. Groups of guests that he conducted up Longs Peak he called Nature Schools. He was a born conservationist, and, about 1909, developed the idea of a large national park. His vigorous efforts to preserve the country he loved so other people could enjoy it were most influential in the formation of Rocky Mountain National Park.

When his busy life as hotel host, guide, and lecturer gave him any time to himself, he spent long winter evenings reading the books he had missed in his youth; then, drawing on his own experiences in the wilds, he wrote books that have brought pleasure to generations of young people. Twelve books were published in his lifetime, four post-humously.

Milner Pass (10,758')   NEVER SUMMER

Trail Ridge Road crosses the Continental Divide at Milner Pass. Motorists stop to read the sign at Poudre Lake, look northeast down a long green valley to see the little stream start its trip to the Mississippi River, then return to their cars to follow Beaver Creek west to the Colorado River.

T. J. Milner was prominent in railroad circles in Colorado, though no record has been found of where he came from or where he died. He first appears as city engineer for Leadville in 1880, when that town boomed. He then moved to Longmont, where he was one of the organizers of the Denver and Salt Lake Western Railroad Company (not to be confused with Moffat's Road that came twenty years later). Milner's Road was designed to run from Denver to Fort Collins, thence "through the cañons and narrows of the Cache La Poudre" to the head of its south fork (Milner Pass) and west to the Bear (present Yampa) River, with the privilege to extend to Utah. Because Milner surveyed this ambitious route, Willis Lee of the U.S. Geological Survey named Milner Pass.

When this railroad did not materialize, Milner became the chief engineer for the Denver Tramway Company. In May 1902 he resigned to survey another railroad route to cross the mountains at Devils Thumb Pass. This, a scheme of David Moffat, was to be an electric interurban, and two short branches were built on the plains, one to Golden, one to the coal fields at Leyden.

Suddenly, David Moffat changed his mind. He would build a broad gauge, steam-powered railroad across the Colorado Rockies. He hired another surveying engineer who laid out the line up South Boulder Canyon, crossing the divide at Rollins Pass. The only part of Milner's original survey to be retained was the spectacular double curve south of Rocky Flats, still used by the Denver & Rio Grande Western Railroad. In order to gain enough altitude to cross Coal Creek at the entrance to its canyon, the railroad circles the arena and executes the Big Ten Curve, a portion of the road still called the Milner Line by faithful admirers of T. J. Milner.

Mirror Lake   INDIAN PEAKS

Mirror Lake   MUMMY RANGE
The Rocky Mountain National Park jogs around this lake in such an unreasonable manner because, in 1926, Superintendent Roger Toll traded eighty acres here for eighty acres of land south of Twin Sisters. Lee and Parker of Johnstown wanted Mirror Lake for water rights, but built no dam.

Monarch Lake (8,340')   LAKE GRANBY
When Frank H. Wolcott, long the comptroller of the University of Colorado, was a young man, he camped on the South Fork of the Grand River (see Arapaho Creek) near a cabin belonging to a prospector named Tad Danforth whose mining claims, the Copper King and Copper Queen, were at the head of the Roaring Fork. Frank told his brother Charles about these claims, and Charles and the Waltemeyer brothers of Boulder formed a company to acquire the mines in September 1903. They also bought Tad Danforth's homestead which included the present sites of Petes Cove and the Roaring Fork Ranger Station. The Boulder men called the company the Monarch Gold & Copper Mining & Smelting Company. When asked where they got the name Monarch, Wolcott replied, "They picked it out of the sky."

Soon the Boulder men decided that lumbering the great stands of timber on the slopes of the South Fork held surer promise of riches than copper mining and organized the Rocky Mountain Lumber Company. In the fall of 1904 they brought in enough men, Frank Wolcott supervising, to throw a rock dam across the Roaring Fork and build a sawmill. Run by hydro-electric power, this turned out enough lumber to construct a company town below the mouth of the Roaring Fork. The town included a three-story boarding house, a store, an office shack, slab cottages, and an assembly hall with hardwood floors on which the neighbors loved to dance. Families of stockholders, current and prospective, flocked from Kansas and Nebraska to spend their vacations in this town named Monarch. One of the sights visitors enjoyed was the Big Tree, sometimes called the Monarch, publicized as the largest tree in the county, the last of many large spruces that had sheltered pioneers from sudden rain storms. So we have two origins for the name Monarch—a spruce tree and a mining company.

The small sawmill of the Rocky Mountain Lumber Company busily cut lumber, enough to build a larger sawmill and then a box factory. Amazing is the tale of how a husky Swede with twelve-horse teams brought five large boilers and other machinery for the new mill and factory from Arrow, the railhead of the Moffat railroad, fifty miles away.

Experienced lumberjacks from Michigan soon were cutting logs too fast for horses to snake them to the mills. To solve this problem the ingenious management manufactured a lake. First they bought 160 acres of land from I. L. Killie (his upper meadows) who had bought the land from William H. ("Commodore") Bryant who had acquired it in 1902 through the Timber and Stone Act. Then the company hired Bulgarian workmen to dam South Fork a mile and a half above the town of Monarch, creating Monarch Lake. On the lake plied a homemade steamboat with a rear wheel paddle. To get the logs to the lake, wooden chutes were built in strategic locations on the steep hillsides. The steamboat pushed the logs across the lake. To get the logs out of the lake, the company hired Japanese laborers to dig a canal from Monarch Lake to the mills.

The next problem was to get the boxes and boards to the Moffat railroad, now only thirteen miles away at Granby. A private railroad was the solution. The Rocky Mountain Railroad Company built a broad gauge line from Granby to Monarch, with plans to extend to Grand Lake. So confident was the company of its expansion that tickets and waybills were printed with the names of both destinations. The thirteen miles of rails that were actually laid and used ran from the town of Monarch through the upper meadows of I. L. Killie's ranch, through a section of school land, through Killie's lower ranch, and then across the Lehman hay meadows. The rails crossed the Grand River about where the present spillway of Lake Granby stands. Then the railroad ran on the west side of the river through a short gorge, crossed over to the east side of the river above the present Camp Chief Ouray, and took a big curve into Granby.

Starting in January 1907, the little Mogul-type engine nicknamed "Old Huldah" pulled out of Monarch whenever a load was ready. One stop was always made, at the west property line of the Killie Ranch. Here the engineer had to stop the train, jump from the cab, let down three wooden bars of a gate, and put them back after he had run the train through. The railroad officials complained because the landowner would not let them build a cattle guard; the landowner, according to his daughter, Mabel Killie Hamlin in 1966, agreed to let the railroad build a cattle guard when the company paid for its right-of-way.

In the fall of 1908 the South Fork was a noisy place. Logs bumped down the chutes and splashed into the lake, the steamboat whistled as it pushed them across the lake to the mouth of the canal, saws in the mills whined, box factory machinery clanked to keep pace with the conveyor belt, and "Old Huldah" occasionally let off steam. Overnight, a night luminous with the flames of the burning box factory, the noise stopped. After the fire the company dissolved. Buildings not burned were sold and moved to Murray Camp, half a mile east of the old town of Monarch, and ex-stockholder Edgar L. McDonald ran a "Galloping Goose" over the rails from Granby to his resort near the site of old Monarch.

Moomaw Glacier—West of Frigid Lake in Wild Basin

A snow-ice field clings to the side of the Continental Divide and drips its milky waters into Frigid Lake. The Moomaw children, five girls and four boys, who knew Wild Basin from childhood, called it the Dresden China Glacier because the stones that dotted it resembled flowers on Dresden china. One of the boys, Jack, became a national park ranger especially interested in Wild Basin. The U.S. Geological surveyors named Moomaw Glacier for him on the 1958 Isolation Peak quad map, though it was not copied on the 1961 Rocky Mountain National Park map.

Jack Moomaw was born in Nebraska in 1892. In 1893 his family moved to a farm near Lyons but spent much of their time in the Estes Park mountains. When Jack wanted to see the world he joined the Navy. Disliking the service intensely, after two years he came home to his mountains. He took various jobs in the Estes Park area, guiding on Longs Peak before he became a national park ranger. He has seen superintendents of the Park come and go, capably serving each in turn, on horseback in summer, on skis in winter. As guide to world-famous scientists, Jack acquired an education, especially in archaeology. From Thunder Lake to Table Mountain, his trained eye can pick up flint chips wherever the Indians fashioned arrowheads.

Jack married Lila Weese and they had one daughter. Their home was in Horseshoe Park. Now retired, Jack lives on the bank of the St. Vrain River. He has written two books, and satisfies his curiosity in extensive travel, but always comes home to his mountains.

Moore Park   ESTES PARK

Moraine Park   ESTES PARK
Because glaciers carved its valleys, the Rocky Mountain National Park is studded with moraines—accumulations of rocks and earth piled up by the grinding movement of glacial ice. A glacier leaves at its side lateral moraines; at its lower end a terminal moraine; and as a rearguard action during its retreat other terminal moraines called recessional moraines. Marking the north and south boundaries of Moraine Park are two lateral moraines; the South Lateral Moraine especially presents a graphic remnant of glacial action. Abner Sprague said his father named Moraine Park when father and son homesteaded 380 acres on the northern slopes of the South Lateral Moraine.

Mosquito Creek   NEVER SUMMER
Until the 1961 map this appeared as Lost Creek. Who decided to memorialize the insect so prevalent in early summer in the mountains is not known. Though insect repellent has alleviated human suffering from these pests, cattle still suffer, and horses seek the smoke of campfires, sometimes so close as to burn themselves. One old-timer of the Park wrote a nature note about a local mosquito that successfully fought an eagle.

Muggins Gulch—East of Estes Park
Although it lies east of Estes Park, Muggins Gulch is intimately connected with local history. Here lived Rocky Mountain Jim Nugent and his dog Ring and his white mule (Jim's spring is below the present buildings of the Meadowdale Ranch); here lived Israel Rowe, mighty hunter, in his nine-room house; here lived Charles Denison, Estes Park's first (unintentional) man-killer. Each successive road starting up the North St. Vrain through the foothills, from Joel Estes's first cart track to the latest paved highway, converged at the foot of Muggins Gulch, then climbed up the nine-mile slope and came to Park View.

The name has been spelled different ways: Isabella Bird wrote McGinn's Gulch; Elkanah Lamb used Mulgins Gulch. Lord Dunraven did not approve of the name. He wrote: "I do not know who Muggins was—no doubt an honest citizen; but he should have changed his name before bestowing it upon such a pretty spot."

Actually it is a nickname. (The word "muggins," according to the dictionary, is sometimes used as an affectionate diminutive and means simpleton.) Milton Estes wrote:

> Muggins Gulch was named for George Hearst, whose nickname was Muggins. He was given the name by Dan Gant, who, with a man named Sowers, had some cattle in the Park, and Muggins was their herder. Muggins built a cabin at the head of the gulch, so he could watch the cattle, lest any should try to leave and go back down the valley.

Mummy Pass, Mummy Pass Creek, Mummy Range; Mummy Mountain (13,425')—MUMMY RANGE
This spectacular range was called White Owls by the 1914 Arapahos because the snow lying on Chiquita, Ypsilon, and Fairchild seemed whiter than other snowfields. Perhaps the artist Bierstadt named the range when he came to Estes Park in 1876 with the Earl of Dunraven; perhaps William Hallett, cattleman, used his imagination to name it. Authorities give both men the credit.

Presumably, the range resembles an Egyptian mummy lying on its back. "Its name was derived from an alleged resemblance requiring an active imagination to perceive," wrote historian Jerome Smiley in 1901. You may use Mummy Mountain or Hagues Peak for the head, with Fairchild representing the drawn up knees, Ypsilon the feet, Chapin and Chiquita the footstools. Or you may make up your own silhouette as you chant the names of the mountains in the Mummy Range—Chapin, Chiquita, Ypsilon, Fairchild, Mummy, and Hagues. The Rowes are not visible from the Estes Park village area, and if you add Dunraven it spoils the rhythm. (See each of these names.)

Murphy Lake   GRAND LAKE
Who was this man Murphy? He had a set of lakes, now known as Haynach Lakes, named for him, and later this lake.

Nakai Peak (12,216')   FOREST CANYON, GRAND LAKE
The 1965 chairman of the Navajo Council is Raymond Nakai, and one Navajo clan is called Nakai Denih, meaning Spanish people. This information came from the public relations director of the Navajo Tribe at Window Rock, Arizona, in July 1965; but he added in answer to a question about the clan's being descended from a white woman captured by Indians near Socorro, New Mexico, "We cannot verify the statement."

This is probably one of the names given by the Colorado Geographic Board, and just as probably one suggested by Harriet Vaille who produced so many Indian names from her reading. She often consulted Hodge, the Indian authority. He wrote that Nakai means "white stranger, i.e., Spanish," and that Nakaydi referred to the Mexican way of walking with the toes turned out. (Any Boy Scout knows that Indians walk with feet parallel.)

Nanita, Lake (Pronounced Na´·ni·ta)   GRAND LAKE
Hodge gives two origins for this word: one, that Nanita was the Navajo word for the Plains Indians, collectively, meaning aliens, or many tribes;

the other, that a tribe of Texas Indians used the name Nanita for Comanches. If this is true, three names in the Park area—Comanche, Mahana, and Nanita—commemorate the Comanches.

Navajo Peak (13,409')   INDIAN PEAKS
This proud peak with its tremendous northwestern face bears the name of a proud people who not only survived their harsh treatment by the conquering white men but have increased on their reservation. The word means very great farmers, and they were known as such by the Spaniards of the seventeenth century. After the Navajos acquired horses they no longer farmed; they raided.
The name followed one of Bethel's suggestions for calling a certain area of the Front Range mountains after Indian tribes.

Needles, The (10,068')   ESTES PARK, MUMMY RANGE
These cliffs, part of the Lumpy Ridge of the 1914 Arapahos, were named either by James of the Elkhorn Lodge or MacGregor of Black Canyon. The Estes Park Needles are fatter than the spires which mountaineers often call needles, or aiguilles.

Neota Creek; Neota, Mount, (11,734')   NEVER SUMMER
The 1914 Arapahos said their word for this mountain—*Hota-neo-tah*—meant mountain sheep's heart. From Thunder Pass the mountain looked like that to Indians, who must have known what a mountain sheep's heart looked like. Does its shape differ from the hearts of other animals?

Neva, Mount (12,814')   INDIAN PEAKS
The prospector who discovered gold near Idaho Springs, George A. Jackson, jotted down in his diary of 1858-59, "Niwot has moved up the South Fork of the St. Vrain. Neva is with him. Gave Neva his dinner and they moved on."
Ellsworth Bethel honored this Neva, an Arapaho, by naming a mountain for him. Evidently Bethel tired of people misinterpreting the name because he wrote a statement saying that Neva was an Arapaho Indian; that the name did not derive from the Latin meaning white; nor from Mount Neva in Switzerland. Nor, it should be added, is it from neve (pronounced nevay), a granulated form of snow which compacts under pressure to become ice, as in glaciers.

Never Summer Mountains   NEVER SUMMER
The 1914 Arapahos called this serrated range, which rises over three thousand feet abruptly from the floor of North Fork Valley, *Ni-chebe-chii,* translated as Never-No-Summer. The Colorado Geographic Board considered the word difficult for the American tongue to pronounce, and preferred not to use the double negative in English, so settled on Never Summer Mountains.

Before this name was chosen, the range had been identified as part of the Medicine Bows, or was called the Rabbit Ear Range, often confused with Rabbit Ear Pass, on the far side of North Park. The Never Summer Mountains were added to the Rocky Mountain National Park in 1929.

Nimbus, Mount (12,706')   NEVER SUMMER
One of the Cloud Peaks named by James Grafton Rogers of the Colorado Geographic Board. Meteorologically, a nimbus is a uniformly gray rain cloud which covers the entire sky. Mythologically, a nimbus means the luminous vapor surrounding a god or goddess when on earth.

Nisa, Mount (10,788')   GRAND LAKE
Here was another mountain with two almost identical summits. What should the Colorado Geographic Board name it? Not Twin Peaks—not Doublehead! Ellsworth Bethel had been studying Arapaho vocabularies; he produced *Nisi-two; Nisah-twins*. The board approved his clever substitution.

Niwot Ridge (13,023')   INDIAN PEAKS
At the end of this great ridge that runs east from Navajo Peak stands Niwot Mountain, originally called Bald Mountain. For the 1961 map, the U.S. Geological Survey did not entirely endorse the new name—they compromised, printing Niwot (Bald) Mountain. The survey surely agreed that too many Bald Mountains dot the map of Colorado—in 1923 the count was nineteen Balds and ten Baldys—but hesitated to replace the old name because so many mining claims specify this Bald Mountain as their reference point.

Niwot (sometimes spelled Nawat) is an Arapaho word meaning left-handed. Only one of many photos of the Chief indicates that the fingers of his right hand had been cut off between the second and third joints. Goldrushers who arrived at the site of Boulder in 1858 found Niwot and his men camped nearby. By the 1860s, although he was only twenty-three or twenty-four years old, he had become an influential leader among the Southern Arapahos. A settler of that time wrote, "Chief Left Hand was the finest looking Indian I have ever seen. He was over six feet tall, of muscular build and much more intelligent than the average Indian. . . . When wearing his war bonnet and full warrior's regalia he looked every inch a chieftain." He had learned to speak English in boyhood, when traveling in the East, and often acted as interpreter for other Indian chiefs.

He was reportedly killed at the Sand Creek Massacre in November 1864. Legend even tells how he stood with his arms folded, saying "I will not fight. Whites are my friends." He may very well have been at Sand Creek—he was in that eastern Colorado neighborhood, seeking peace, a few weeks earlier—and he was considered by the whites to be friendly, "a good chief." However, he lived to kill Major Joel Elliott and his band of nineteen men four years later in Oklahoma in the battle of Washita, in which fight the Cheyennes and Arapahos were decisively defeated by General G. A. Custer. This was Niwot's last stand. He later said of himself, "All of my time was taken up on the warpath. It was my aim that my name should become great among my people. I had a brave heart." He was principal chief of the Southern Arapahos from 1889 until the early 1900s when he was succeeded by his son, Grant Left Hand (named for President U.S. Grant, the great warrior).

Converted to Christianity in his closing years, Niwot told of his experience in simple forceful language at a great meeting of the Baptists in Oklahoma City in 1908, although he was old and blind and had to be led. He died in 1911.

An historical confusion resulted when Niwot Mountain was named, because on its east side rises Lefthand Creek. The creek was named not only years before the mountain, but years before Chief Niwot of the Arapahos was known to white men—probably before he was born. Andrew Sublette, fur trader of the 1830s, was a "south paw"; the creek was named for him.

Nokhu Crags (12,485') NEVER SUMMER
An American name for these rocks was Sawtooth, certainly not a distinctive name, so the Colorado Geographic Board abbreviated the name used by the 1914 Arapahos, *nea ha-noXhu* (Rocks Where the Eagles Nest). Watch these crags flash into view from Trail Ridge Road.

Nokoni, Lake GRAND LAKE
One of the leading chiefs of the Comanche tribe was named Nokoni, according to the Colorado Geographic Board who named the lake for him.

North Fork of the Big Thompson River MUMMY RANGE
The Rowe Glacier gives birth to this fork, once called Cow Creek.

North Fork of the Colorado River GRAND LAKE, NEVER SUMMER
In the days when the Colorado River was called the Grand, and up to the time of the Colorado-Big Thompson Project, four forks joined together to form the headwaters of the Grand River. Now the Lake Fork is under Shadow Mountain Lake; the East Fork is called Buchanan Creek; the South Fork is under Lake Granby. That leaves only the North Fork, which is smaller than it was before the Grand Ditch caught waters that formerly belonged to it. The North Fork rises east of the Never Summer Mountains in the inverted "U" made by the Continental Divide, and ends in the southern part of Shadow Mountain Lake.

North Inlet GRAND LAKE
As early as 1882, Abner Sprague was urging that a trail be built from Flattop down the North Inlet to Grand Lake, a much shorter route than

the long-established Big Meadows Trail. Ten years later when Charles Hanington, summer resident of Grand Lake, descended from Flattop via the North Inlet, he noted with regret that the trail had been neither blazed nor cleared but that the canyon had plenty of thick timber, fallen logs, and steep and slippery slopes.

In 1901 Franklin I. Huntington, the same engineer who helped survey the Fall River Road, and Fred Sprague blazed a trail down the North Inlet. They managed to get themselves and their pack horse from Bear Lake to Grand Lake in four days. Today a seventeen-mile trail, one of the park service's best, connects the two points, but even this wide path has a long history of disasters and near-disasters during blizzards or sudden summer storms.

North Ridge   WILD BASIN
This appeared first on W. S. Cooper's 1911 map, "as the most prominent feature of the north wall of Wild Basin."

North Saint Vrain Creek—See Saint Vrain Creek.

Notch, The   GLACIER GORGE, WILD BASIN
The Notch cuts into the ridge south of the East Face of Longs Peak. The name dates back at least to 1868. L. W. Keplinger, first man on the summit of Longs Peak with the Powell party of August 23, 1868, wrote in 1919 of his attempt to make a solo climb the evening before.

> Wouldn't it be a bully thing to go ahead and get a scoop on the other boys? I went ahead, into and through the Notch; the distance is only a few yards, not to exceed twenty-five, as I now remember. At the northerly edge of the Notch, Estes Park was before me for the first time. . . . I started up on the Estes Park side, using hands and feet. All was well until I paused and looked down. . . . A lonesome feeling came over me. I started back. . . . Finally I got where I could let go without slipping over, and dropped a short distance onto an ice formation in the northwest corner of the floor of the Notch. I feel quite sure that ice has not melted yet.

Notchtop Mountain (12,129')   FOREST CANYON, GLACIER GORGE
This name was suggested by Dr. W. J. Workman who built the Fern Lake cabins.

Nymph Lake   GLACIER GORGE
Dr. C. C. Parry found the type specimen of the yellow pond lily on a tarn, which he called Osborns Lake, near Gold Hill, west of Boulder, in 1864. Botanists called it *Nymphae Polysepala.* Perley A. Smoll, park naturalist, 1924-1926, simplified this to Nymph Lake. Later botanists substituted *Nuphar* for *Nymphae,* but the lake retains its name and its lilies. Nymph Lake formerly had more mundane names—Lily Pad Lake and Grant Lake.

In mythology a nymph was a divine and beauteous maiden who dwelt in forests. The Rocky Mountain National Park actually had one of these— at least she was a beauteous maiden who ran around in a leopard skin, appearing occasionally to unwary tourists. As to her divinity, the *Denver Post* merely claimed she was "a modern Eve."

If L. C. Way, the second superintendent of the Rocky Mountain National Park, really did think up this publicity stunt to advertise the beauties of the Park, he certainly went to the right man to manage it. Al Birch, an old-timer in Estes Park, was the promotion manager of the *Denver Post,* and the campaign he waged for the Modern Eve is a sample of his expertise.

The July 29, 1917, *Post* spreads pictures of Agnes Lowe all over the front page. She, a Michigan coed whose family has a summer cottage near Estes Park, wants to prove that the modern girl can live in the wilds. July 30—a picture shows her standing lonely by a tree waving farewell to her mother. She is wearing a leopard skin, ample according to 1966 standards, daring in 1917. The next day she is back in the *Post* because she had sought shelter from the pouring rain at a cottage. (Most unusual weather, said Superintendent Way.) August 6—more pictures. Front page. Leopard skin. She is going back to the wilds. More than two thousand people see her off! (Quite a crowd for the Park in 1917. The publicity was working.)

The *Post* does not mention the Modern Eve for four days. Perhaps it was during this time that Ranger Dixie McCracken, under orders from the superintendent, delivered her to an inn where she rested for a day or two, then returned her to Wild Basin dressed in a dry-cleaned leopard skin.

August 10—Enos Mills and Superintendent Way have lunch with her. She serves nature's food. Menu: pine bark soup, mountain trout, mushrooms, chipmunk peas, wild honey, chokecherries. "Every one of these articles, of course, had been obtained in the wilderness about the lake." On August 13, Agnes Lowe, the Modern Eve, triumphantly returns to Longs Peak Inn after a week in the wilds near Thunder Lake. Movies of her will be shown at Denver theaters.

A month later the *Denver Post* runs the first of a three-part serial written by the Modern Eve herself. Double-page spread in the Magazine Section. With pictures. The last installment tells of her terror as she flees from a pursuing Adam. The Park rangers rescue her from a fate worse than death. A picture of this Adam, known to the rangers as the Crazy Greek, shows a sheepish youth in a bearskin.

An hilarious version of this tale appears in *Timberline,* a book written by Gene Fowler about the *Denver Post.* He gives the modern Eve's real name as Hazel Eighmy. In the Denver directories from 1913 through 1920, Mrs. Hazel Eighmy's name appears as receptionist for a photographic studio at 1425 Washington Street.

Odessa Gorge, Lake   FOREST CANYON, GLACIER GORGE
On the shore of Odessa Lake, W. J. Workman, who ran Fern Lake Lodge, built a cabin for his daughter, his second child by his second wife. The daughter said her real name was Dessa, but "guessed her father used the longer name because he thought it more poetic." (She herself used the full name in the Denver directory of 1904 when she was teaching school in that city.)

Ogalalla Peak (13,138')   WILD BASIN, GRAND LAKE
The Oglala (the name has a variety of spellings) were the principal division of the Teton Sioux. Bethel says, "They were the terror of the frontier, under the leadership of Sitting Bull and Crazy Horse." The tribe now lives at the Pine River Agency in South Dakota.

Oldman Mountain (8,310')   ESTES PARK
The rock that squats west of the village of Estes Park resembles the profile of a sitting man, which is the direct translation of the name used for it by the 1914 Arapahos. The name Oldman predates 1914 by decades; the first settlers used it. The U.S. Board on Geographic Names at the suggestion of the National Park Service, sanctioned the name on February 9, 1965.
At the foot of this rock sits Elkhorn Lodge, for many years run by the James family. Their guests used this rock as an evening climb, but did not remain on top for days, fasting, as did the Arapahos.

Olive Lake, Ridge   WILD BASIN
The Olive Mining and Milling Company, organized by a group of men from Omaha, sank a shaft 120 feet deep on this ridge. It was not deep enough to find gold. By 1906 the Olive Corporation was defunct and the shaft house demolished. The lake, spring-fed, is still there except when it dries up in long hot summers.
Opposite Olive Ridge, west of the highway, the Clara Belle Mine operated at about the same time. With local stockholders, its annual meetings were held at Allenspark. In 1903 it was building a two-thousand-foot flume to carry water for power from the North St. Vrain River, the mill was just about completed, the tramway finished, and both day and night shifts worked the main lead of the Clara Belle. It had no more success than the Olive operation, and folded about the same time.

Olympus, Mount (8,808')—East of Estes Park village
The 1914 Arapahos called this mountain and two adjacent hills by words which translate as Faces to the Wind.

By naming Mount Olympus, Fernando C. Willett is given credit for bringing Greek mythology to the Park area. Willett was a school teacher who had served with great success as the principal of the high school in Evansville, Indiana, from 1866 to the spring of 1870. He resigned because of ill health. After staying in Denver, he came to Estes Park in May 1873, where he tutored Griff Evans's children and lived with his cousins, Mr. and Mrs. John Hubbell, in a two-story house over a mile from Evans's cabins. In Estes Park that summer of 1873 were other educated people—two geological survey parties whose leaders were Ivy League graduates, titled British sportsmen, Miss Anna Dickinson of the lecture circuit, Miss Isabella Bird, world traveler, and Rocky Mountain Jim Nugent. Surely Fernando Willett's classical allusion to Mount Olympus, the home of the gods, was not only applauded but comprehended.

Both John Hubbell and Fernando Willett had hoped to find health in the mountains. Mr. Hubbell's seven months' stay did him no good; he died the following January. Willett recovered sufficiently to become secretary of the American legation in Mexico City, where he died somewhat later.

Onahu Creek (First and last syllables accented)   GRAND LAKE

The 1914 Arapahos used this name for Fish Creek, a tributary of the North Fork of the Colorado River. It means "warms himself," and refers to one of the Indian race horses who on cold evenings came up to the fire to warm himself. This horse died on Fish Creek, whose undistinctive name the Colorado Geographic Board changed to Onahu.

Opposition Creek   NEVER SUMMER

Some old-timers think the 1961 map misplaced this creek. They claim that Opposition Creek runs in what is called Red Gulch on the 1961 map. Others say the map correctly places it in Hells Hip Pocket, and the reason the Grand Ditch ended here for so many years is that an especially obdurate boulder opposed its strength to that of the ditchdiggers, stopping the ditch and naming the creek.

Orton, Mount (11,724')   WILD BASIN

Professor Edward Orton, Jr., of the Chemistry Department of Ohio State University, conducted a survey of Mills Moraine and the Longs Peak area one summer in the early 1900s. Dean Babcock, a summer resident, who joined Orton's Ohio students, remembers that they wanted to name a peak in honor of their leader. Professor Orton declined the honor, but offered his father, Edward Orton, Sr., as a worthy candidate. Orton, Sr., was president, first of Antioch College, then of Ohio State University (1873-1881) and was a state geologist for twenty years. Babcock saw to it that Mount Orton appeared on the Cooper-Babcock map of 1911. The younger Orton commissioned Dean Babcock to paint a portrait of the mountain and presented the painting to Ohio State University as a memorial to his father.

Otis Peak (12,486') GLACIER GORGE, GRAND LAKE

Edward Osgood Otis, M.D., was born in New Hampshire in 1848, attended Phillips Exeter and Harvard, and received his degree from the Harvard School of Medicine in 1877. He became a prominent physician in Boston. In the 1880s he climbed with Chapin in the Estes Park region, and Chapin named the mountain south of Hallett Peak after him. Dr. Otis wrote in 1915, "Under what circumstances my name was given to the peak I do not remember."

Ouzel Creek, Falls, Lake; Ouzel Peak (Pronounced oo·z´l) (12,716')—
GRAND LAKE, WILD BASIN

The water ouzel, a chunky gray bird, is sometimes called a dipper. He bobs up and down on water-washed rocks, then plunges headlong into the swift stream to catch his insect bill of fare.

In the early 1900s when young William Cooper came to climb in Wild Basin, he saw a great peak towering above a certain lake. He knew that Enos Mills had named Ouzel Lake so, by association, he called the mountain Ouzel Lake Peak. Enos Mills probably had first named Ouzel Creek and then, by association, Ouzel Lake, for Mills was a naturalist who knew that water ouzels frequent swift water, not still lakes.

The Colorado Geographic Board wanted to change the name of Ouzel Lake Peak to Tawawa Peak, though it left no record of the meaning of the name. R. B. Marshall used Tawawa on his map of the newly created National Park, but Washington decided on Ouzel Peak.

Pagoda Mountain (13,497') GLACIER GORGE, WILD BASIN

The name first appears on the Cooper-Babcock map of 1911, and Dean Babcock wrote in 1965 that he gave the name because to him the mountain looked like a pagoda. Few people have known the Rocky Mountain National Park as well as Dean Babcock, artist. Born in Canton, Illinois, in 1888, where he grew up, he started summering in the Park area when he was fifteen. With his cousin, Louis Levings, he took an extended walking trip from Boulder to Boulder by way of Estes Park, Grand Lake, and the Arapaho Peaks country. (See Spectacle Lakes.) By 1908 he had won two scholarships at the New York Art Institute and had traveled in Spain, but he returned to the Park in 1908 when he was with Edward Orton in Wild Basin, and helped Cooper survey that area the same summer. That fall Babcock's mother bought eighty acres of land under the Stone and Timber Act and they started their mountain home—the Ledges—in 1910. That was the first winter he spent in Estes Park. From 1918 to 1921 Babcock was a ranger-naturalist for the park service. Babcock's ability as an artist is shown in the maps he drew of the Estes region, but more especially in his paintings, his water colors of aspens being particularly pleasing.

Paiute Peak (13,088')   INDIAN PEAKS
    The U.S. Board on Geographic Names refused to let Bethel use Ute for any point in the Indian Peaks because many other mountains in Colorado bear that name. This upset Bethel—the Utes were the most important tribe in the Colorado Rockies—but he compromised by using Paiute, the common name for several tribes related to the Utes. The word means either Water (pah) or True (pai) Ute.

Paradise Creek, Park   GRAND LAKE, LAKE GRANBY
    Without even a trail crossing its wilderness, Paradise Park (once misnamed Hell Canyon) shows no marks of man. Ecologists think that the Engelmann spruce and alpine fir here form the climax of a forest which has developed without disturbance since the last glaciation. This means that when the last glacier melted, leaving the valley covered with bare boulders, the natural succession of plant life began, from rock to soil to forest. First lichens and mosses gained footholds; they gave way to plants, then shrubs, then to aspen and lodgepole pine; finally the climax growth of spruce and fir took over. Evidence of the undisturbed growth is the uniformity of the stand of spruce and fir, and the regularity of the forest floor, covered only with blueberries. A welter of fallen timber and rotting logs makes it virtually impassable. No elk and few deer venture through this jumble. Hikers traverse the park through soggy subalpine meadows and sphagnum bogs which, like the forest, represent a succession uninterrupted since the Ice Age.

Park Hill—East of Estes Park, head of Muggins Gulch
    When the motorist on the North St. Vrain highway drives up Muggins Gulch to the crest of the hill, he suddenly sees Estes Park lying at the foot of the Mummy Range. Today this is "a grand sight and a great surprise," just as it was in October 1859 when Milton Estes and his father Joel first saw it. An old pine tree used to stand south of the old road at the crest of Park Hill. Every traveler, on horseback, in carriage, or in classic car, had his photograph taken here with the Mummy Range as a backdrop. Today the Highway Department provides ample parking space from which to see the Park.

Patterson, Mount (11,424')   GRAND LAKE
    In January 1915 the Colorado Geographic Board asked that the name Mount Senator be substituted for Bald Mountain. "Bald Mountain is not well established locally, is objectionable, and Mount Senator has been

used somewhat in the Grand Lake country as a memorial to Senator Patterson, who was influential in establishing the National Park and is now seventy years old." The U.S. Board on Geographic Names agreed that Bald Mountain was a poor name, but chose Patterson instead of Senator.

Thomas M. Patterson (1817-1916) was a power in Democratic politics from the time he arrived in Denver in 1872, when almost immediately he became city attorney. He was territorial delegate to Congress when Colorado became a state in 1876, returning to Washington the next year as representative. Proof of his political influence lies in his return to Congress as senator in 1901, a quarter-century later. In 1890 he bought the *Rocky Mountain News*. Through it, he fought for what he believed were people's rights, too long abused by corrupt politicians and untouchable corporations. Specifically he fought Bonfils of the *Denver Post;* Robert Speer, mayor of Denver; and the Colorado Supreme Court. He was instrumental in making Denver an independent county, freed from the control of the state legislature.

Tom Patterson's log cottage still overlooks Grand Lake on Campbells Point, which was named for the Senator's son-in-law and business manager of his newspaper, Richard Crawford Campbell.

Pawnee Lake; Pawnee Pass (12,541')　　　　INDIAN PEAKS

A forest service trail from Brainard Lake to Monarch Lake crosses Pawnee Pass. Topping the divide south of this pass, another and earlier trail bears an interesting name—Breadline Trail. In 1882 engineers for the Union Pacific, ubiquitous in their search for possible railroad routes across the Rockies, surveyed a line west, planning a tunnel above Lake Isabelle to pierce the Continental Divide. Like the newly built Georgetown Loop on which the Colorado Central Railroad crossed above its own tracks by means of a high trestle, the proposed Union Pacific line was to gain the needed altitude by two double loops.

Canadian Indians, hired by the Union Pacific, carried supplies to the engineers working on the Western Slope. The supplies included bread— hence the Breadline Trail. The Indians walked from Brainard Lake past Long Lake and Lake Isabelle, then left the present route over Pawnee Pass to cross the divide at the next saddle south. Thence they found a way down the only passable gulch in the steep cliffs east of Crater Lake. Members of the Boulder group of the Colorado Mountain Club still use the Breadline Trail occasionally, but it is unmarked and hard to find, and sometimes they miss the western gulch. Then they climb back up, using ropes and pitons, knapsacks heavier at every step, to regain the regular Pawnee Pass trail which is longer but easy to follow.

Pawnee Peak (12,943')　　　　INDIAN PEAKS

In this name Ellsworth Bethel commemorated the Pawnees, an Indian tribe which roamed between the Platte and Arkansas rivers in eastern

Colorado. They now live in Oklahoma. This name derives from parika, meaning a horn, because the Pawnees stiffened their scalp lock with paint and grease to make it stand up like a horn, daring their enemies to remove it.

Peacock Pool   GLACIER GORGE
Kent Dannen, Y.M.C.A. hike-master, said that someone in every party he guided along the Chasm Lake Trail asked him if he had noticed how much this pool looks like the eye of a peacock's tail.

Pear Reservoir (10,582')   WILD BASIN
Joe Mills, as a boy camping alone in Wild Basin, amused himself by naming lakes according to their shapes. "This one that bulged out at one end was surely a plump 'Pear.'" Pear is one of the Arbuckle reservoirs filed on in 1902. (See Bluebird Lake.) The 1906 amended filing for Pear (Arbuckle #4) specifies a lake depth of fifteen feet and a dam eleven feet high, at an estimated cost of $400. (When the city of Longmont bought Pear Reservoir along with Bluebird and Sandbeach lakes in 1933, during the economic depression, it paid $92,000 for the three—down from an asking price of $200,000.) Today the dam at Pear Reservoir, badly deteriorated, holds no appreciable amount of water and the pond has reverted to its original shape—a plump pear.

Peck Glacier   INDIAN PEAKS
A group of photographers, led through the Crater Lake country by Fred Fair in 1922, decided to name the glacier southwest of Lone Eagle Peak after the supervisor of the U.S. Forest Service in Denver.
Allen Steele Peck (1880-1951) graduated in forestry from the University of Michigan. After World War I, Colonel Peck came to Denver as regional director for the Rocky Mountain Region of the United States Forest Service, where he served twenty-four productive years. His many activities connected with the enjoyment and preservation of the outdoors included a directorship in the Colorado Mountain Club.

Pennock Creek   MUMMY RANGE
Charles Pennock of Bellvue was a pioneer fruit-grower in the Cache la Poudre Valley. He planted the first orchard in 1889, and his homestead was a mecca for horticulturists because of his successful experiments.

Petes Cove   LAKE GRANBY
Pete Youngblood served for many years as caretaker, alone in the winter, for various buildings around Monarch Lake.

Pettingell Lake   GRAND LAKE
In 1942 the Rocky Mountain National Park staff officially recommended for this lake the name local people had long used—the name of Judge J. N. Pettingell. Originally from Boston, he settled at Hot Sulphur

Springs in the 1880s. During a long and useful life he held several public offices in Grand County, including that of county judge. Pettingell Peak, 13,553 feet, on the Continental Divide in the southeast corner of Grand County, is the county's highest point.

Phantom Creek   NEVER SUMMER

Years before Lester Scott bought Squeaky Bob Wheeler's ranch, he rode one evening at twilight downstream from the ghost town of Lulu City; both he and his horse seemed to sense the phantoms of Indians, trappers, surveyors, Chinese coolies, fishermen, and miners who once had peopled the North Fork Valley. He thought at that time that if he owned Squeaky Bob's camp he knew what he would call it. When he and his partner bought Bob's place in 1926 he remembered his ride and changed the name to Phantom Valley Ranch.

Scott had three partners in succession; the last one, an attractive young easterner, Milton Statler, was the son of the tycoon of the Statler Hotel chain. Scott and Statler planned expansion for the ranch, but Statler was killed in an automobile accident in Arizona before the plans materialized. The ranch was sold to Irwin Beattie in 1941. In the early 1960s the National Park Service bought the establishment and tore it down in order to recreate the wilderness—adding to the phantoms of the valley the many guests who had stayed at the ranch. The North Fork owes a debt of gratitude to the person who, by naming Squeak Creek and Phantom Creek, has kept history alive.

Pierson Park   ESTES PARK

Pierson was "kind of a prospector or trapper," remembers Emma Moomaw Hutchins, "and his name was already on Pierson Park when we camped there one summer about 1905. Dad was sawmilling, but when we had an earthquake Dad was scared and got out the next day. (It was time for school to open anyway.)"

Pilot Mountain   WILD BASIN

Pine Ridge   GLACIER GORGE

W. S. Cooper noted the fine stand of lodgepole pines covering this ridge and named it on his 1911 map. Nature, who fashioned these trees thin, with small, easily chopped-off branches, obviously designed them for the use of Indians to prop up their lodges—lodgepole pines. One can recognize the lodgepole by its short needles, about two inches long, which grow in bundles of two, and its solid little cones. These stick to the branches years after they have dropped their seeds.

Along with aspens, these pines often spring up on fire-burns. Perhaps the warmth of the fire helps germinate the pine seeds lying below the charred ground. Thousands of the baby trees will appear in one season, fifty or more to a square yard. In their adolescence they look like perpendicular matchsticks, all practically the same size. The lodgepoles in older forests stand so close together that the sun scarely penetrates to the forest floor. This needle-covered ground provides an ideal nursery for shade-loving spruce and fir seedlings which, in a few decades, crowd out the lodgepoles that sheltered them in their youth. The lodgepoles, without sun, die. On Pine Ridge even now, small stands of spruce and fir mingle with the dominant lodgepoles, as the story of unrelenting forest succession unfolds. In the year A.D. 2000, accuracy will demand that the name be changed to Spruce-Fir Ridge. Later, perhaps, a fire will come, and aspens and lodgepoles will start all over again.

Around Grand Lake today the lodgepoles are being killed by dwarf mistletoe. No chemical is available to control its spread, but hope is held that such will be found soon. The forest service recommends speeding up the natural succession by planting spruce among the dying trees so that the shores of Grand Lake will not be bare when the lodgepoles die.

Two other kinds of pine trees grow in the Park—limber pines above the zone where the lodgepoles flourish, and ponderosa in lower altitudes. Limber pines also have short needles, but with five in a bundle instead of two. On windswept ridges where weather thwarts their normal growth, the grotesque trees may spread horizontally instead of vertically, and put one inch on their girths while their protected neighbors add ten. Climbers caught in a timberline storm sometimes crawl under the roof made by their matted branches. The thick-trunked limber pines at Emerald and Haiyaha lakes may be the oldest living things in the Park.

A typical stand of the third pine that grows in the Park surrounds the Beaver Meadows Entrance Station. The ponderosa, or western yellow pine, grows in open forests in lower regions of the east side of the Park. Unlike the lodgepoles, they grow far, far apart, with plenty of room to develop character. These striking red-trunked trees have needles four to six inches long in clusters of twos or threes. Children gather their large open cones for starting fires or making Christmas decorations.

These three—lodgepole, limber, and ponderosa—are real pines, not to be confused with spruce, fir, Douglas-fir, and juniper. When a name is needed to cover all mountain evergreen trees, many people mistakenly say "pine trees." The accurate covering term is conifers, meaning cone-bearers.

Pinnacle Pool   NEVER SUMMER

An especially high pinnacle juts above this small pond southeast from Mount Howard.

Pipit Lake   WILD BASIN

This is one of the lakes William Cooper named in Wild Basin. A high mountain lake like this most appropriately bears the name of the water pipit, one of four birds that nest above timberline. (The others, all of which are commemorated by lake names in the Park, are ptarmigan, horned lark, and rosy finch.) Resembling a slim sparrow, the water pipit is striped brown with inconspicuous white sides on its tail. When standing on the ground it wags its tail; it flutters into the air and sings on the wing. Its song consists of *chwee* repeated seven times.

Pisgah, Mount (8,630')—East of Estes Park
In the Bible, Mount Pisgah was the name of the mountain east of the Dead Sea from whose summit Moses looked down on the Promised Land just before his death. The name appears on various heights all over the West, a pathetic symbol of the high hopes of many early settlers.

Placid Lake   ESTES PARK

Pole Creek   GRAND LAKE, LAKE GRANBY
Probably named for trees which were cut along its course by Indians for lodge poles, or by whites for cabins.

Pool, The   FOREST CANYON
Of course many pools form in the streams of the Park, and many ponds are called pools, but the Pool is always this one, just as the Saddle refers only to the saddle near Rowe Glacier.

Frederick K. Funston spent the summer of 1889 in Moraine Park with a biological expedition including journalist William Allen White, naturalist Vernon Kellogg, Chancellor Snow of Kansas University, and a group of fun-loving boys. Funston and another boy found a pool below Fern Falls from which they netted 312 trout in one day! When Funston fell into the pool, the boys claimed he was frightened by a bear and dubbed the place Funston Pool. The U.S. Board on Geographic Names shortened this to the Pool.

Funston became famous as a general in the Philippines during the Spanish-American War. He brought order to San Francisco when federal troops were called after the fire and earthquake. Camp Funston in Kansas bore his name during World War I.

Potts Puddle   MUMMY RANGE
Ranger Jack Moomaw once dumped about two thousand rainbow fry into this high pond. Three years later Merlin Potts came upon the pond. He was a ranger officially assigned to study mountain sheep but somehow he managed to carry on his survey near fishing holes. When he threw a line into this lake, his excitement about the size and quantity of the fish that rose caused fun-loving Jack Moomaw to name it Potts Puddle. The name appears on the 1961 map. Mr. Potts retired as chief naturalist of Rocky Mountain National Park, 1965, died 1966.

At one time this lake and another near by were known as Clara and Emma lakes, names connected with the MacGregor family.

Poudre Lake   NEVER SUMMER
The old maps specify two lakes here at Milner Pass. Folklore has it that one drained toward the Eastern Slope, the other toward the west. Whatever happened to the other lake? It is all one lake now, thanks to a bulldozer. In July 1965 the U.S. Board on Geographic Names changed the name from the plural to the singular. (See Cache la Poudre River.)

Powell, Lake   GLACIER GORGE, GRAND LAKE, WILD BASIN
This, a recent name, is presumably for John Wesley Powell, leader of the first party to climb Longs Peak. In 1868 Powell and his group came from Grand Lake, and, leaving their horses when the going got rough, climbed the peak from the Wild Basin side. Accounts of their trip appear in reports by Powell, Byers, Keplinger, and others, but their specific route is hard to trace. The lake was named for the one-armed leader of the expedition who later became famous as the first navigator of the Colorado River. In 1960, Ranger Ritterbush wanted the lake named for Clarence King, after the campaign to change Copeland Mountain to Mount Clarence King had failed. (See Copeland Mountain.)

Powell Peak (13,208')   GLACIER GORGE, GRAND LAKE
The February 1961 decision of the U. S. Board on Geographic Names states that this name was proposed by the National Park Service because of a nearby feature, meaning, probably, Lake Powell. This mountain should not be confused with Mount Powell in the Gore Range, climbed by Powell in 1868 after his Longs Peak climb. (See Gore Range Overlook.)

Prospect Canyon   GLACIER GORGE
The name comes from an old tunnel made by a prospector in his unsuccessful search for rich ore.

Prospect Mountain (8,900')   ESTES PARK
The 1914 Arapahos called this the Shirt, because on its northern slope four or five hostile Indians had been killed, one of whom was wearing a shirt. The American name comes, of course, from the splendid view from the top, gained today by riding a cable car, but on August 30, 1873, W. H. Jackson lugged what he called his "traps," meaning the paraphernalia needed to take pictures with glass plates, to the top of Prospect Mountain without benefit of cable car.

Prospect Mountain Tunnel   ESTES PARK
The third, and last, tunnel of the Colorado-Big Thompson Project pierces Prospect Mountain.

Ptarmigan Creek, Lake, Pass; Ptarmigan Point (12,363')—Grand Lake

The ptarmigan, probably the best-known, certainly the best-publicized bird of the tundra country, is an alpine grouse. It changes color with the season; snow-white in winter, only its black eyes and bill betray its presence; in summer its mottled brown blends with the rocks. Trusting in its camouflage, it usually lets intruders approach quite close; a little too close and it walks away, still believing it is invisible.

The abundance of ptarmigan on the Flattop peneplain gave the name to the pass. Roger Toll proposed the name Ptarmigan Point in 1924 because of its proximity to the pass; the name also attaches itself by association to the creek that drains the area, and to its lake.

Ptarmigan Mountain (12,324')   Grand Lake

Arapaho National Forest files show that this mountain was named as early as 1860 because of the numerous ptarmigan on its slopes. Although the forest service had officially ceded jurisdiction of this territory east of Grand Lake to the park service, in 1916 it recommended retaining the name in order not to confuse "innumerable land-office records," since the mountain had long served as a tying point for mineral rights.

Rainbow Bay   Lake Granby

Rainbow trout bear a brilliant reddish "rainbow" streak on their sides. Introduced from the West Coast years ago, these sporty fish now make up more than half the trout caught in Colorado.

Rainbow Curve   Forest Canyon, Mummy Range

When the clouds are right, this parking place makes a splendid viewpoint for rainbows, often double.

Rainbow Islands   Grand Lake, Lake Granby

Rainbow Lake   Forest Canyon, Grand Lake

The north edge of this lake shines through the water like a rainbow. Until the 1961 map, this and Irene Lake together were known as the Rainbow Lakes.

Rams Horn Mountain (9,314')   Estes Park

Early settlers called this Sheep Mountain, for the same reason others called it Rams Horn Mountain. The authorities, in an effort to avoid the commonplace Sheep Mountain, approved Rams Horn. A note in the Arapaho National Forest files states that this name was given either because bighorn sheep are seen on this hill every year, or because a great quantity of their horns were found here. Mountain sheep do not lose their horns every year; then why so many on one mountain? Was this a slaughter house like Milton Estes's Sheep Rock?

In his memoirs, Milton Estes wrote a description of what pioneers did when they saw sheep on Sheep Rock:

> There was a rocky mound which we called "Sheep Rock" about 150 feet high. There was a crevice or seam running from the bottom to the top, on the north side of the rock, by which the sheep could climb to the top of the rock, single file. On the top of Sheep Rock there was a large basin which filled with water when it rained. In winter or during the hunting season, there was not much water in the basin. The sheep used the rock for a place of safety; after feeding they would climb to the top of the rock and lie down to rest. But we always knew when a flock was on the rock, by seeing one lone sheep standing guard on top, on the rim of the rock. He would be looking out for danger while the sheep were in the basin. That was the way father (Joel Estes) first discovered that the rock was a retreat for sheep; so he named it "Sheep Rock." From that time, the rock has been called "Sheep Rock." (Not on 1961 map.)
>
> When the sheep were in the basin, you could not see them from the ground, but they would walk up to the brow or edge of the rock, to look at us; and we would pick them off. When they fell outward, which they often did, the fall mashed them to a jelly. On the west side, where they nearly always fell, the rock was perpendicular. That rock was the cause of the mountain sheep, except a few stragglers, being exterminated in the Park. When we saw a flock of sheep within a mile or two of the Sheep Rock, we had a trained dog that we set on them, and they would strike straight for the Sheep Rock, then we would get the whole flock.

Rams Horn Tunnel ESTES PARK

The second tunnel of the Colorado-Big Thompson Project was bored through Rams Horn Mountain.

Ramsey Peak (11,582') MUMMY RANGE

This peak was named for Hugh B. Ramsey by his son-in-law, Frank R. Koenig, one of the first National Park rangers. In answer to inquiries about Hugh Ramsey, his daughter Hazel B. Koenig, wrote a letter on August 11, 1965, saying:

> Yes, Ramsey Peak was named for my father. He was born in Cass County, Nebraska, Dec. 17, 1862, and moved from there to Loveland, Colorado, where he built a brick plant and built the first brick houses in Loveland. He also played his violin for dances in Loveland.

Mr. Ramsey came to Pingree Park to homestead a ranch in 1890. There were no roads at that time, only a trail. He built the first road from the Ranger Station (which in those days was the Mac Hammond place), over the Pennock Pass to Twin Lakes, then down to Pingree Park. (Pingree was the name of an early trapper.)

He built two sawmills in Pingree Park. The first one was with a steam engine, the second run by the power of water brought down off the hill from Fall Creek by a pipe line. He sold the lumber in Loveland. He built Lawn Lake in Estes Park, and after moving to Pingree Park, he built Hour Glass Lake and Twin Lakes.

I can remember my father speaking the Arapaho Indian language when I was a little girl. He had a young Arapaho Indian friend and this is perhaps where he learned their language. (Hugh Ramsey helped the Nomenclature Committee of the Colorado Mountain Club with the 1914 Arapaho words.)

Ranger Creek   GRAND LAKE

Raspberry Park   FOREST CANYON
The tasty wild raspberry grows on sunny rocky slopes up to 10,000 feet. In 1864 Byers noted "inexhaustible" fields of raspberries on his way to Longs Peak but he reckoned without the population explosion. Housewives intent on raspberry shortcake try to time their berry-picking expeditions when the berries are ripe but before the bears have eaten them.

Red Gulch; Red Mountain (11,605')   NEVER SUMMER
Old-timers told Arapaho National Forest men that Indians used earth from this mountain for war paint.

Ribbon Falls   GLACIER GORGE
The Park records state that the name was suggested by Roger Toll in 1922, although until the publication of the 1961 map these falls were known to Park personnel as the Silver Slide.

Richthofen, Mount (12,940')   NEVER SUMMER
Here follows the case of Ferdinand vs. Walter, both Barons von Richthofen from Silesia in eastern Germany, but not close kin. (They were descended from two brothers who lived in 1660.) The question is—which baron left his name on handsome Mount Richthofen in the Never Summer Mountains?

Counsel for Ferdinand rises first and calls to the witness stand the ghost of Henry Gannett, chief topographer of the U.S. Geological Survey, and president of the National Geographic Society. Gannett is shown a book called *The Origin of Certain Place Names in the United States,* published in 1902. He admits he wrote it, and reads from the book a flat statement: "Richthofen, a mountain in Colorado named for the geologist." Counsel enters this book as Exhibit A.

Counsel asks the witness what geologist he had in mind. The answer is Ferdinand Paul Wilhelm, Freiherr von Richthofen (1833-1905). This man worked from 1862 to 1868 as a volunteer with the Whitney Survey in California where Gannett knew him. Baron Ferdinand developed theories about volcanic rock, and recorded in his treatises on the Comstock lode. Later the Baron penetrated into central China where he made the first map of its mountains. He was encouraged by Josiah Dwight Whitney, who had become interested in the young German in California. Their friendship lasted a lifetime, the Baron writing Whitney in 1895, "I never forget what you have been to me in California," signing himself, "I remain in ever grateful memory."

Counsel for Ferdinand continues the examination of the witness, Henry Gannett. Q. Did Josiah Whitney name Mount Richthofen? A. No, Whitney was not in Colorado with the King Survey. Q. What was the King Survey? A. The Survey of the 40th Parallel under the direction of Clarence King. They worked the Estes Park region in the early 1870s, and named mountains. Q. Was Baron von Richthofen with them? A. No, he was in China, but surveyors had a habit of naming mountains after fellow scientists. I cite the highest mountains in four western states: Mount Whitney in California, Wheeler Peak in New Mexico, King Peak in Utah, and Gannett Peak in Wyoming.

Counsel then hands Gannett a copy of the atlas of the King Survey. Gannett opens it and points to two mountains—Hagues Peak named for Arnold Hague who was in Estes Park with the King Survey; Mount Richthofen, named, Gannett maintains, for the geologist who was in China. Counsel for Baron Ferdinand von Richthofen enters the atlas as Exhibit B and rests his case.

Opposing counsel intends to prove that Walter, Baron von Richthofen, was an important man in Denver and therefore commemorated by the Colorado mountain. He calls various witnesses to the stand, living and dead, who knew this red-bearded Junker, twenty-seven years old when he arrived in Denver in 1877. Their testimony proves that Baron Walter used his tremendous energy to promote south and east Denver. Near Exposition Avenue and South Broadway he built Sans Souci, a beer garden where ladies were served strawberries and cream. He had stock in the Denver Circle Railroad that ran to present Overland Park where he raced his blooded horses. Tiring of south Denver, he turned east to the little town of Montclair. Here he built a lonely castle for his second wife whom he had met at the horse races, and a Molkerie where health-seeking consumptives sat on porches drinking milk furnished by imported cows stabled on the ground floor of the milk parlor. Both of these buildings still stand. The Baron planned to create a German Spa on the high plains, piping water—"ginger champagne," he called it—about twenty miles from a well near Barr Lake to the site of the present headquarters building of Lowry Air Force Base.

Before this scheme materialized, the Baron died, in 1898, two weeks after he personally had presented a bouquet to each of 1,200 soldiers as they marched down Seventeenth Street en route to the Spanish-American War. How proud this military-minded man would have been of his nephew, Manfred von Richthofen, the ace aviator of World War I, known as the Red Knight of Germany!

The last witness for Baron Walter is Edward Ring, teller of Colorado tales. He testifies that Richthofen was president of the Corkscrew Club of Denver to which the Earl of Dunraven belonged but cannot prove that the Baron was ever with the Earl in Estes Park.

Baron Walter's counsel submits two exhibits to prove the superior claim of his client: *Cattle Raising on the Plains of North America,* a book written by his client; and a street-sign from east Denver reading "Richthofen Place."

Counsel for Baron Ferdinand, in rebuttal, introduces a new exhibit: a newspaper obituary of Baron Walter von Richthofen. He points to the date Baron Walter arrived in Denver—1877. Then he flips open his Exhibit B, the King atlas, first to the map showing Mount Richthofen; then to the date of publication—1876.

With this conclusive evidence against the red-bearded promoter, counsel for Ferdinand moves for a directed verdict. The judge grants the motion and directs the jury to bring in a verdict in favor of the geologist, Ferdinand von Richthofen, who knew well the Chinese mountains but never saw his Colorado Rocky.

Roaring Fork (of Arapaho Creek)—LAKE GRANBY; **Roaring Fork** (of Cabin Creek)—GLACIER GORGE; **Roaring River** (tributary to Fall River)—MUMMY RANGE
What a noisy place the Park must be! Roaring is used in mountain nomenclature almost as much as fork.

Rock Creek WILD BASIN

Rock Cut ESTES PARK, MUMMY RANGE
When Edmund Rogers, as superintendent of Rocky Mountain National Park, was closely supervising the building of Trail Ridge Road, he arranged to blast the route through this spectacular cliff.

Rock Lake, Little Rock Lake FOREST CANYON
Rock Lake was formerly Big Rock Lake; Little Rock Lake was called Primrose Pool by Dr. Workman.

Rocky Mountain National Park
Herbert N. Wheeler was the first superintendent of the Colorado National Forest. According to his memoirs he moved his headquarters

from Estes Park to Fort Collins in June 1908, but before he left he talked to the Estes Park Improvement Association. "If you want to draw tourists," said he, "you should establish a game refuge where tourists can see the wild life," and he produced a map of four townships stretching northwest toward North Park, which the forest service could probably control as a game refuge.

Many people—too many to mention by name—took up the idea. For example, according to Wheeler, Gifford Pinchot of the U.S. Forest Service hired Enos Mills at a salary of $1,600 a year and travel expenses to make a lecture tour advertising the beauties of the region to women's clubs.

Gradually the idea of a game refuge administered by the forest service under the Department of Agriculture changed to the thought of a national park administered by the newly created National Park Service under the Department of the Interior. As the idea grew, so did the boundary lines of the proposed Estes National Park. The first bill presented to Congress designated Rollins Pass as the south boundary line. The final bill (all the bills were drafted by members of the Colorado Mountain Club) that passed January 26, 1915, had moved the line up to the Middle St. Vrain, but Robert Sterling Yard of the National Park Service in Washington continued to have a larger vision. He wrote:

> My dream is to see it (the Park) eventually in three sections, with general headquarters in Denver; the Longs Peak section enlarged to include the Arapahoe Peaks; the Mount Evans section, to add which there is already (in 1919) a bill before Congress; and the Pikes Peak section.

To cover such a dream, obviously the original name—Estes National Park—had to be replaced. R. B. Marshall of the U.S. Geological Survey suggested in his report on the proposed national park that

> it should bear a name of broader significance and it is certainly fitting that this striking park section of the Rocky Mountains—the backbone of the country—should be honored in the naming of this proposed park . . . it should be called the "Rocky Mountain National Park."

In 1915, Rocky Mountain National Park became the tenth national park. The revolutionary national park idea, a concept described by Freeman Tilden as "successfully impractical," is preservation. Americans since Pilgrim days have fought to tame the wilderness; the national parks preserve it. The parks are designed to remain in their natural state in order to perpetuate America's natural heritage.

Man disturbs the park as little as possible. No commercial enterprises which consume resources operate within its boundaries—no logging, grazing, farming, or mining, nor hunting and trapping. (The forest service, operating on the principles of multiple use, accepts these uses as well as recreation, and tries to conserve in spite of the uses.) But the park service confines the works of man to the minimal necessary to handle human visitors: campgrounds, a few ranger stations and back-country shelters, museums in Moraine Park and on Fall River Pass, and roads to Bear Lake and over Trail Ridge. Ghost towns, irrigation ditches and dams, and two or three resorts now in the Rocky Mountain National Park boundaries were there before the creation of the Park. Other resorts, like Steads Ranch and Phantom Valley Ranch, have been bought by the park service and razed. The National Park Service itself has interfered with naturalness by fighting blights and forest fires, an action questioned by some naturalists. If they stop forest fires, will they doom to extinction the after-fire succession of raspberry bushes, spindly lodgepole pines, and autumn-spectacular aspens?

Rocky Point   LAKE GRANBY

Roosevelt National Forest   INDIAN PEAKS, WILD BASIN
Most of the land within the boundaries of the Roosevelt National Forest was withdrawn from settlement from 1902 to 1905. On May 17, 1905, it was added to the Medicine Bow Forest Reserve. On July 1, 1910, the name was changed to Colorado National Forest. On March 28, 1932, President Herbert Hoover announced that the name was changed to Roosevelt National Forest in honor of President Theodore Roosevelt, the champion of forestry and conservation who first established the forest.
The Roosevelt National Forest is adjacent to the Rocky Mountain National Park on the north, east, and southeast. The eastern slope of the Indian Peaks is under its jurisdiction.

Round Pond   FOREST CANYON

Routt National Forest (Rhymes with shout)   NEVER SUMMER
On June 12, 1905, President Theodore Roosevelt established the Park Range Forest Reserve. In 1908 the name was changed to honor a governor of Colorado, John L. Routt. He was appointed by President U. S. Grant as territorial governor in 1875. The next year, when Colorado became a state, Routt was voted into the office of governor, serving until 1879. From 1891 to 1893 he was again governor, having served as mayor of Denver in the interim (1883-85). In 1877 the western part of Grand County was made into a separate county, called Routt. Later Routt helped develop the rich coal mines of the county that bears his name.

Rowe Glacier, Peak; Rowe Mountain (13,184') (Rhymes with how)—
MUMMY RANGE
In the fall of 1875, Israel Rowe came to Estes Park to work on MacGregor's toll road, his wife cooking for the road gang over an open

fire. He eventually built a nine-room house on land which later became the Crocker Ranch. Rowe discovered Gem Lake, but his discovery of Rowe Glacier should really be credited to dead grasshoppers and black bears. In 1880 grasshoppers flew over the Rockies in great clouds, myriads of them dying on the high snowbanks of the peaks. (Thawed, they smell like long-dead whales.) Bears consider grasshoppers a delicacy worth climbing high to secure, and Israel Rowe liked to hunt bears. Hunting, he came upon what he thought was the largest snowfield in the Rockies.

Rowe took two other hunters to see this marvel, and also told William Hallett about it. In 1884 Hallett investigated, alone. He fell into a fissure two feet wide and thirty feet deep, its bottom filled with water and its sides made of clear, crystalline ice. He extracted himself by the grace of God and extreme exertion. Convinced that such a crevasse could occur only on a true glacier, Hallett told Professor G. M. Stone of Colorado College about his experience. Stone, through scientific channels, publicized the discovery of a glacier so far south in the Rockies. Thereupon glacialists from east and west swarmed to measure and admire Hallett Glacier.

Hallett Glacier was its name from 1888 until Abner Sprague tired of explaining to his guests that Hallett Peak was south of Flattop, above Tyndall Glacier, whereas Hallett Glacier was across the Park, nowhere near Hallett Peak, but in the Mummy Range. Sprague suggested in 1924 that Hallett Glacier be renamed Rowe Glacier. Many people objected. Charles Hanington, friend of Hallett in the Rocky Mountain Club, wrote a letter of protest to the Colorado Mountain Club. Finally Roger Toll, noted for his ability as a peacemaker, suggested that the glacier keep the name of Hallett but that a certain mountain, hitherto unnamed, be called Rowe Mountain. The suggestion backfired. In June 1932 the U.S. Board on Geographic Names not only changed the name of the glacier to Rowe but also pinned the name on two mountains. Now we have Rowe Glacier (formerly Hallett Glacier), Rowe Peak just to the north of it, and Rowe Mountain north of Rowe Peak. The latter pair is the only duplication of peak names in the Park area. Perhaps correspondence explaining this may someday be found in the files of the U.S. Board on Geographic Names. One hopes that either Rowe Peak or Rowe Mountain commemorates Mrs. Israel Rowe who camped, took care of two small children, and cooked for a road gang over an open fire.

Saddle, The   MUMMY RANGE
    Any low place between two mountains may be called a saddle, but this is the Saddle, a name in use by 1913. Willard H. Ashton of Horseshoe Park

Lodge used to send his guests to Lawn Lake where he had built a shelter cabin, then across the Saddle, and on north until the western side of Hagues Peak flattened out enough for them to describe a U-turn and come south to Rowe Glacier. (See Lawn Lake.)

Saint Vrain Creeks, Glaciers; Saint Vrain Mountain (12,162')—
INDIAN PEAKS, WILD BASIN

This name dates back to fur-trading days, but the creek had a previous name. On the night of July 3, 1820, Major Long's expedition camped on the South Platte River nearly opposite the mouth of the St. Vrain, which he called

> Potera's Creek, from a Frenchman of that name who is said to have been bewildered upon it, wandering about for 20 days almost without food. He was found by a band of Kiawas, who frequent this part of the country, and restored to his companions, a party of hunters at that time encamped on the Arkansas.

The name of the bewildered Potera gave way to the name of a store-keeper. Since any efficient storekeeper locates his store in a solvent community, successful merchants of the fur trade era, such as the brothers Bent and the brothers St. Vrain, built stores near where their customers, the Indians, could kill buffalo and bring robes to trade for luxuries like looking-glasses or a slice off a sugar loaf. Bent's Fort stood on the Arkansas River; another store financed by Bent and St. Vrain rose about 1837 on the east bank of the South Platte River, one and one-half miles below the mouth of St. Vrain Creek, three miles west of the present town of Gilcrest. This, the heart of the Arapaho country, was frequented also by Sioux, Cheyenne, Shoshoni, Pawnee, and other tribes whose names Ellsworth Bethel tried to affix to the peaks that tower on the skyline to the west. The store, or post, was first called Fort Lookout, then Fort George in honor of one of the Bent brothers, then gradually became Fort St. Vrain; the stream that joined the river near the fort became known as St. Vrain Creek.

Ceran St. Vrain was the capitalist of his family; but his younger brother Marcellin reigned as bourgeois (storekeeper) of the fort. He was a pleasant host with cultivated St. Louis manners and a Sioux wife, who brought trade from the Plains Indians. In 1843 John Charles Fremont and William Gilpin celebrated the Fourth of July with Marcellin St. Vrain, eating fruit-cake shipped from St. Louis, and ice cream made with snow from Longs Peak. Gilpin's note on this feast did not explain how the snow was transported without melting.

How appropriate that the three branches of St. Vrain Creek have their origins in the Indian Peaks, since the Indians were the source of the success of St. Vrain's store!

Sandbeach Creek, Lake (10,283') WILD BASIN

Dr. Cooper remembers that this lake was named by Enos Mills. The sandy beach was covered up when the dam was built which turned the natural lake into a reservoir. The Supply Reservoir Company, in its filing in 1902, called the lake Supply Reservoir #1, and called the creek on which it lies Big Cascade Creek, but these names never became general. By 1916 the road to the lake had deteriorated into a trail. (See Bluebird Lake.)

Satanta Peak (11,979') INDIAN PEAKS

Another way of spelling this name of a Kiowa warrior is S*et-T'ain-te* (White Bear). Satanta (1830?-1878), known as the Orator of the Plains, lives in the memory of his people as one of the irreconcilables who strewed the path of white conquest with as much cactus as he could. Despite his hostility, he was a favorite with U.S. Army officers—in war, an able antagonist; between wars, a man of humor. When they visited his camp, he spread factory-made carpets on the ground and served them meals on tables of painted boards twenty inches wide by three feet long, ornamented around the edges with bright brass tacks (an early version of TV tables). To announce dinner, Satanta blew vigorously on a trumpet.

Kit Carson captured Satanta, holding him hostage in a vain attempt to subdue the Kiowas. Two years later the Indian brave left Fort Sill, but the prison cell had drained the gaiety from his heart and filled it with hatred for the white conquerors. Henceforth, the only times he played his trumpet was to confuse the U.S. Cavalry; when their bugler sounded "Charge," Satanta played "Retreat."

On a friendly visit to General Sherman, Satanta boasted of a recent murder of white settlers. General Sherman had him seized. An eyewitness described this six-foot Kiowa as he arrived at the Huntsville, Texas, jail, his feet lashed together under the belly of a small pony: "His muscles stood out on his gigantic frame like knots of whipcord, and his form, proud, erect in the saddle, his perfectly immobile face, and his motionless body, gave him the appearance of polished mahogany."

Three years in the Texas prison were enough for this vigorous man. One day he chanted the Kiowa death song, folded his arms, and plunged to death on the stone pavement three stories below the prison hospital windows.

Sawmill Creek NEVER SUMMER

A sawmill built on this stream provided lumber for the construction of the Grand Ditch.

Sawtooth Mountain (12,304') INDIAN PEAKS

As seen from the Boulder Turnpike this mountain stands against the sky between Mount Audubon to the south and Ogalalla Peak to the north, both much higher. The precipitous south face of the ripsaw tooth of this mountain makes it easy to recognize from the plains. Sawtooth has the distinction of marking the extreme eastern point reached by the Continental Divide in the United States.

Seven Utes Mountain (11,458')—Four miles west of Nokhu Crags
This is the only mountain in the Park region that bears the name of the Ute Indians who inhabited the western mountains of Colorado, and this name was given to the mountain not to commemorate the independent Ute nation but to mark the place where the Utes suffered a tragedy. The 1914 Arapahos had a long name for this mountain which meant where-the-Arapahos-killed-seven-Utes. The Colorado Geographic Board struggled with the original Arapaho words, hoping to use them or part of them for this mountain, but decided to use "the translation of an unpronounceable word from the 1914 Arapaho trip meaning Seven Utes."

Shadow Mountain (10,155') GRAND LAKE
The 1914 Arapahos knew this mountain as Pine Ridge. When George Barnard and Jim Rogers asked local people what they called it, everyone gave a different answer. Some called it Lookout Mountain but, according to Charles Hanington, no true Grand Lake resident ever used that name. They preferred Wooded Mountain, except those who used Echo Mountain. In the summer of 1915 James Cairns pointed to this mountain opposite his store window and told Harriet Vaille it had three names, a middle and two sides. The central part was Cornstalk Mountain because of fire-killed timber sticking up like stubble in a cornfield. To the west the ridge was Echo Mountain; to the east the ridge was the Lady of the Lake.

Official approval by the Colorado Geographic Board of any one of these would inevitably antagonize someone. Lawyer Rogers, chairman of the board, formulated a policy for such contingencies: In case of altercation, all old names should be replaced with an entirely new one, and he noted, "Old names replaced were in no case undisputed names." But what name should replace Lookout-Wooded-Echo-Cornstalk, and Lady of the Lake? George Barnard suggested Shadow Mountain because the ridge cast its shadow on Grand Lake.

Shadow Mountain Lake (8,367') GRAND LAKE
George Barnard could not have dreamed that Shadow Mountain would someday also cast its shadow on a man-made lake that covers the sagebrush flats through which the Colorado River once meandered and children hunted Indian arrowheads among the gentians. Made by damming the river below the confluence of the Lake Fork and the North Fork of the Colorado River, Shadow Mountain Lake is part of the Colorado-Big Thompson Project. Water pumped by electricity from Lake Granby, also man-made, to Shadow Mountain Lake flows to Grand Lake;

thence, via the thirteen-mile Alva B. Adams Tunnel to the Eastern Slope. Here the fall of water creates electricity which is carried back by power lines across the divide to the pumps at Lake Granby, a system which approaches perpetual motion.

In an effort to preserve the especially attractive shoreline of Grand Lake, the U.S. Bureau of Reclamation agreed with the Grand Lake community that the water should rise no higher than its natural level when the big project was completed. The levels of Grand Lake and Shadow Mountain Lake are quite constant, while Lake Granby rises and falls with the runoff and with irrigation demands.

Shadow Mountain Lookout (9,923')   Grand Lake
Although this lookout is over two hundred feet lower than the top of Shadow Mountain, the view is ample. In the forest service lookout building, well protected against lightning, the summer firewarden watches for forest fires, augmenting the modern air patrol. The warden's job is eagerly sought and often held by honeymooners, whose only contact with the world below is by telephone, except for forest service men on horseback who bring them supplies, and for hikers.

Shadow Mountain Recreation Area   Grand Lake, Lake Granby

Lake Granby and Shadow Mountain Lake, man-made reservoirs linked by channel to Grand Lake, Colorado's largest natural body of water, comprise the "Great Lakes" of Colorado. The recreational potential of the area, recognized as one of the greatest in the United States, is being developed by the National Park Service through agreement with the Bureaus of Reclamation and Land Management, U.S. Department of the Interior.

So reads the official folder of this area. Boating, water skiing, and lake fishing on a lake as large as Lake Granby, about eight miles long, are unusual for a state full of what easterners call ponds, but few states can supplement the boating with a mountain view such as that of the Indian Peaks on the Continental Divide seen from Lake Granby.

Sharkstooth, The (12,630')   Glacier Gorge
The Walter Fricke book on technical climbing states, "The summit of this superb fang . . . is accessible only to the fifth class rock climber. The *hoi polloi* never reach it." Even Warren Gorrell, who made the first ascent in 1936, admitted that "the toe holds were not too obvious." Surprisingly, the top is a flat fifteen by thirty yards.

Sheep Lakes   Estes Park, Mummy Range
Mountain sheep often come to these lakes today as they did in 1917 when Willis T. Lee wrote, "This lake has long been a favorite resort for the

bighorns. . . . They come down to Sheep Lake nearly every day for water. A supply of salt placed here has tempted them to frequent the spot." (See Bighorn Mountain, Rams Horn Mountain.)

Sheep Mountain   Mummy Range

Sheep Rock   Never Summer
Surprisingly often, bighorn sheep look down from this rock at the motorists who have stopped at Milner Pass to read the Poudre Lake sign. Look up to them!

Shelf Creek   Glacier Gorge

Shelf Lake   Glacier Gorge
This lake in Glacier Gorge is an example of the ice-action that leaves lakes—hanging lakes—perched on shelves above the valleys.

Shelter House   Glacier Gorge, Wild Basin
There is good reason for a mountain shelter-house to be marked on a map; it can mean survival. The shelter at Chasm Lake marks the end of the horse trail. Climbers often spend the night there before attempting the ascent of the East Face; and it houses the park service rescue equipment—litters, ropes, bandages, emergency food.

At the Keyhole on Longs Peak is another, smaller shelter, erected by her family near the spot where Agnes Vaille died on January 12, 1925. This structure was designed by Arthur A. Fisher, Denver architect, along lines suggested by some ancient dwellings in Apulia, southern Italy. The heavy walls, the floor, the bench, even the bee-hive roof are stone.

On the Boulder Field stood for many years still another shelterhouse, run by Robert Collier and his wife Dorothy—at 12,500 feet, the highest tourist hotel in Colorado! Though built on rock, it proved to have a precarious foundation. The alternate freezing and thawing of water below caused the huge boulders to shift their positions slightly; the walls cracked and finally fell.

Shelter Island   Grand Lake, Lake Granby
On Lake Granby, shelter from eccentric winds and forceful whitecaps can be as important to the boatman as shelter on a mountain is to a climber.

Shipler Park; Shipler Mountain (11,317')   Never Summer
Joseph L. Shipler, a Civil War veteran, built a cabin in Shipler Park in 1876, the first cabin in the valley of the North Fork. Shipler was a forerunner of the mine rush, one of the discoverers of the Wolverine Mine on Bowen Mountain. In December 1882 he located the Collins Lode in the

Lead Mountain Mining District; its enormous mine dump on Shipler Mountain is conspicuous from Shipler Park.

Mr. Shipler was still living in his cabin when the Colorado Mountain Club camped in his park in August 1914. One of the thirty members of the Prairie Club of Chicago who came on this outing wrote an account of his cabin, reached at the end of a long walk from Grand Lake. Her report of the lonely walk on a dirt road contrasts with motor travel on today's paved highways:

> The walk of 16 to 18 miles to our Shipler Park camp, which was 1,000 feet higher than Grand Lake, was one of the finest trips of the whole outing. A wagon road leads from Grand Lake to Shipler Park, and we followed it all the way, through seas of flowers of every hue imaginable. The fringed blue gentians grew so thick that one swoop of the hand would have secured a large bunch, and they formed pools of blue, first on one side and then on the other side of the road. . . . We also found quantities of wild strawberries, and you know how sweet they were. . . . The only people we saw that day were two forest rangers, for we were in the Arapahoe Forest Reserve; Squeaky Bob, who kept a fishing resort a mile and a half below our camp; and a Prairie Schooner drawn to one side of the road. . . . by 3:30 we arrived at Squeaky Bob's Camp which he called the Hotel de Hardscrabble. It is a pleasant looking log cabin resort surrounded by tents, and much frequented by trout fishing enthusiasts, as the trout fishing in Grand River is very good. (The next day, George Barnard, leader of the Colorado Mountain Club outing, caught 127 brook trout for the group's breakfast.) Squeaky Bob is considerable of a character, having been everything from a cow puncher, horse thief, and guide, to a resort keeper, and he got his name from his voice which is high pitched and has a falsetto note in it. . . . I was anxious to see the camp so I pushed on, and I was well rewarded. It was really the most beautiful camp of the whole trip . . . this park was adorned by the finest grove of Engelmann Spruce and Fir Balsam trees I have ever seen, and bounded on the one side by the Grand River and the other by a swift running mountain brook.
>
> The only person up there was an old miner, Mr. Shipler, who had several claims in that region, and from whom the Park as well as a mountain looking down upon it, got their name. Mr. Shipler proved to be the soul of hospitality, and when the wagons and provisions did not arrive, gave us all the coffee he had, so we secured a hot drink at least. Then hearing that one of the girls was sick, he fixed up the other bed in his cabin and came out to offer it to her, as it began to look as though we would have to spend the night outdoors. The sick girl, however, had already been sent down to Squeaky Bob's, so Mrs. Pettengill who was beginning to feel cold, made a dicker with Mr. Shipler whereby she and I obtained the much coveted bed, and it was quite an experience I can assure you.

The bed was made from four wide slabs of rough wood put together to form a square box into which spring and mattress had been placed, and this bed with another of similar make occupied one side of the cabin, the only other furniture being a kitchen table, small stove and two chairs. Tiny windows high up on either side, together with a glass pane set into the upper half of the one door, let in the light of day, and we could peer out through chinks from which the clay had fallen as well. The inscription on the door was the best part of the cabin though, as it read as follows: "Everybody welcome here, except a low down cur of a thief who belongs in the Penitentiary, and I have his name and number and will get him. G. Shipler."

Ships Prow GLACIER GORGE, WILD BASIN

The lower end of Glacier Ridge "ends abruptly in a 400-foot cliff whose majestic upward sweep from the valleys . . . led to the appellation Ships Prow," Walter Fricke wrote, and then listed eight distinct routes used by rock climbers, routes with (unofficial) names like the Nose, Stromboli, Nexus Corner, Half Days Work, Gangplank.

Shoshoni Peak (12,967') INDIAN PEAKS

In 1965 a young man from Chile named Evilio Echevarria, a teacher at the University of Colorado, and a mountaineer, proposed that an unnamed peak on the Continental Divide between Apache Peak and Pawnee Peak, 12,967 feet high with a precipitous southeast face, be named Shoshoni Peak. The U.S. Board on Geographic Names sent out inquiries concerning it in January 1966 and accepted it in July. How pleased the spirit of Ellsworth Bethel must be that the Shoshoni tribe has taken its place among the Indian Peaks, fifty years after he heatedly tried to have Mount Alice changed to Shoshone Peak. (See also Mount George.)

Signal Mountain (11,262'); **South Signal Mountain**—MUMMY RANGE

White pioneers who watched smoke rise in spurts from the top of Signal Mountain wondered what the redmen's signals meant, and later told their children of seeing the smoke. The 1914 Arapahos did not remember signaling from the mountain; they called the two mountains Wolf Ridge. (See Bulwark Ridge.)

Skeleton Gulch NEVER SUMMER

Two men caught in a snowslide were carried far down this gulch where their skeletons were found in the late spring.

Skull Point (12,026') MUMMY RANGE

On August 9, 1927, Charles R. Hughes of Denver found a human skull in rocks near the summit of this point. Roger Toll and others, investigating, found animal bones there, and concluded that mountain lions had denned on this point long, long ago. Toll proposed the name on September 15, 1927.

Sky Pond   GLACIER GORGE

By eastern standards, Sky Pond is just a small pond; by western mountain standards, Sky Pond is big enough to be called a lake. It was named by an easterner, Robert Sterling Yard, who fully appreciated the spectacular scenery when Abner Sprague guided him to the head of Loch Vale. Yard was investigating the area in order to prepare the first official pamphlet for tourists about the newly created Rocky Mountain National Park.

Robert Sterling Yard (1861-1945), after securing a B.A. from Princeton in 1883, was connected with both *Scribners* and *Century* magazines. From the inception of the National Park Service in 1914 to 1919, he was chief of the educational section. In 1919 he organized the National Park Association, and in 1935 helped establish the Wilderness Society. It is pleasant to think of Sky Pond and Lake of Glass, probably Icy Brook, too, as names given by this dedicated conservationist.

Snow Lake   NEVER SUMMER

Snowbank Lake   WILD BASIN

Janet Neuhoff Robertson recalls that Dean Babcock sat in the Neuhoff living room in Allenspark and wondered if Veronica Lake, movie star, had taken her name from Veronica Lake which he had named for the wild flower, alpine speedwell, and put on a map of Wild Basin. The lake later became either Lion or Snowbank Lake.

Snowdrift Lake   GRAND LAKE

The sizable cirque enclosing this lake shelters a snowdrift; Ferrel Atkins, park ranger-naturalist, "suspects a glacierette." Before this lake had a distinct name all its own, it and Murphy Lake to the north of Snowdrift Peak were called Murphy Lakes.

Snowdrift Peak (12,274')   GRAND LAKE

This was labeled Mount Fisher by R. B. Marshall on the map he drew for the Denver Chamber of Commerce about 1915, but the Colorado Geographic Board "could find no local authority whatever for the name and it seemed meaningless." (One wonders if they asked Marshall if he named this peak for Arthur Fisher, his guide, with John Baker, on his tour of the proposed national park area in 1913. Because of a snowdrift conspicuous from the Flattop Trail, the Colorado Geographic Board asked to have Fisher Peak renamed Snowdrift Peak in February 1915, the U.S. Board on Geographic Names making the change official in 1932.

Soda Creek, Spring   LAKE GRANBY

Solitude Lake—GLACIER GORGE; **Solitude, Lake**—GRAND LAKE

South Fork of the Colorado River—See Arapaho Creek.

South Lateral Moraine—See Moraine.

South Saint Vrain Creek—See Saint Vrain Creek.

Spearhead, The (12,575') GLACIER GORGE, WILD BASIN
Dean Babcock knew this name in 1922, and Roger Toll recorded it officially in July 1923 after he and a group of Colorado Mountain Club members had climbed it. "This sharp wedge-shaped spur running north from Chiefs Head is a prominent feature of Glacier Gorge," Toll wrote. Superintendent Toll fancied balanced names like Arrowhead and Spearhead, Knobtop and Notchtop.

Specimen Creek NEVER SUMMER
Before the 1961 map, this was called Volcano Creek.

Specimen Mountain (12,489') NEVER SUMMER
The 1914 Arapahos, with no hint from Oliver Toll or Shep Husted that the area was of volcanic origin, said they knew this mountain as Mountain Smokes. One of the Indians, Sherman Sage, told a legend, illustrating it by arranging eight stones on the ground, each representing a generation of his ancestors. As he placed the last stone he said, "This man, when he was a boy, saw smoke coming out of the mountain."
Geologically speaking, Sherman Sage should have spent all day heaping up stones to represent the generations of man that have lived and died since smoke came out of Specimen Mountain; but smoke it did, once. Its appearance today, so entirely different from that of other mountains in the Park, testifies to its volcanic origin. Specimen Mountain is formed in layers laid down by eruptions—volcanic, glass, ash, lava, mud-flows, breccia, and pumice. The cone probably once stood thousands of feet higher than the present summit of the mountain, and what is called the Crater on its southwest side is not a crater. The name Specimen Mountain appears on an 1882 township map. The specimens are gemstones, like opal, agate, chalcedony, and black obsidian. All these and more may be observed on the mountain, especially in the Crater. Observed, but NOT collected. Collecting is prohibited in national parks.
Frank Byers, son of William Byers who climbed Longs Peak in 1868, remembered that when he was a boy at his father's ranch at Hot Sulphur Springs this mountain was called Geode Mountain. A geode is an ordinary looking stone with a crystal center. Young Frank doubtless spent happy hours breaking open stones with the hope of finding beauty within.

Spectacle Lakes MUMMY RANGE
Named by Roger Toll in 1922, not for their spectacular appearance at the foot of Ypsilon's cliffs, but for their shape, which resembles a pair of eye-glasses.

Above the lakes is the grave of a twenty-one-year-old youth who was killed on August 2, 1905. Louis Raymond Levings and his two cousins, George Black and Dean Babcock, had climbed Fairchild Mountain that day. Dean returned to camp but the other two youths wanted a picture of one of the snow cornices that protrude over the arms of the "Y" on Ypsilon Mountain. About six hundred feet down, Louis fell when a rock he was using as a hand hold gave way. His body was left on the mountain, cement being poured over the grave. By 1929, when the cement started to disintegrate, iron plates for a coffin were packed up the trail, then bolted together, and he was reburied about seven hundred feet above and to the north of Spectacle Lakes.

Spirit Lake   GRAND LAKE
This was the Ute name for Grand Lake. (See Grand Lake.) The name Spirit Lake was ignored by white settlers. Fortunately someone saved the Ute name from oblivion by moving it upstream on the East Inlet of Grand Lake.

Sprague Glacier, Pass; Sprague Mountain (12,713')—FOREST CANYON, GRAND LAKE; **Sprague Lake**—ESTES PARK
Before he died in 1943, Abner Sprague was the patriarch of Estes Park. His two manuscripts on the Park's history are gold mines. Abner Sprague had come in 1864 by covered wagon from the Midwest with his family to settle on a farm near Loveland. In 1875 young Abner braved the animosity of Dunraven's overseer to squat on land in Moraine Park. Later Sprague found that the Earl, in grabbing his huge hunting preserve, had filed on the South Lateral Moraine, but had neglected to claim the valley floor of Moraine Park. There Abner and his father acquired two quartersections of land. Soon Mother Sprague was cooking for hungry hunters who appeared at the only door within miles to ask for food and shelter, and the Spragues became innkeepers. About 1900, Jim Stead, a dairy man from Chicago, whose wife was kin to the Spragues, bought the hotel and changed its name to Steads Ranch. After a while Abner built another hotel, this time in Glacier Basin. He who owned wild Mills Lake and the Loch traded them for land on which to build a pretty fishing lake for his guests—Spragues Lake. Sprague sold his hotel to the National Park in 1932 for $35,140, but he and his nephew continued to operate it until 1957 when the Park razed the buildings. The nephew bought Steads, sold that to the Park in 1963 for $750,000 and it, too, was razed.

Abner Sprague delighted in taking discriminating guests to the head of Spruce Canyon. He led a group in August 1898 to examine an ice field previously noted by Chapin, and found it indeed to be a glacier. The party named it Sprague Glacier. Sprague knew this terrain as well as any man will ever know it. Enos Mills acknowledged this when his 1905 map appeared with Sprague's name on the glacier that feeds Spruce Creek. Whoever applied Sprague's name to the adjacent mountain and pass, on the 1961 map, paid a little of the debt the Park owes Abner Sprague.

Sprague himself made maps. He ran lines for railroads and private property-owners, and, for three years around 1890, was official surveyor for Larimer County. In trying to map the Estes Park area, he found his sketch a confusion of hachures denoting many nameless mountains between Longs and Hagues, between Richthofen and Mount Olympus. Because a map without names lacks character, Sprague set about naming the natural features of the land he loved. He honored old-timers, neighbors, and guests at his hotel whom he had guided across the mountains, reserving a beautiful waterfall for his wife, Alberta.

Spruce Canyon, Creek   FOREST CANYON
These features originally were called Willow. Abner Sprague changed the name to Spruce because of the splendid Douglas spruce that grew in the canyon upstream from the Pool. It was not his fault that dendrologists later changed the name of the tree to Douglas fir. The name of the canyon, however, need not be switched to fir, as Engelmann spruce grow there, too. Chapin in 1886 noted this forest. "Fires have never ravaged it, it is truly primeval." It still is.

Douglas fir is really neither spruce nor fir. A young Scot, David Douglas, went to Oregon in 1824 to collect for the London Horticultural Society. (Later he went to Hawaii where he was killed by a bull.) He found the tree popularly identified by his name. Its Latin name for many years was *Pseudotsuga taxifolia.* (Literal translation—*pseudo,* Greek word for false; *tsugo,* Japanese word for hemlock; taxi, from *taxus,* Latin word for yew; *folia,* from Latin word for leaf. This means the tree is a false hemlock with leaves like a yew.) However, Douglas was not the first man to identify the tree. Another Scottish botanist, Archibald Menzies, discovered it on Vancouver Island in 1791. In an effort to give credit where credit is due, dendrologists have recently changed the Latin name of the Douglas fir to *Pseudotsuga menziesii.*

What is the amateur botanist to do among this confusion of spruce, fir, hemlock, yew, Greek, Japanese, Latin, and two Scots? He can call the Douglas fir a Christmas tree, and identify it by its soft, flat needles and hanging cones with three-pronged tongues protruding between the scales.

Spruce Lake   FOREST CANYON
Besides the Douglas fir, which is neither spruce nor fir, real spruce and real fir grow in the Park. One way to tell them apart is to feel the needles. The spruce needle is sharp and four-sided; the fir needle soft and flat. The Boy Scouts remember this by four words: spruce—square; fir—flat.

Two kinds of spruce grow in the Park. The Engelmann spruce dominates the subalpine zone, and the Colorado blue spruce groups along streams in the lower mountains. The Engelmann spruce was named for the same St. Louis botanist for whom the mountain with the great cirque, south of Berthoud Pass, was named.

The blue spruce is the official state tree of Colorado. This tree emigrated from Colorado to the Midwest in the 1860s, carried by the turn-backs of the Pikes Peak Gold Rush who loaded small silver-blue spruce instead of gold nuggets into their empty prairie schooners before turning their backs on the Rocky Mountains. The gardens of Iowa, Missouri, Illinois have been ornamented by Colorado blue spruce for a hundred years. Spruce Lake was named by Cliff Higby in 1914, probably because it lies in Spruce Canyon. Cliff Higby and his brother Reed were first boys and then businessmen in Estes Park, enthusiastic about all aspects of the mountains. After serving in Europe during World War I, Cliff refused to come home until he had climbed the Matterhorn. In Colorado he not only climbed with the Colorado Mountain Club but was instrumental in forming the club's Estes Park group (now incorporated by chapters in Boulder and Fort Collins). Later Higby homesteaded in North Park near the Wyoming border, running a guest ranch called the Skyland Ranch.

Before 1914, Dr. Workman had named Spruce Lake for Fred Dille, naturalist, for whom Ed Andrews assiduously collected bird eggs. At the age of nineteen Fred Dille was the second school teacher in the Estes Park school. His reminiscences are in the library of the Rocky Mountain National Park. On June 30, 1932, the U.S. Board on Geographic Names recognized Spruce Lake, "Not: Dilly."

Squeak Creek NEVER SUMMER

Robert Wheeler (1865-1946) arrived at his brother's ranch in North Park in 1885 in a silk hat, striped coat, and kid gloves. To acquire this correct traveling outfit young Bob had saved for months. He soon learned how to dress and how to hold his own in a world of men, despite his short stature and high-pitched voice. During the Spanish-American War he had charge of the horses for a troop of Rough Riders who never got out of Florida. He worked in mines at Encampment, Wyoming, and at Lulu City, then in 1907 homesteaded 160 acres on the North Fork of the Grand River. Here he built a tenthouse resort. It went by three names: formally it was Camp Wheeler; its owner always referred to it as Hotel de Hardscrabble; and to sportsmen it was Squeaky Bob's place. The last was inevitable because in excitement Robert Wheeler's high, thin voice rose to a falsetto squeak.

His guests took for granted the first-class hunting and fishing, but never Squeaky Bob's tales interlaced with wit and inventive profanity. Though he had housekeepers, Bob usually did the cooking himself, for what did a woman know about cooking wild game? Bob married the last of his housekeepers, and in 1924 sold his camp for a life in the lowlands. The new owner, Lester Scott, changed the name to Phantom Valley Ranch and tore down the tent houses, but among the new buildings he erected was a cabin where Squeaky Bob and his wife might spend the summer. (See Phantom Creek.)

Stanley Park ESTES PARK

Freelan O. and Francis E. Stanley, identical twins (with identical beards) from Maine, invented the Stanley Steamer, one of which, in June 1903, F. O. drove to Estes Park. He was used to mountain roads, since he was the first man to drive a horseless carriage, in 1899, up New Hampshire's Mount Washington. Tradition in Estes Park maintains that Stanley's car was the first to arrive in that town, but tradition forgets. In June, 1901, two Denver doctors, H. T. Pershing and W. H. Bergtold, started to drive their Locomobile steamer to Estes, but above Lyons the ruts in the road were so deep and the center so high that the rear axle dragged. They retreated and hired a Lyons man to work on the road. The following week they left Denver at 2:15 PM, spent the night in Longmont, and, by pushing the car most of the way up Rowell Hill, made Estes Village at 6:30 PM, July 3, 1901.

In 1903, a month before Stanley arrived, the first mechanical stage arrived in Estes. On May 7, the Burlington Railroad unloaded a twelve-passenger, thirty-horsepower touring car at Lyons for a test run for a fleet of stages. "The machine worked first class," reported the Lyons newspaper, "with the exception of where it encountered mud holes on heavy up-grades . . . but not once did it refuse to act or a single break occur. And the 20 and 25 percent grades were easily ascended where the roads were in good condition."

Nor did Stanley's steamer "refuse to act." Not waiting for the young man who was to help carry water for the steam engine, Stanley left Denver at noon, missed the road to Longmont, and sundown found him somewhere north of Boulder. He arrived late that night at Welch's Resort. Next morning, Billy Welch refused to sacrifice a man to the dangerous machine, so Stanley set forth alone. Arriving at Estes Park an hour and fifty minutes later, he telephoned Welch, who couldn't believe the contraption had not blown up.

The troubles Stanley encountered on the road decided him to reroute and improve it. Except for the state's contribution of $2,500, he raised the money himself—some say $50,000, some $16,000, and some $9,000. In late August of 1907 it was finished. He planned a fleet of four Stanley Steamers, each equipped with a telephone which could be attached at any point to the roadside telephone line. He guaranteed a trip of no more than an hour and a half from Lyons. The next summer, and many summers thereafter, his twelve-passenger steamers hissed up the new road with ease. No more was recorded about the phones.

F. O.'s first invention was a mechanical drawing set. F. E. turned to photography. In 1886 the brothers patented their Dry Plate Machine and made photographic plates; on January 5, 1904, they sold the patent to Eastman Kodak for $565,000. Then came the Stanley Steamer. In 1898, just as they set up a plant to produce two hundred of these cars (the first mass production plant for cars), the Locomobile Company—organized by John Brisben Walker, another Colorado character, expressly to buy the Stanley Steamer—paid them $250,000 for their works. By 1902 the Stanleys had invented a new steamer, one so vastly superior to the Locomobile that in 1904 the latter company turned to internal combustion engines. Stanley Steamers were still bringing in money to the twins in 1917 when they retired from the company.

Given three months to live by his doctor, F. O. Stanley came to Colorado to slow up and rest. Spending summers in Estes Park and winters in Massachusetts, he lived thirty-seven years more, but he did not slow up. First, he built a summer home in Estes Park for himself and his wife. In the evenings he would sit on its wide front porch, playing his homemade violin with its professionally sweet tone, and describing the sunsets over Longs Peak to his wife, who was blind. (Stanley's hobby was making violins; by the time he made his last one in 1937 he had given away twenty-four fine instruments.) For a man who had invented an automobile, Stanley had a singular quirk: he refused to drive backwards. To avoid it he installed a turntable in his garage.

After he had built his home, Stanley acquired half of the Dunraven Ranch, and built a hotel there in 1908. This he planned to call the Dunraven but the *Mountaineer* protested the name all summer long. Stanley offered a prize of $10 for a better name. Who got the prize is not recorded, but the hotel was officially the Stanley when it opened in 1909 with a Drivers' convention.

The power plant Stanley built supplied electricity not only to his hotel but to the village of Estes Park until the Public Service Company bought it in 1926. Through his efforts the village acquired a water system; through his generosity land for its sewage disposal plant. Stanley helped pick up the tab for transporting elk from Montana to repopulate the big game herds of the Park region, and deeded to the village the seven acres of land now known as Stanley Park.

Static Peak   NEVER SUMMER

In 1942 the Rocky Mountain National Park staff suggested that, since Thunder Mountain stood east of Thunder Pass, Lightning Peak should stand to the west. Why the authorities refused this suggestion is not recorded, but Static was substituted—a good name, as any mountain

climber will testify. Caught in a lightning storm above timberline, he compacts himself into as small a bundle as possible, while his hair rises, his
fingers tingle, and his ears buzz until lightning discharges the static,
which soon starts the demonstration all over again.

Steep Mountain   ESTES PARK
This hill had an Indian name with the same connotation as steep. The
name translates into Where-the-Buffalo-Was-Chased. Old Gun Griswold
of the 1914 Arapahos could even date the year it was thus named—1860.
That summer he was camped with many other Arapahos in Tuxedo Park.
Boys herding the camp's horses chased a buffalo part way up the mountain, noteworthy because the mountain was steep.
Abner Sprague thought that the name came from a map of a subdivi-
sion of Estes Park on which a surveyor had noted "a steep mountain." The
name appears on the 1874 township map.

Stillwater Creek   LAKE GRANBY
Placid Stillwater Creek runs into Lake Granby, which has inundated
the old Stillwater Ranch, once a landmark on the stage road to Grand Lake.

Stone Lake   INDIAN PEAKS

Stone Man Pass   GLACIER GORGE, WILD BASIN
Dean Babcock, on September 8, 1922, wrote a letter to Roger Toll
telling of a rock forty feet high which he had seen from Glacier Gorge. It
looked like the upper part of a man's figure—hat, face, and coat. The next
month Roger Toll climbed McHenrys Peak and agreed that the rock
looked like a man "when seen from Flattop Pass, like an old woman of the
Dutch Cleanser form when seen from Frozen Lake, and at other times it
looks like anything you please."

Stones Peak (12,922')   FOREST CANYON
G. M. Stone (1841-1912) was a professor of geology at Colorado College from 1881 to 1888. He invented surveying instruments, also devices
to aid helpless invalids. In 1884 Hallett reported his discovery of a glacier
to Professor Stone. (See Rowe Glacier.) In 1886, G. M. Stone stayed at Ferguson's Hotel and climbed with Chapin and Hallett.What more natural
than, at the end of the summer when Chapin and Hallett took their final
climb of the season and discovered a glacier, that they name the mountain
on which it lay after Stone?
"It will be a long day's tramp," said Hallett, as they left their horses on
Fern Creek to spend a carefree day—strong climbers traveling light. They
stalked mountain sheep, they observed a lion's tracks, though no bear
tracks. (Odd, because the 1914 Arapahos called Stones Peak and Mount
Julian the"Bear Paws.") After a snowstorm on the first false summit, they

rejoiced in a rainbow; and, at 3:30 PM, on the top, admired "a view destined to become famous." Then, at a running gait, they descended to a snow-field—a true glacier because it squeezed blocks of ice into the lake below. At 5:30 they remembered they should go home. In the dark, after fifteen hours of activity, Hallett, true mountain man, stepped lightly along the slippery log at the last stream crossing, but Chapin admitted that he "basely straddled the log."

Storm Pass; Storm Peak (13,326')   GLACIER GORGE

Enos Mills, observer of nature, knew where the clouds gathered when the elements prepared to battle. He named both Battle Mountain and Storm Peak.

An earlier name for Storm Peak was Velies Peak. Jacob W. Velie (1829-1908), at one time curator of the Chicago Natural History Museum, in 1864 came from Rock Island to explore with Dr. C. C. Parry, tireless botanist of the Front Range. In August they joined William Byers's and George Nichols in Byers's first attempt to climb Longs Peak. Byers called Velie "an ornithological sportsman." After climbing part way up the mountain together, the four men parted, Byers and Nichols to climb Mount Meeker. Parry and Velie, according to Parry's account of the climb, "winding around the western face toward the south, came upon a rugged ridge that connects Long's Peak with the main range. On one of the highest points of this ridge, named (after one of the party) Velie's Peak, the barometer was set up." Besides estimating the altitude, the men closely observed the water courses of Longs Peak and decided that the mountain was definitely east of the Continental Divide.

Stormy Peaks Pass: Stormy Peaks (12,148')   MUMMY RANGE

Lester Scott is credited with naming these peaks. He took dudes on horseback trips up the North Fork, over Stormy Peak, and down Pingree Park to spend the night at Koenig's place.

Stratus, Mount   NEVER SUMMER

After Roger Toll led climbers up this mountain on August 4, 1921, he proposed this name to conform to its neighbors, Mounts Nimbus, Cumulus, and Cirrus. Stratus is a cloud-form characterized by its horizontal extension and low altitude.

Strawberry Bench, Lake   LAKE GRANBY

On the steep mountain slopes in the Monarch Lake area the walker can pick quantities of wild strawberries without bending down.

Sugarloaf Mountain   MUMMY RANGE

Have you ever puzzled over the shape of the many mountains named Sugarloaf in eastern America, western America, or Rio de Janeiro? They do not resemble the shape of our lump sugar, cube sugar, domino sugar, or any other angular shape of modern pressed sugar. Most Sugarloaf Mountains are cone-shaped.

This leads us back to the days before granulated sugar was sold in bulk. Loaf sugar was a fully refined crystallized sugar which, while hot and in liquid form, was run into molds of terra cotta or iron, and allowed to cool and solidify. The syrup either dripped out of a hole in the bottom of the mold, or was sucked out by vacuum. A favorite size was conical in shape, five and one-half inches in diameter at the bottom, three inches at the top, thirteen inches high. It weighed slightly over seven pounds. This was called cone or loaf sugar. It was wrapped in heavy paper—usually blue paper to counteract any yellow tinge in the sugar that was supposed to look like a piece of white marble.

The sugar brought west in prairie schooners was loaf sugar, and was a luxury, which accounts for so many Sugarloaf Mountains being named by men who craved sweets.

Summerland Park GRAND LAKE

Ezra Kauffman homesteaded this land on the North Inlet of Grand Lake. He later built the Kauffman House at Grand Lake. When his widow sold the homestead for the Summerland Park development, she retained two lots, but the National Park bought them from her.

Sundance Creek; Sundance Mountain (12,400')—FOREST CANYON, MUMMY RANGE

Bill Currance used to watch the early morning play of sunlight on this mountain so he named it Sundance. (Do not confuse it with a whitish yellow hump of rock on the western end of Lumpy Ridge which, in 1956, technical climber Layton Kor called Sundance.) Bill Currance's cabin stood above Fall River about two miles upstream from Chasm Falls on Mount Zion, the local name for the southern slopes of Mount Chapin. Here he sank his ore shaft in the summer of 1908, and here he lived, undisturbed by the Rocky Mountain National Park, or by people who called him "Miner Bill" or "Crazy Bill." About 1940 he moved to the mental hospital at Pueblo. Thereafter, although he visited in Estes Park, he was always anxious to return to the hospital's security. On one of the summits of Sundance Mountain is the Toll Memorial with its mountain indicator.

Sunset Point LAKE GRANBY

Surprise Beach LAKE GRANBY

Table Mountain (8,830')   LAKE GRANBY
Spaniards call them mesas, these flat-topped mountains with steep sides; Americans call them tables. On the top of this Table Mountain, Indians sat in the sun to fashion arrowheads and axheads, scattering so many scraps of rock that archaeologists consider this one of the more important Indian factories in northern Colorado.

The 1914 Arapahos used a more distinctive name than Table—*Haa konon*—but even less poetic; translated it means the Lungs. According to Oliver Toll, the Arapahos thought the color of jasper anagate found on this mountain resembled the color of animal lungs freshly drawn from a carcass. Chalcedony and petrified wood are also found here. Remember— neither rocks nor artifacts may be collected. Table Mountain is in the Shadow Mountain Recreation Area where the rule holds that specimens may be admired but must be left.

Tahosa Creek   WILD BASIN
This creek that runs through Tahosa Valley was known as Cow Creek until the U.S. Board on Geographic Names changed it to the poetic Tahosa Creek in March 1961.

Tahosa Valley   WILD BASIN
The Colorado Geographic Board had nothing but trouble naming this valley. Five names they considered. The first was Longs Peak Valley, an early name for the strip of land east of the great peak. The second was Glacier Valley, used by Enos Mills on his 1905 map. A surveyor suggested Meridian Valley, noting that the land lay on a north-south line. None of these names seemed distinctive. Then a certain faction in the community produced Elkanah Valley as a name, which upset the easily upset Enos Mills.

In the Bible, Samuel's father was called Elkanah (El·kay´·nah). The name means Whom God Possessed. It was the Christian name of the tall preacher-climber, the first guide on Longs Peak, the first owner of Longs Peak House—Parson Elkanah Lamb. One evening the Bitners of Columbine Lodge gave a party which was attended by the elderly minister and other members of the Front Range Settlers League. One of the Hewes brothers, of Hewes-Kirkwood Inn, suggested that Lamb's first name be given to the area he had homesteaded. Many of the neighbors approved the name; by 1913 Clatworthy had inscribed it on his map; in 1914 Charles Edwin Hewes published a poem called *'Tis Evening in the Valley of Elkanah.*

Enos Mills objected, militantly. (Basically, the fight was not over a name for the valley, but was one of the skirmishes in the long war waged between Enos Mills and the Front Range Settlers League over the establishment of a national park in the area—national park vs. forest service.) Enos Mills spoke to Harriet Vaille, secretary of the Colorado Geographic Board. She dutifully reported to the board that "Mr. Mills, for personal reasons, very much resented the name Elkanah, saying that the name had no particular connection with the valley." Though the minutes of the board report nothing further, surely Miss Vaille must have pointed out that Mills well knew Lamb's first name. They had traveled together in Europe, and Mills not only had bought Longs Peak House from Elkanah Lamb, but in 1905 had written an introduction to Lamb's book. Lamb had settled in the region ten years before Mills saw it. Elkanah no connection with the valley, indeed!

Seeking peace, the Colorado Geographic Board, as was its wont in intramural wars, produced an entirely new name—Tahosa (Ta·ho´·sa), meaning Dwellers of the Mountaintops. The name, once seriously considered by Congress for the territory admitted to the Union under the name Colorado, was probably of Kiowan origin, since a Kiowa had signed a treaty in 1837 as "Tahosa, the Top of the Mountains."

Believing in democratic processes, the board canvassed families in the Longs Peak vicinity, tallying votes for Elkanah or Tahosa. The count was about even, so the board still had to decide. Not wishing to offend Enos Mills who was working for the establishment of the National Park, and fancying the appropriateness of a name that meant Dwellers of the Mountaintops for this high valley, the Colorado board recommended Tahosa to the U.S. Board on Geographic Names.

But peace did not spread over the valley. A member of the Front Range Settlers League, Burns Will, who was county commissioner and owner of Copeland Lake Lodge, wrote the Colorado Geographic Board in March 1915, denouncing Tahosa in particular and Indian names in general. He wrote that these were "due to the efforts of Miss Harriet Vaille, a very sentimental young lady of Denver who does not know the country in question." Following up the letter, Burns Will headed a three-man delegation that waited on the board to complain about Tahosa. Chairman Rogers opened the meeting by reading a letter from the U.S. Geological Survey stating that the Longs Peak quad of 1915 had gone to press with the name Tahosa Valley on it. Because of this *fait accompli,* Rogers observed that any discussion of the matter would be academic. Whereupon the delegation discussed the matter all evening, with the chairman murmuring every now and then that the map had gone to press. The meeting finally broke up after the board agreed to spread the whole matter over the minutes, where it could be consulted before the next printing of the map.

The U.S. Board on Geographic Names in March 1916 decided for Tahosa Valley, a decision that has not changed.

Tanima Peak (12,420') (Pronounced Ta·ni´·ma)   WILD BASIN
The name was proposed to the Colorado Geographic Board by Roger Toll, who said it was the name of a Comanche chief. It was also the name of a tribe. The Tanima tribe (the name means liver-eaters) was one of the

thirteen recognized tribes of Comanches when white men first came west, but by 1892 only one old man survived.

Tanima Peak had at least one previous name—Kirkwood. When the Hewes brothers and their mother, Mrs. Kirkwood, ran the Hewes-Kirkwood Inn, Charley Hewes went into Wild Basin with W. S. Cooper, and the young men had fun putting family names on unnamed peaks. Kirkwood appeared on Cooper's 1911 map for what is now Tanima, and Hewes for a mountain to the south, either the present Isolation or Mahana.

Taylor Glacier; Taylor Peak (13,153')—GLACIER GORGE, GRAND LAKE

Albert Reynolds Taylor, president of Kansas State Normal School in Emporia, and his family spent the summer of 1895 in Colorado. "He does not grow weary," reported the school's monthly magazine that September, "of telling of thrilling scenes, of crossing rivers on logs, mountain climbings and tumbles, broncho rides, and trout fishing." Evidently Sprague gave his guest much attention that summer, and liked him well enough to name a peak for him.

The name is also applied to the glacier on its southeast face. Taylor Glacier is a true, living glacier, the others in the Park being Andrews, Rowe, Sprague, and Tyndall; lying to the south of the Park are the St. Vrain glaciers; Peck, Fair, and Isabelle glaciers; and the Arapaho glaciers, the southernmost remnant of the Ice Age in the Front Range of the Rockies.

Before the arrival of white men, the 1914 Arapahos called Taylor Peak by a word that means the Bangs. They had killed a man, probably a Pawnee, near the summit on the south side. What made this memorable was that the foe wore his hair cut straight across his forehead, like a girl!

Teddys Teeth   ESTES PARK

A mountain topped with granite cliffs stands east of the Y.M.C.A. Camp. The boys at the camp called it Teddys Teeth because of the protruding rocks. The name dates from Theodore Roosevelt's presidency, 1901 to 1909, when cartoonists pictured him with his face full of teeth. Flippant, the authorities found this name, and not appropriate for a great green mountain they gave the ridge the name of Rams Horn Mountain, but they kept Teddys Teeth as a name for the rocks.

Ten Lake Park   GRAND LAKE, LAKE GRANBY

Tepee Mountain   NEVER SUMMER

Named by Frank Wright, a wrangler at the Phantom Valley Ranch who was interested in Indian lore.

Terra Tomah Mountain (12,718')   FOREST CANYON

In the summer of 1914, George Barnard topped a rise in the rough country of the Gorge Lakes and exclaimed, "Oh, there's the lake they told us about!" Turning toward his friends who followed him, members of the Third Annual Outing of the Colorado Mountain Club, he sang out his usual expression of delight—"He ne Terratoma, ne terratoma," and the others answered with an echo.

Since this lake had no name, James Grafton Rogers, president of the club and chairman of the Colorado Geographic Board, assigned the name Terra Tomah to it. He printed the name on the advance sheet of the U.S.G.S. map. "Evidently we didn't write very plainly," remarked Jim Rogers in 1965, recalling the episode, "because, when the map came back from Washington with the approved names added, Terra Tomah was on a mountain, not the lake." (The lake later became known as Doughnut Lake.) Since the name Terra Tomah had an Indian flavor, the board let it remain on the mountain.

The history of the name concerns the Cohuila Indians who lived on the slopes of the San Jacinto mountains in southern California. The remnant of their band—by 1902 only 159 members survived—in 1892 held their last fiesta. Two youths from Pomona College, near Los Angeles, spent their vacation with these Indians and one night, from a hiding place, listened to a war chant accompanied by tom-toms and the low moaning of women around the fire.

The young men, David P. Barrows and E. P. Brackett, took the haunting melody back to Pomona College. There, in 1894, George Barnard, later of Denver, and climber-extraordinary, was a student. He heard Barrows lecture on the Cohuila Indians and chant the war song. The students took it up as a college yell. In 1902, A. D. Bissell incorporated the chant into a song called the Ghost Dance. Singing it, the Pomona Glee Club won national awards, so many that the judges of at least one convention ruled out the song as unfair competition. The Ghost Dance, re-written in 1930 as "The Torchbearers," still inspires Pomona College students.

What do the words He ne Terratoma, ne terratoma mean? Dr. Barrows asked some Cohuila Indians. "We do not know," they replied. "The words are archaic." Dr. Barrows surmised in 1936 that "this may have been so, or they may not have wished to tell me, or the ones I asked to interpret the lines may not have known."

Today, old-timers of the Colorado Mountain Club still chant "He ne Terratoma, ne terratoma" across high valleys, and listen for the echo.

Thatchtop (12,668')   GLACIER GORGE

Brinton W. Woodward, chancellor of the University of Kansas, who spent many summers at Spragues Hotel, arranged one autumn to stay until the aspens turned yellow and the tundra changed to orange, red, and brown. He was especially impressed with the ground cover on the roof-shaped mountain west of Glacier Gorge, noting that as it turned from green to brown it matted down like a thatched roof. Sprague adopted this name for Thatchtop.

The 1914 Arapahos called this mountain the Buffalo Climb, in memory of the year many buffalo were caught by a storm on its top, enabling the Indians to kill them with ease.

Thousand Falls   FOREST CANYON, MUMMY RANGE

Thunder Falls, Lake   WILD BASIN

Charles Edwin Hewes, in his book of poems with historical notes, called *Songs of the Rockies,* states that this lake in the upper end of Wild Basin was "named by Harry Cole, an early settler, on account of the deep reverberations of thunder which roll grandly from Kirkwood's (Tanima's) mighty slopes and boom tempestuously across the lake." Eleanor James Hondius bought her first horse from this Harry Cole, who had a ranch south of Longs Peak Inn. Mr. Cole put on a skirt in order to break the pony to side-saddle. He was evidently a cattleman with a ranch on the plains as well as one in the mountains, since the *Lyons Recorder* of May 21, 1903, states that he had driven his cattle through Lyons to his mountain ranch.

Archaeologists find indications that the shores of Thunder Lake held Indian camps, one of at least six such sites in Wild Basin. On its shores in 1917 the Modern Eve spent part of an idyllic week. (See Nymph Lake.) The National Park has a patrol station at the lake, used often by Jack Moomaw who knows the Boulder-Grand Pass country so well. St. Pat's Cathedral is his unofficial name for the rocks that tower above Thunder Lake.

Thunder Mountain, Pass   NEVER SUMMER

The pioneers called the pass Lulu Pass. (See Lulu City.) The Arapaho words for Thunder Pass were *bohah ah ah* (thunder) *netheson* (pass). Although their word for thunder, pronounced explosively, is positively onomatopoetic, the Colorado Geographic Board chose the English translation. "The Arapahos said that there was always a black cloud over it," reported Oliver Toll. A non-official story about the name tells that by the time the two older Indians of the 1914 Arapaho party got to Squeaky Bob's ranch they were exhausted and tired of answering questions. After Squeaky administered to their needs with a little "red-eye," they were willing to answer questions but had no interest in historical accuracy. Noting a thunder cloud over Lulu Pass, they stated that their people always called it Thunder Pass.

Thunderbolt Peak (11,938')   INDIAN PEAKS

Surveyor Jenkins named this peak Electric Peak because he had seen lightning strike it. The Colorado Geographic Board considered this name in February 1915. Noting several Electric Peaks in Colorado, they thought "Thunderbolt Peak more graceful and would still satisfy his idea."

The next month an Arapaho National Forest man agreed: "I think it is perfectly satisfactory to everyone concerned to rename Electric Peak—Thunderbolt Peak."

Tileston, Mount (11,254')   MUMMY RANGE
This name came from the Colorado Geographic Board, proposed by Ellsworth Bethel at the suggestion of Enos Mills. So far, information about this man Tileston has come in shattered bits. Name—Merrill Tileston, or Henry Merrill Tileston; profession—"a noted preacher or author," according to a note in the Park files; summer residence— "cottage at James's, now Elkhorn Lodge"; hobby—"he made cinder glasses"; publication—*Chiquita: The Romance of a Ute Chief's Daughter;* date—1902; publisher—Merrill of Chicago.
Amplification of these facts is sought. Where was he noted as a preacher? No references to him can be found at the library of the Denver Iliff School of Theology, nor in the historical societies of Colorado, Kansas, or Illinois. Who published the book? The present day publishers Merrill of Chicago and Bobbs-Merrill of Indiana firmly deny responsibility. And what are cinder glasses? Optical or receptacle? Finally, does the fact that Tileston was the maiden name of Mrs. Freelan Stanley have any connection with the mountain's name?

Timber Creek   NEVER SUMMER
This name obviously must date back to pre-National Park days when lumbermen delighted in the board feet of fine timber available on the Western Slope of the Continental Divide.

Timberline Falls   GLACIER GORGE
Named by Robert Sterling Yard, author of the earliest information brochure on Rocky Mountain National Park. He was a good publicity man who knew that timberline is an interesting phenomenon of mountain scenery. Timberline marks the level on mountains above which trees cannot grow. The height of this treeline depends on the climate, timberline in Mexico being thousands of feet higher than timberline in Alaska. In northern Colorado it usually runs along the 11,500-foot contour, give or take a few yards depending on exposure.

Timberline Pass (11,484')   FOREST CANYON
At the head of Windy Gulch, this pass leads to Tombstone Ridge. Roger Toll named it in 1914, noting it as the only pass on the Ute Trail that is not above timberline.

Toll Memorial (12,310')   MUMMY RANGE
A mountain indicator was erected in 1941 on Sundance Mountain in memory of Roger Wolcott Toll, superintendent of Rocky Mountain

National Park from 1921 to 1929, who was killed in an automobile accident in 1936. The 360-degree view from the memorial includes many mountains, most of which he had climbed, many of which he had named.

Roger Toll (1883-1936) and his three brothers, Charles, Henry, and Oliver, spent their childhood summers at Tolland, their winters in a home east of Cheesman Park in Denver. For this house the architect had been instructed to make three bays, one facing Longs Peak, one Mount Evans, and one Pikes Peak. After Roger was graduated from Columbia University he and his brother Charles made a round-the-world tour, stopping longest for climbs in Switzerland. In 1908 Roger worked with the Coast and Geodetic Survey at Cook Inlet, Alaska; then came home to be chief engineer of the Denver Tramway Company.

With mountains in his blood, Roger was of course interested in the Colorado Mountain Club. In 1915 he invented for the club a cast bronze container to hold a pencil and registration book for climbers to record their achievement of reaching the summit of a mountain. This is much neater than scribbles on scraps of paper enclosed in empty tomato cans. Roger put the first of these registers on top of Mount Blaine near Kenosha Pass in 1915.

On Estes Park summits, Professor Arnold Emch placed many registers. This man—his son, now living in Estes Park, describes him as "a passionate pioneer of mountaineering"—was born in Switzerland in 1871. A great mathematician, he taught at the University of Colorado from 1900 to 1905, later at the University of Illinois. He wrote up his climbs for American newspapers, for the *Jahrbuch* of the Swiss Alpine Club, for a book published in Switzerland in 1908, and for a guidebook to Estes Park summits which he sent to the Colorado Mountain Club early in 1918. In 1917 a club committee had compiled a similar guide but the club was too poor to publish it. These two efforts culminated in a book called *Mountaineering in Rocky Mountain National Park*. It was signed by Roger Toll, edited by Robert Sterling Yard, and published by the Department of the Interior in 1919, after Major Toll returned from World War I. In that year Toll climbed in Hawaii, and Stephen Mather, director of National Parks, was also in the Islands. One day Mather was driving along a road when he caught sight of Roger Toll. Mather stopped the car. When he drove on, Roger Toll was the new superintendent of Rainier National Park.

Both Toll and Colorado were delighted in 1921 when he was transferred to Rocky Mountain National Park as its third superintendent following C. R. Trowbridge and L. C. Way. The new superintendent inherited a quarrel over the Rocky Mountain Transportation Company's monopoly of Park roads. Roger Toll had a gift for making peace, but this dispute ended in the U.S. Supreme Court.

The Colorado Mountain Club published a list of mountain peaks in Colorado with their altitudes, compiled by Roger Toll in 1923. Although some of the names have been changed and a few added, and although the altitudes have grown or shrunk with each new survey, this is still a unique reference tool. One of Roger Toll's dreams was to enlarge the Rocky Mountain National Park. To the west he was instrumental in adding the Never Summer Mountains in 1929, but was unable to acquire the Indian Peaks south of Wild Basin. Now, almost half a century later, Congress is considering a proposal to annex part of the Indian Peaks area to the Park. This area is now part of the Indian Peaks Wilderness Area.

Roger Toll's final contribution to the Park came in 1929 before he was transferred to Yellowstone. He persuaded Edmund Rogers, a born outdoorsman then working in a Denver bank, to accept the position of superintendent of Rocky Mountain National Park. Edmund Rogers, brother of James Grafton Rogers, had served as president of the Colorado Mountain Club and been active in its climbs, and had worked for the U.S. Geological Survey. On all of his experiences he would draw in his new position. Edmund Rogers was superintendent of Rocky Mountain National Park from 1929 to 1936, then succeeded Roger Toll as superintendent of Yellowstone National Park.

Toll, Mount (12,979') INDIAN PEAKS

On July 24, 1915, Arnold Emch and his son Arnold F. set out from Brainard Lake to climb the thick hump south of Paiute Peak. That day they got cliff-hung on the crags of Pawnee Peak, so they camped at timberline. The next day, by 8 AM, they had made the first ascent of what they christened Paiute Horn. Roger Toll wrote that later he and Charles Buckingham in "one much too long day" traversed from Paiute (summit at 10:10 AM) south to Apache (4:30 PM), slogging back to Brainard Lake in the rain by 7 PM Toll decided, probably in an effort to get the Ute name on an Indian Peak, that Ute Horn would be better than Paiute Horn. Neither name stuck.

Toll's interest in the Indian Peaks led to naming one of them in his memory. The Colorado Mountain Club and forest service suggested changing the name of Paiute Horn to Mount Toll. The U.S. Board on Geographic Names accepted the recommendation on November 14, 1940, four years after Toll's death.

Tombstone Ridge FOREST CANYON

The rocks on Tombstone Ridge reminded some early traveler of gravestones. Of this name the Colorado Geographic Board approved, then searched for a name for the whole stretch of the Ute Trail from Windy Gulch to Milner Pass. J. G. Rogers recommended Tombstone Ridge for the whole. The other members of the board disagreed, especially since to them the rocks "scarcely looked like tombstones." They voted for Trail Ridge, Chairman Rogers dissenting. He had a flair for drama. If today's highway across Trail Ridge were called Tombstone Ridge Road, the name would be more dramatic though the road might not be so attractive to tourists.

Tonahutu Creek (Pronounced To·na·hu´·tu)   GRAND LAKE
The 1914 Arapahos used this word which means Big Meadows, and the Colorado Geographic Board adopted it.

Tourmaline Gorge, Lake   FOREST CANYON
Dr. Workman named this lake, not for a girl, but for the tourmaline, a gem stone usually black.

Trail Ridge—See Tombstone Ridge, Ute Trail.

Trail Ridge Road
One of the many acrimonious fights connected with the early years of the Rocky Mountain National Park was settled in February 1929 when the Colorado State Legislature voted to cede jurisdiction over the roads in the Park to the United States. (When the Park was created, Colorado had retained jurisdiction in order to finish Fall River Road.) The very day Governor William H. Adams signed the bill, the head of the National Park Service announced the government would build a "wonder road" to be called Trail Ridge. Immediately the Bureau of Public Roads advertised for bids on a new road, in two sections: one from Estes Park to Milner Pass, to replace the steep Fall River Road; the other from Milner Pass to the North Fork of the Colorado River more or less following the old road.

A seventy-three-year-old contractor from Las Animas, Colorado, took on the eastern end of the job, from Deer Ridge to Milner Pass. William A. Colt (1856-1955) was an experienced earth mover. He graded the Missouri Pacific railroad bed from Kansas to Pueblo in 1887, using eight hundred mules and one thousand men. He built the eastern slope of the Wolf Creek Pass road in 1922 and in 1924 the nine top miles of the Independence Pass road. Starting in October 1929, he completed his part of the Trail Ridge Road (which he preferred to call the "Rendezvous with the Clouds Highway") in four hundred instead of five hundred days allowed in his contract. He was said to have lost money on his $500,000 bid.

Meanwhile, another contractor, L. T. Lawler of Butte, Montana, rebuilt the western section of the road. The whole spectacular highway was completed by the fall of 1932.

Trap Creek   NEVER SUMMER
Up to the 1930s when bear trapping was still legal in Colorado, at least six bear traps—the pit type—were dug along this creek. One or two may still be located. Who knows when they were dug? Trap Creek is named on early maps.

Another explanation for the name is that mines seep poison, perhaps arsenic, into the water of Trap Creek; but the mines on Iron Mountain are too shallow to produce seepage, and no one remembers seeing dead fish, game, or cows. Miners admit that mines can poison water; nature, unaided, can too. Near Crested Butte, the Rocky Mountain Biological Laboratory proved that sulfides, dissolving out of rocks near a small stream and mixing with water and oxygen, formed sulfuric acid, so that, for a half mile, the stream had no insects or fish.

Triangle Lake   INDIAN PEAKS

Trio Falls   WILD BASIN
Named by Jack Moomaw, park ranger, in 1921.

Triple Lakes   INDIAN PEAKS

Tundra Curves   MUMMY RANGE
Tundra, a Russian word, designates the treeless land of the Alpine Zone, whether it be in the Colorado Rockies or the Arctic Circle. In both, tundra plants are the same—the forget-me-nots are as blue and smell as sweet on Trail Ridge as in northern Alaska. In a fifty-mile-drive from Lyons to the Tundra Curves, the motorist passes through the same vegetation zones as he would in an eight-thousand-mile trip from Colorado to the Arctic Circle. These zones include the semi-arid Foothills Zone; the lush growth of the Montane Zone; the brilliant plants of the Sub-Alpine Zone; and the dwarf growth of the Alpine Zone in the tundra.

Tuxedo Park   ESTES PARK
A Delaware Indian named P'Tauk-Seet (meaning wolf or bear) lived east of the Hudson River centuries before 1886 when Pierre Lorillard IV founded a millionaires' community about forty miles northwest of New York City, borrowing the Indian name for his Tuxedo Park. Here commuting Wall Street executives stepped from the Albany Express to carriages waiting to carry them to their twenty-room cottages; there they changed to sport clothes for fishing or tennis or ice skating, then expressed their appreciation of the informal life by dining at the club dressed not in their customary tails but in English dinner jackets. These jackets soon acquired the name tuxedo. The ladies dressed simply for dinner in last year's Newport gowns, according to Emily Post's 1911 account of Tuxedo Park.

F. O. Stanley transferred the name Tuxedo Park from New York to the Estes Park area. Perhaps he planned some day to create a hunting and fishing preserve for tired executives in the West, like the New York club, but his only use of his Tuxedo Park was when he took his friends camping there, causing the R.M.N.P. superintendent to report in June 1922 that "such camps must be controlled."

Twin Creek—LAKE GRANBY; **Twin Lakes**—WILD BASIN

Twin Owls, The   ESTES PARK, MUMMY RANGE
"The two sculptured figures . . . appearing almost exactly like two great
owls" were noted by Chapin in 1887. His observation may have established the name, but more probably he heard it from an earlier settler. No
such name had been used by the Arapahos.

Twin Peaks (11,957')   LAKE GRANBY

Twin Pines Point   LAKE GRANBY

Twin Sisters Peaks (11,428')   ESTES PARK
On March 7, 1907, Ellsworth Bethel wrote the Geographic Board in
Washington that the name Twin Sisters Peak was well established. "Not Lil-
lie," he urged. (See Lily Mountain.) Later, in 1915, Bethel changed his mind.
He wanted this mountain named Tahosa. "Not Twin Sisters nor Lillie Moun-
tain," he wrote, stating that the peak showed twin tops only from one angle.
But this name was rejected, Twin Sisters retained. (See Tahosa Valley.)

Two Rivers Lake   FOREST CANYON, GLACIER GORGE
The "rivers" that theoretically originate in this lake are Fern and Mill
creeks. Although the lake has no visible outlet, its water percolates under-
ground to both creeks.
An undocumented rumor credits Dr. Workman with using the same
name for this lake as he used for Lake Helene. A girl named Helen and a
girl named Mary, having heard he often named lakes for girls, teased him
into naming one for them. He obliged—Helmary Lake.

Tyndall Creek, Glacier, Gorge   GLACIER GORGE
Enos Mills thoroughly educated himself by intensive reading during
the long winter evenings he spent alone in his cabin. He read much about
John Tyndall (1820-1893), the great English physicist and student of
glacial phenomena. Mills wanted to rename the present Copeland Mountain after Tyndall. The Colorado Geographic Board raised the objection
that Tyndall had no direct connection with Colorado. After Mills's suggestion for a Tyndall Mountain was rejected, the naming of Tyndall Glacier may have been a compromise, although the name was not adopted by
the National Park Service until June 30, 1932.

Ute Trail   FOREST CANYON
The 1914 Arapahos spoke of three trails leading from Estes Park
toward Grand Lake—the Big Trail (Flattop), the Dog Trail (Fall River),

and the Childs Trail. This last trail went up Windy Gulch to the head of Hidden Valley, then went approximately where Trail Ridge Road goes now, crossing it at various points on the Tundra Curves.

The trail was called the Childs Trail because the Arapahos said it was so steep in places that children had to dismount and walk, according to Oliver Toll—yet it is the gentlest of the three trails. A more logical explanation of the name Childs Trail is found in an 1890 book by H. Beaugrand, mayor of Montreal, *Six Mois dans les Roches Montagnes*. He wrote that French-Canadian trappers called Ute Indians "la tribe des Enfants," because they were short, like children. Were the 1914 Arapahos unsuccessfully trying to explain to Oliver Toll that this trail was used by the short people, the Utes?

How much this trail was used by the Indians is hard to tell. Abner Sprague, who came to the Park in 1875, stated definitely that he saw no trace of an Indian trail across Trail Ridge at that time. In the 1870s, Ferguson and Farrar cut a trail at the mouth of Windy Gulch to bring out the carcasses of three elk they had killed. However, miners headed for Lulu City or Gaskill, and hunters headed for Squeaky Bob's soon wore ruts deep into the tundra across the alpine meadows. They called it variously North Fork Trail, Specimen Mountain Trail, Poudre Lakes Trail, Squeaky Bob's Trail—whatever its name, it was the standard trail from Estes Park to the North Fork of the Colorado River. It may have been named Ute Trail by the Colorado Geographic Board in 1915. Today, the Rocky Mountain National Park officially calls it the Ute Trail, and has marked it by small, neat cairns.

Verna, Lake   GRAND LAKE
Five lakes stretch along the East Inlet of Grand Lake—Lone Pine, Verna, Spirit, Fourth, and Fifth lakes. The five are called the Shoestring Lakes by some Grand Lake old-timers; Charles Hewes knew the three lower lakes as the Trinity Lakes. The longest lake, extending between steep granite walls with hardly enough shoreline for a fisherman to stand on, is Lake Verna, named for the sweetheart of a member of the U.S. Geological Survey. Neither authority for this statement, George Barnard or John King Sherman, state what survey, what member, or what sweetheart.

War Dance Falls   GRAND LAKE
Clement Yore, novelist and hotel keeper of Estes Park, wrote in 1922 that Sherman Sage of the 1914 Arapahos had pointed to these falls,

performed a war dance, and said, "I call him War Dance Falls." Toll's official report of this trip, however, does not state this.

Watanga Creek, Lake; Watanga Mountain (12,375') LAKE GRANBY
This name was probably proposed by the Colorado Geographic Board because of its vast interest in Indians. Watanga (Black Coyote) a Southern Arapaho, lived in Darlington, Oklahoma. E. A. Burbank painted his portrait with scarlet crosses scattered over his body; these marked the scars from the day Watanga offered pieces of his own flesh as sacrifice to the Sun to save his children from death. Watanga, with one of his wives, signed the Cheyenne-Arapaho Treaty in 1890; he was captain of Indian police, a delegate to Washington, deputy sheriff of Canada County, Oklahoma. Artist Burbank stated that Watanga was

> of considerable importance to his tribe and in his own sight. . . . Black Coyote once received $800 in cash from the government for some service. He immediately bought a new team of horses for his carriage and hired a coachman. . . . It was an amusing sight to see Black Coyote with his squaw and children step out of the carriage in style and crawl into the tepee, after which the carriage rolled on to the barn, where the coachman slept with the horses.

Wescott, Mount (10,421') GRAND LAKE
Named for Judge Joseph L. Wescott, pioneer of Grand Lake, who was born in Nova Scotia in 1838. In Colorado his Civil War service with Company G, First Colorado Cavalry, left him with rheumatism. Somehow he got to Georgetown, Colorado, and arranged to travel with a group across Berthoud Pass, lying in a hammock slung on poles between two burros. In Middle Park he soaked in the healing waters of Hot Sulphur Springs. In the pool he regained his health but almost lost his life when an Indian shot at him. In June 1867 he settled at Grand Lake, where he lived in a cabin on the southwestern shore of the lake until he died in 1914. He wrote a long poem, called "The Legend of Grand Lake." (See Grand Lake.) He was a good storyteller—children adored his tales. His speech indicated a good education and even culture. Patience Stapleton's book, *Kady,* features Wescott under the name of Judge West.

Some Grand Lake people who appreciated Judge Wescott's unique character thought the most prominent mountain to the east of the lake should bear his name. The Colorado Geographic Board disagreed. They retained Mount Craig for that mountain and named the mountain west of it for Judge Wescott.

West Creek MUMMY RANGE

Wheeler Basin INDIAN PEAKS
Reverend S. R. Wheeler, who was born in England in 1834 and died in Boulder in 1925, brought his family west and established the Seventh Day

Baptist Church in Boulder in 1893. He had three sons and two daughters. One girl married Darwin M. Andrews of the Rockmont Nursery in Boulder. (See Andrews Peak.) The oldest son, H. N. Wheeler, became supervisor of the Colorado National Forest. (See Arapaho Glacier.) The third son, Alfred Truman Wheeler, trapper, prospector, forest service worker, and for some years caretaker of the Boulder water supply at Silver Lake, knew every rock in what is now called Wheeler Basin.

He and James C. Bennett first ventured into that area in search of gold in 1903. They built a cabin and then trails—the first trail to Monarch Lake, and a ten-mile trail to Arapaho Pass. This involved twenty-six bridges and the original switchbacks leading to the pass. About 1915 Wheeler staked two placer claims in the basin southwest of Arikaree Peak. These gave him control of a deposit of rock flour, or glacial milk, which had a certain amount of radioactivity and was said to have medicinal values. Though the claims have never been patented nor the medicine proved, the Wheeler family in Boulder has kept the claims alive by annual assessment work these fifty-odd years. Wheeler Basin was known as Hell Hole. A. T. Wheeler, maintaining that "the devil owns too much of God's beautiful earth," wanted to rename it the Garden of Pinnacles. Asked for help in this campaign, the Boulder Chamber of Commerce countered by suggesting that it be called Wheeler Basin. Fred Fair, county surveyor, tried unsuccessfully to accomplish this. Largely through the efforts of Robert Woolfolk of the Arapaho Valley Ranch near Monarch Lake, the name Wheeler Basin appeared on the 1958 Monarch quad map.

The U.S. Board on Geographic Names in its 1958 Bulletin confused father and son, recording that Wheeler Basin was named for "A. T. Wheeler, pioneer clergyman, now over 90." The father, whose initials were S. R., was the clergyman. No matter—Wheeler Basin honors a Boulder family especially attached to that certain corner of the earth.

Wild Basin   WILD BASIN
When Joe Mills sat on Longs Peak making a rude sketch of Wild Basin in his notebook, he labeled it "Land of Many Waters," an appropriate name for this lake-dotted country drained by the North St. Vrain Creek. Equally appropriate is the official name Wild Basin, which dates back to early days in the Park—perhaps to Elkanah Lamb. That Wild Basin is today still an appropriate name is due to the wise decision of the National Park Service fifty years ago to preserve the southern part of the Park as wilderness. Except for reservoir dams, constructed before the Park regime and now deteriorating, very little of man is noticeable. Wild Basin's trails are used well and often by the kind of people who go beyond paved roads.

The first person to map Wild Basin in detail and name many of its features was William S. Cooper, now living in Boulder after a distinguished career as head of the Botany Department of the University of Minnesota.

Largely because of his study of plant ecology and glaciers in Alaska, Glacier Bay National Monument was created. One of the mountains of the Fairweather Range, the backdrop of the bay, was named Mount Cooper in his honor.

In June 1965, for *Trail and Timberline*, Dr. Cooper wrote about Wild Basin as he knew it in 1904 to 1908:

In July 1904, a botanist of tender age—the undersigned—along with father and mother, by train from Denver to Lyons, by four-horse stage the rest of the way, arrived in Estes Park. We settled at Elkhorn Lodge, but Longs Peak was the main attraction for me. Enos Mills brought down two horses for a companion and me and we rode up to Longs Peak Inn, most of the way at a gallop, with several stops to open and close gates. A few days later Enos guided us to the summit of Longs Peak by moonlight. . . . For me the Longs Peak region brought love at first sight. The mountains themselves I am sure came first, but science was not completely neglected. On the basis of one month's field work I contributed a brief account of the wildflowers to Mills's *The Story of Estes Park and a Guide Book* published in 1905.

In 1906 I returned to the Longs Peak region, this time without parents. For the most part I stuck closely to my scientific duties, varying these with several climbs of Longs and other peaks. From these studies came my first scientific publication: "Alpine Vegetation in the Vicinity of Long's Peak, Colorado" (Botanical Gazette, vol. 45: 319-337, 1908). . . . In 1908 I again returned, planning to continue my scientific work. But I thought it would be fun, in addition, to make a map of the region centering on Longs Peak, which, except for a limited portion covered by the rough Mills map of 1905, had never been surveyed. So I bought myself a small plane table with a simple alidade, taught myself how to use it, laid out a half-mile baseline near the Inn, and gradually developed a triangulation net. Numerous climbs were made to points of vantage for triangulation and the sketching in of topography, represented by hachures. No attempt was made to measure altitudes. Particular attention was given to Wild Basin, the headwaters of the North St. Vrain river system, because it was the least known part of the region covered.

One trip to this area is particularly memorable: personnel, Charley Hewes, the writer, and Pat, the burro. . . . The time was mid-June; snow lay deep in the higher forests, the streams were raging torrents. Pat did not like either condition. Forcing him to cross belly-deep streams required invention of new engineering methods. . . . On that expedition we climbed Mount Copeland and Elks Tooth and enjoyed an exciting glissade to the frozen surface of Pipit Lake.

At summer's end my good friend Dean Babcock, a far better topographer than I, was my prospective companion on a final trip to cover the northwest corner of Wild Basin. Our first night's camp was at Sandbeach Lake. After dark, just about bedtime, a distant shot rang out, and shortly Enos Mills appeared, with the news that my father in Detroit was dangerously ill. I made all haste to return, but was too late. (See Cooper Peak.)

Dean finished the survey, and in 1911 we published our map, which sold for fifteen cents per copy. On it we attached names to various natural features. Some, quite personal, have been rightfully ignored. Eleven were officially accepted, most of them in Wild Basin, and appear on the latest map of Rocky Mountain National Park: Ouzel Peak (Enos Mills had named Ouzel Lake), Meadow Mountain, Mount Orton, Pine Ridge, Bluebird Lake, Junco Lake, Pipit Lake, Chickadee Pond, Calypso Cascades, Mertensia Falls, Columbine Falls.

Willow Creek—NEVER SUMMER; Willow Creek—WILD BASIN; Willow Park—MUMMY RANGE

So many willows grow in the area, it is a wonder that no more than two creeks and one park bear their name. Of the many varieties of willows that grow in the Park, three are easily identified: alpine willows by their enormous catkins; mountain willows of the Montane Zone by their yellow twigs; and the whiplash willows of the lower hills by their shining red stems. Willow colors enliven the winter landscape, growing more vivid as spring comes on. The late spring snowstorm of the mountains is often called the willow bender.

Wind River, Wind River Pass ESTES PARK

The 1914 Arapahos used a long name for Tahosa Valley, literally translated as "woman-log-it-killed-her." They recalled riding through the gap at the head of the valley—Wind River Pass—when a horse bumped a dead tree which fell on a woman and killed her. Interpreter Tom Crispin slowly dictated the Arapaho words for "woman-log-it-killed-her" to Oliver Toll who meticulously wrote them in his notebook: *issā-bes- di - noX - kāh - wah - nāt ôwah ah-nât,* thirty letters divided into twelve syllables. Both the young Coloradan and the interpreter were amused at the end when the Indian remarked, "That makes it short and clear." The Colorado Geographic Board preferred the English translation.

Windy Gulch, Windy Gulch Cascades FOREST CANYON

Perhaps the name for this gulch is as old as the first men who felt its breezes, but the first trail up Windy Gulch can be dated to the early 1870s, when H. W. Ferguson and Hank "Buckskin" Farrar, two early settlers who refused to be intimidated by Dunraven's minions, went hunting. According to the "50 Years Ago" column in an Estes Park newspaper, they "killed three elk on the south slope of Brinwood Mountain in Moraine Park. The trail they had to cut to get these elk out was the beginning of the Windy Gulch Trail"—the eastern end of the present Ute Trail.

Wuh, Mount (10,761')   FOREST CANYON
This Arapaho word means grizzly bear. The phonetic spelling is *woX,*
with the "X" pronounced as an explosive "h." It is more often pronounced
(and often spelled) Mount Woo. Not the 1914 Arapahos but Roger Toll in
1923 named the mountain, even though he must have known the Park no
longer harbored grizzly bears. Naming Mount Wuh settled the problem
of which was Steep Mountain, a name definitely fixed now on the mountain east of Wuh.

Ypsilon Lake; Ypsilon Mountain (13,514')   MUMMY RANGE
This is one of the few mountains in the Rockies that bears its name
clearly written on its face, to be read by those who can read Greek.
Ypsilon is the Greek word for the letter "Y." In 1888 Frederick Chapin
climbed this mountain but he recorded that his wife had christened it the
year before when the two idled away a day on the banks of "the little tor-
rent" called Wind River:

> I had been fishing a little. Later we were looking at the mountains, which
> from here are so beautiful in the west. One great peak with a steep wall fac-
> ing the east, and a long reclining ridge leading toward the southwest,
> especially interested us. A large snow-field lay on the eastern face; two glit-
> tering bands of ice extended skyward to the ridge of the mountain, form-
> ing a perfect "Y." My wife said to me, "Its name shall be Ypsilon Peak." So
> it went forth, and the name was accepted by the dwellers of the valley and
> by visitors to the ranches.

When in 1910 officials of the Young Men's Christian Association,
searching for a spot for their conference grounds, caught a view of
Ypsilon's "Y" from the old Wind River Lodge they felt that "the hand of
God led them to this place." Later, after John Timothy Stone of the
Chicago Presbyterian Church and at least eight other ministers built
houses on the slope east of the Y Camp, the slope was called Holy Hill.

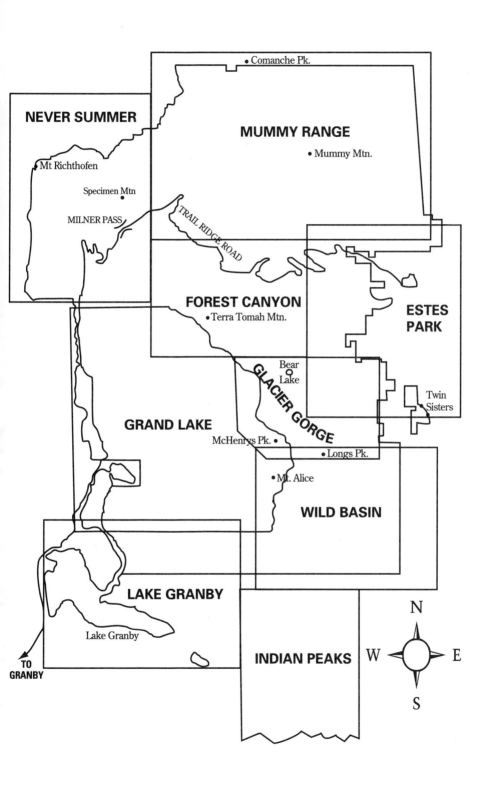

NEVER SUMMER

• Mt Richthofen

Specimen Mtn •

MILNER PASS

Comanche Pk. •

MUMMY RANGE

• Mummy Mtn.

TRAIL RIDGE ROAD

FOREST CANYON
• Terra Tomah Mtn.

ESTES PARK

Bear Lake

Twin Sisters

GLACIER GORGE

GRAND LAKE

McHenrys Pk. •

• Longs Pk.

• Mt. Alice

WILD BASIN

LAKE GRANBY

Lake Granby

TO GRANBY

INDIAN PEAKS

N
W — E
S

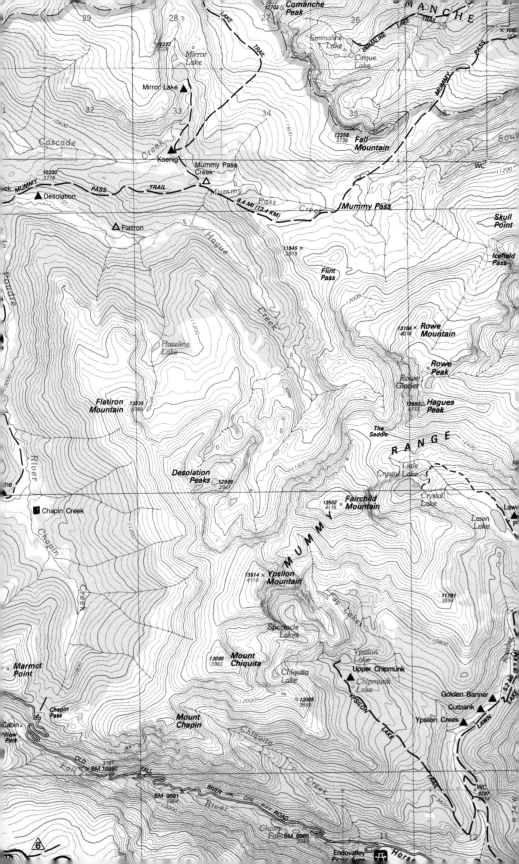

NEVER SUMMER

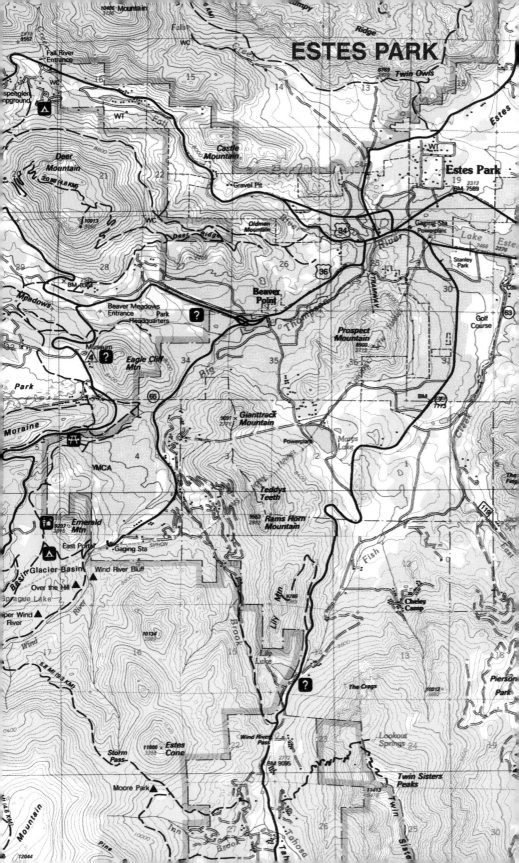

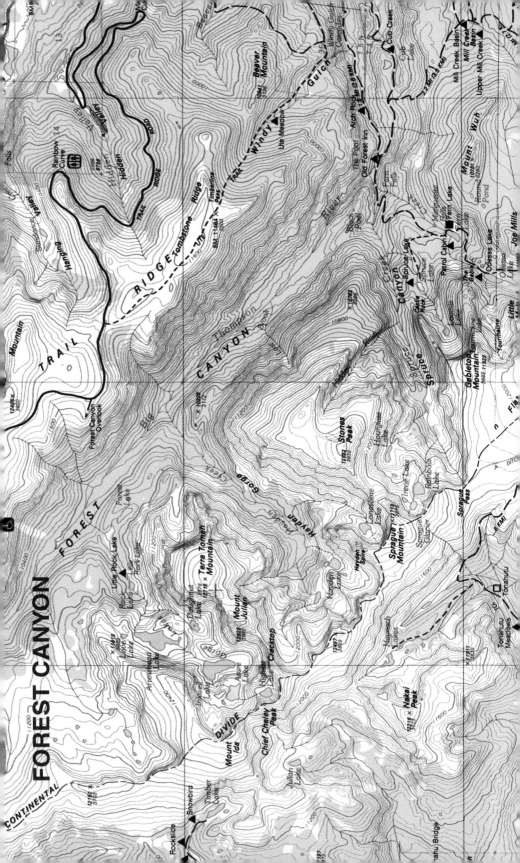

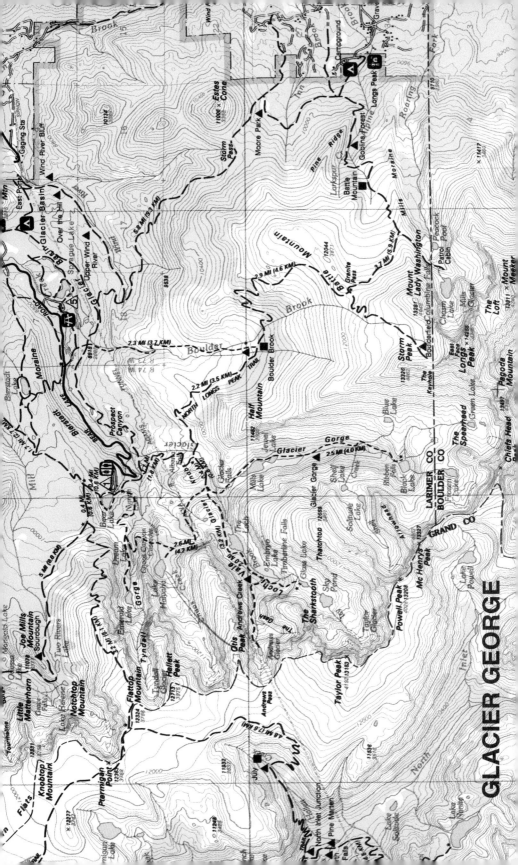

GLACIER GEORGE

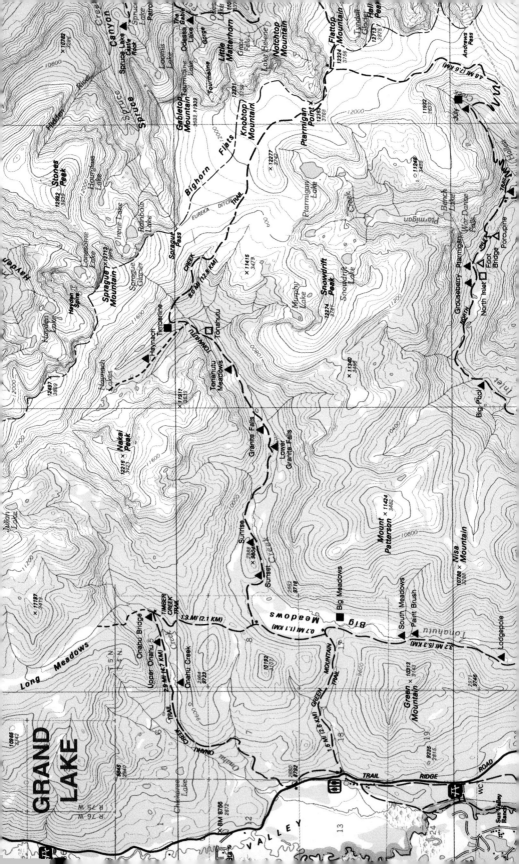

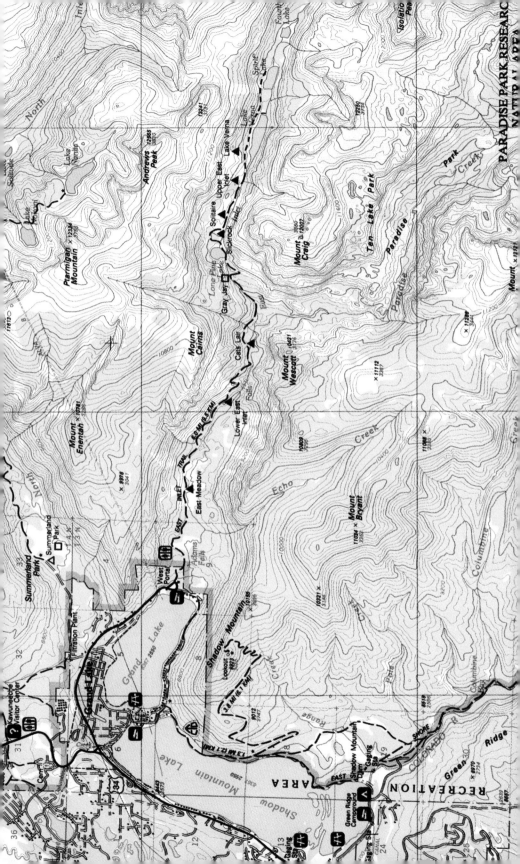

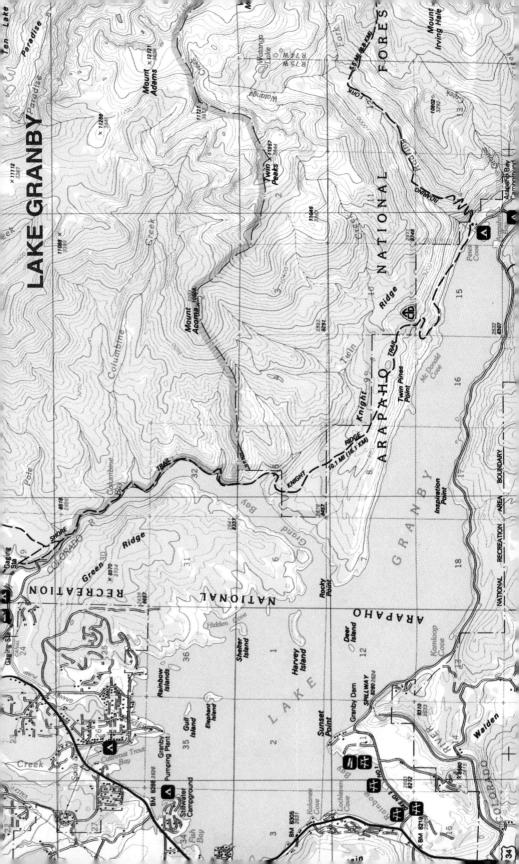

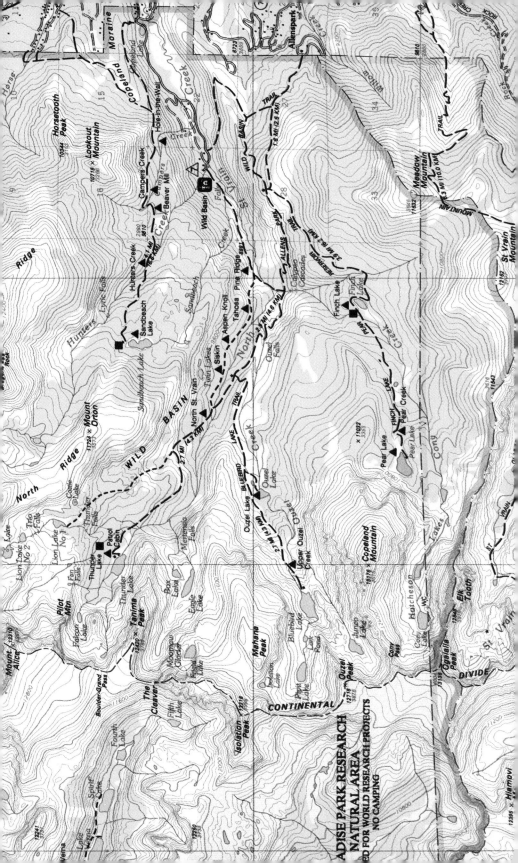

INDEX

NOTE: Dictionary headings are not repeated in index.

ABOUT ROCKY MOUNTAIN NATURE ASSOCIATION

The Rocky Mountain Nature Association is a non-profit organization which supports the interpretive, educational, and research programs of the National Park Service and other allied agencies. Through the sale of interpretive material to visitors, the Rocky Mountain Nature Association funds dozens of programs each year for the National Park Service, state and city parks, and the U.S. Forest Service. The association also offers a wide variety of outdoor field seminars centered around the natural and cultural history of Rocky Mountain National Park. Members in the association receive discounts on publications and seminars and receive the quarterly RMNA newsletter. For more information contact:

Rocky Mountain Nature Association
Rocky Mountain National Park
Estes Park, CO 80517
(303) 586-1258